JUMBLE®

BrainBusters™ Bonanza

A Bevy of Brain-Bending Puzzles

David L. Hoyt and Russell L. Hoyt

TRIUMPH
BOOKS
CHICAGO

This book is available in quantity at special discounts
for your group or organization.

For further information, contact:

Triumph Books
601 South LaSalle Street
Suite 500
Chicago, Illinois 60605
(312) 939-3330
FAX (312) 663-3557

Printed in the United States of America

ISBN 978-1-57243-616-9

CONTENTS

JUMBLE®

BrainBusters™

Beginner Puzzles

PUZZLE 1

JUMBLE® TRIVIA

Unscramble the Jumbles, one letter to each square, to spell words as suggested by the trivia clues.

#1 John ______, a doctor and vegetarian, developed a popular cereal in the late 1800s.

#1 GOKLELG

#2 The ______ made its first flight on March 2, 1969.

#2 NCOCODER

#3 This planet is the fourth-largest planet in our solar system.

#3 NPUNEET

#4 This country was formerly called Northern Rhodesia.

#4 MZAIAB

#5 One variety of this creature can grow to 15 feet in length and up to 650 pounds.

#5 SFCTIHA

Arrange the circled letters to solve the mystery answer.

The first telephone book was published in this U.S. state in 1878.

MYSTERY ANSWER

PUZZLE 2

MOVIES

JUMBLE BrainBusters

Unscramble the mixed-up letters, one letter to each square, to spell movie titles.

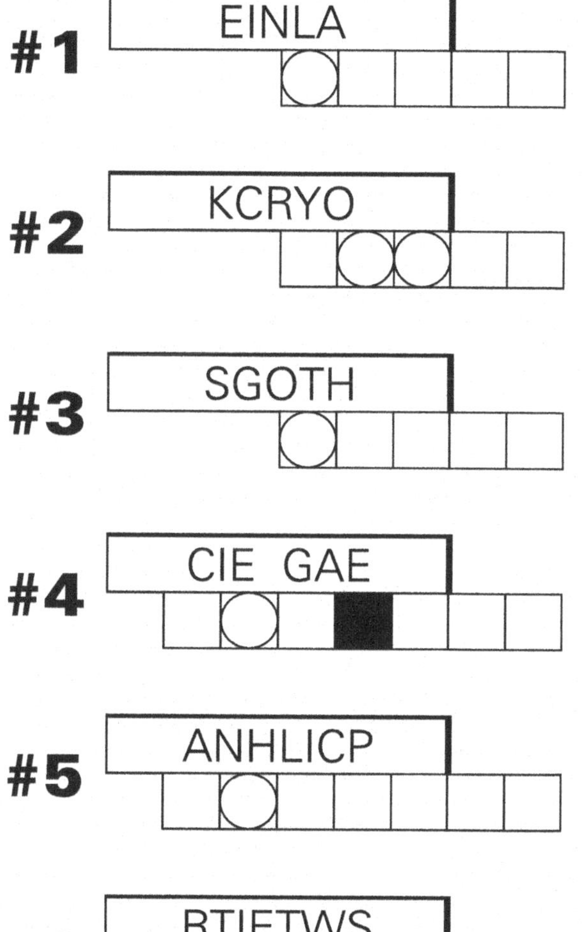

Box of Clues

Stumped? Maybe you can find a clue below.

- -1992 Robert Downey Jr. movie about a famous Charlie
- -1976 Best Picture
- -2002 movie featuring the voice of Ray Romano
- -2002 Best Picture
- -1996 Helen Hunt movie
- -1990 movie starring Demi Moore and Patrick Swayze
- -1979 Sigourney Weaver movie

Arrange the circled letters to solve the mystery answer.

MYSTERY ANSWER

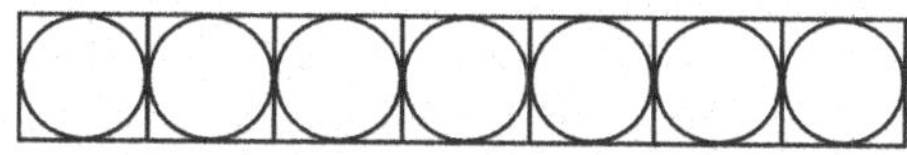

MATH

JUMBLE BrainBusters

Unscramble the Jumbles, one letter to each square, so that each equation is correct.

For example: NONTEOEOW

ONE + ONE = TWO

#1 SXEXSIRIZO

□□□ − □□□ = □□□◯

#2 NTHEOIGNEIEN

□□◯ + □□□□□ = □□□□

#3 NVFTEOSVIEEW

◯□◯□ + □◯□ = □□□◯□

#4 TEEIHRETENHENR

◯□□□□ × ◯□□□□ = □◯□□

#5 EOREESZEVNVSNE

□□□□◯ − □□□□ = □□□□□

Arrange the circled letters to solve the mystery equation.

MYSTERY EQUATION

ANIMALS

Unscramble the Jumbles, one letter to each square, to spell names of animals.

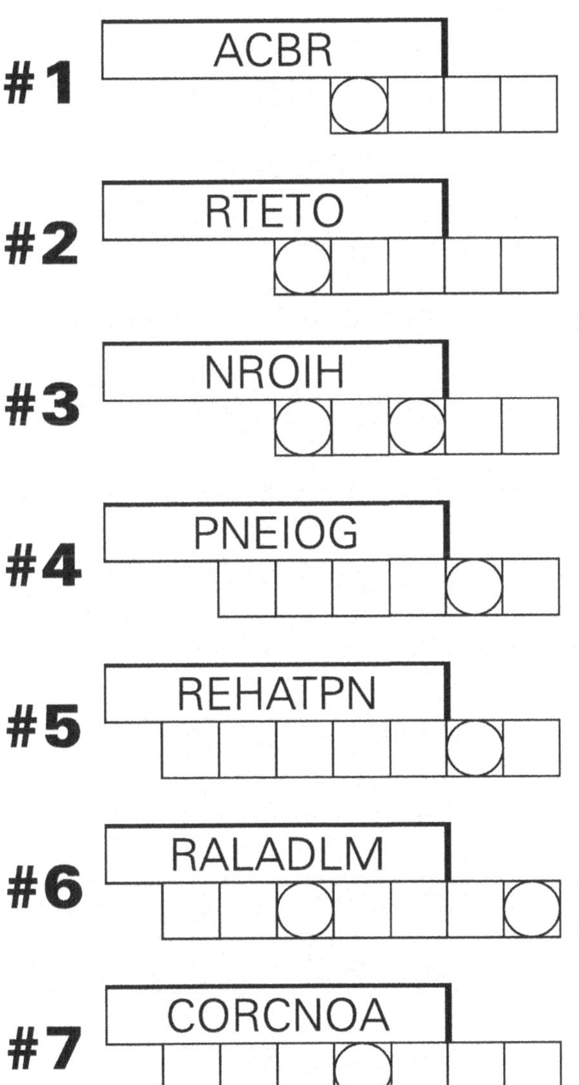

#1 ACBR

#2 RTETO

#3 NROIH

#4 PNEIOG

#5 REHATPN

#6 RALADLM

#7 CORCNOA

JUMBLE® BrainBusters

Box of Clues

Stumped? Maybe you can find a clue below. (No clue for the mystery answer.)

-Starts with *R*; ends with *O*
-Starts with *O*; ends with *R*
-Starts with *P*; ends with *R*
-Starts with *C*; ends with *B*
-Starts with *R*; ends with *N*
-Starts with *P*; ends with *N*
-Starts with *M*; ends with *D*

Arrange the circled letters to solve the mystery answer.

MYSTERY ANSWER

PUZZLE 5

ABBREVIATIONS

JUMBLE BrainBusters

Unscramble the Jumbles, one letter to each square, to spell words that are often abbreviated.

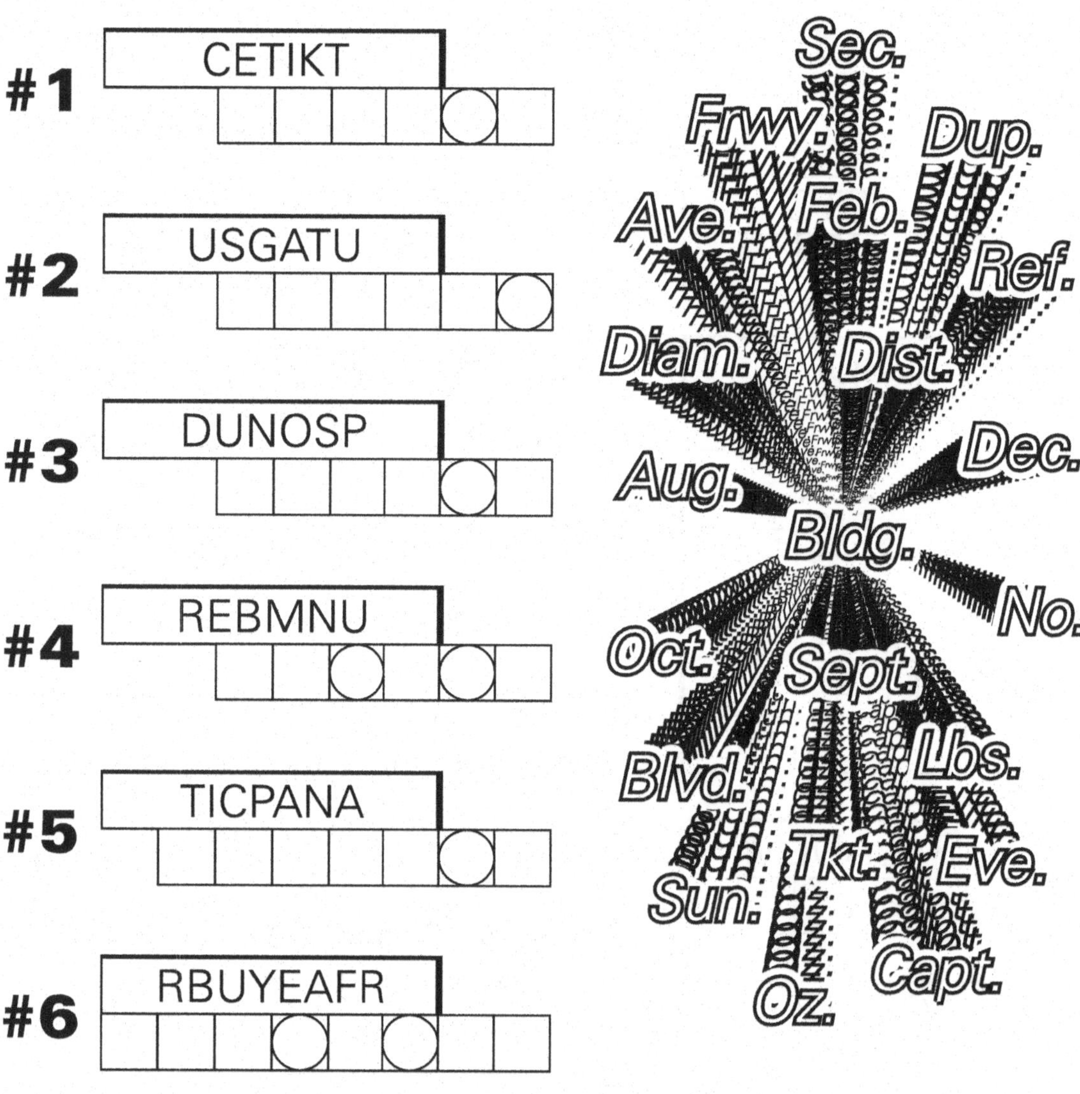

#1 CETIKT

#2 USGATU

#3 DUNOSP

#4 REBMNU

#5 TICPANA

#6 RBUYEAFR

Arrange the circled letters to solve the mystery answer.

MYSTERY ANSWER

PUZZLE 6

STARTS AND ENDS WITH THE SAME LETTER

Unscramble the Jumbles, one letter to each square, to spell words that start and end with the same letter.

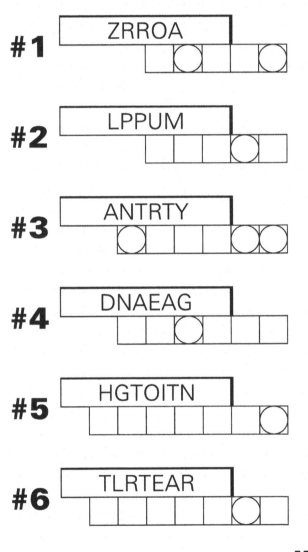

JUMBLE BrainBusters

RADAR ARENA POP GOING RIVER HIGH DICED CRYPTIC

#1 ZRROA

#2 LPPUM

#3 ANTRTY

#4 DNAEAG

#5 HGTOITN

#6 TLRTEAR

Box of Clues

Stumped? Maybe you can find a clue below.

- -Harsh ruler
- -Having a full, rounded form
- -Keen-edged cutting instrument
- -*The ______ Show*
- -The silent ______
- -Type of American pit viper
- -List of things to be done

Arrange the circled letters to solve the mystery answer.

MYSTERY ANSWER

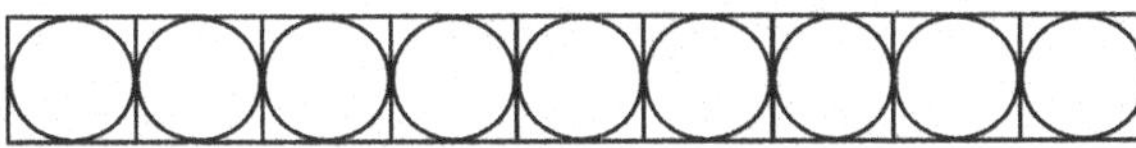

PUZZLE 7

RHYMING WORDS

Unscramble the Jumbles, one letter to each square, to spell pairs of words that rhyme.

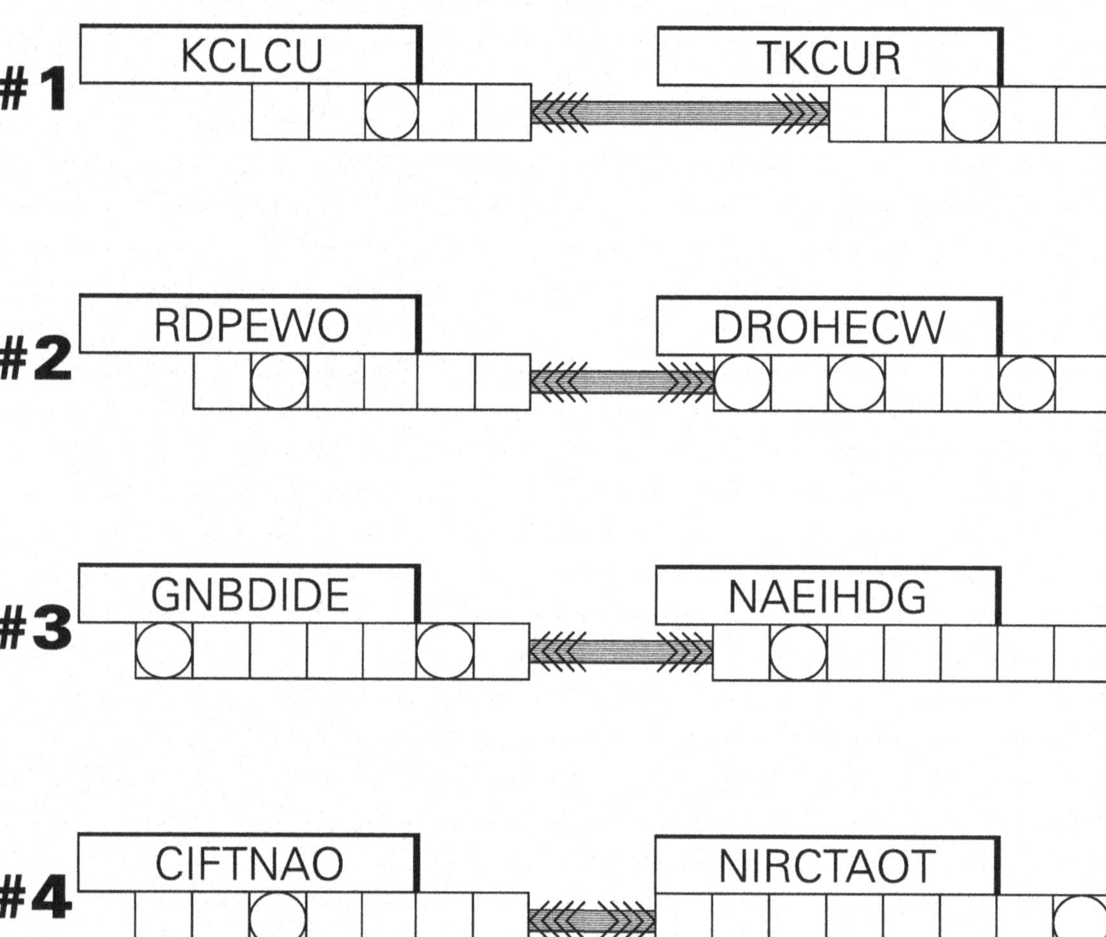

Arrange the circled letters to solve the mystery answer. (Form two words that rhyme.)

MYSTERY ANSWER

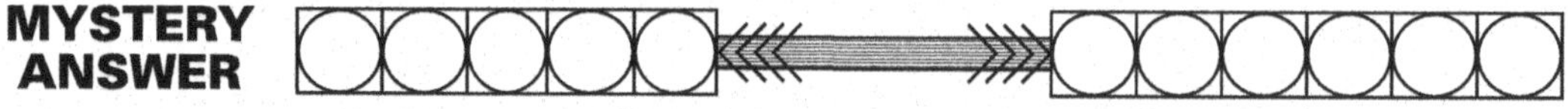

PUZZLE 8

SPORTS

JUMBLE BrainBusters

Unscramble the Jumbles, one letter to each square, to spell words related to sports.

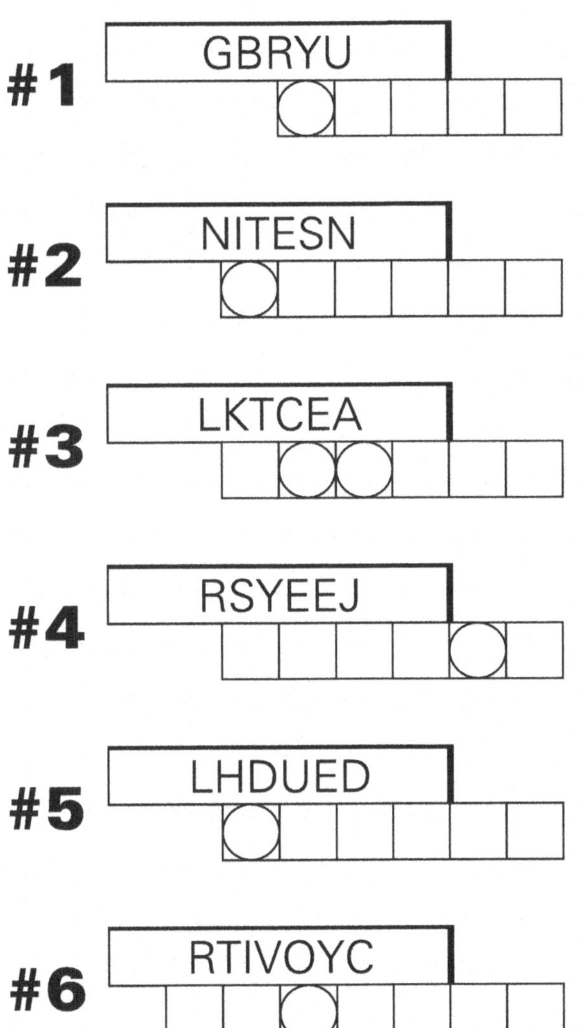

Interesting Sports Facts

In baseball, a "can of corn" refers to a fly ball that's easy to catch.

Kickers tend to score more points over their careers than any other player in pro football.

Arrange the circled letters to solve the mystery answer.

MYSTERY ANSWER

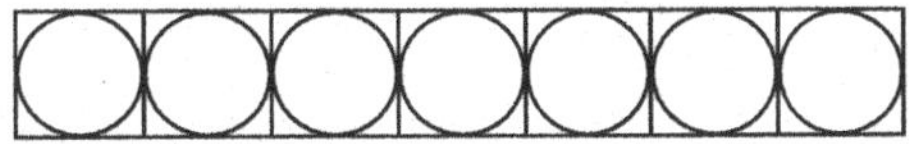

PLANET EARTH

JUMBLE BrainBusters

Unscramble the Jumbles, one letter to each square, to spell words related to planet Earth.

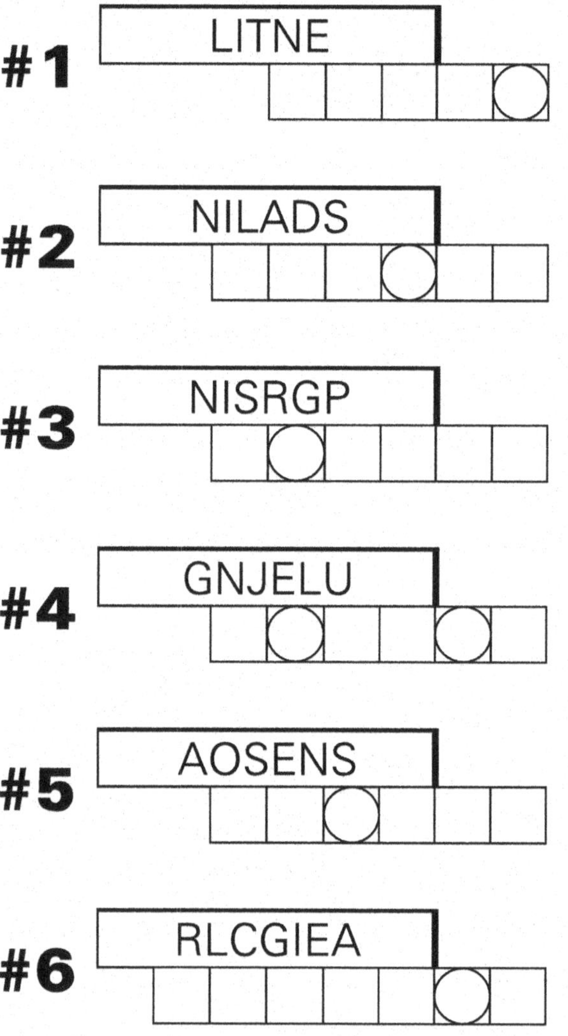

Box of Clues

Stumped? Maybe you can find a clue below.

- -Surrounded land mass
- -Huge mass of slowly flowing ice
- -Land densely overgrown with tropical vegetation
- -Natural division of the year
- -Elevated, comparatively level expanse of land
- -A recess, such as a bay or cove, along a coast
- -Small stream of water flowing naturally from the earth

Arrange the circled letters to solve the mystery answer.

MYSTERY ANSWER

PUZZLE 10

WARS AND THE MILITARY

JUMBLE BrainBusters

Unscramble the Jumbles, one letter to each square, to spell words related to wars and the military.

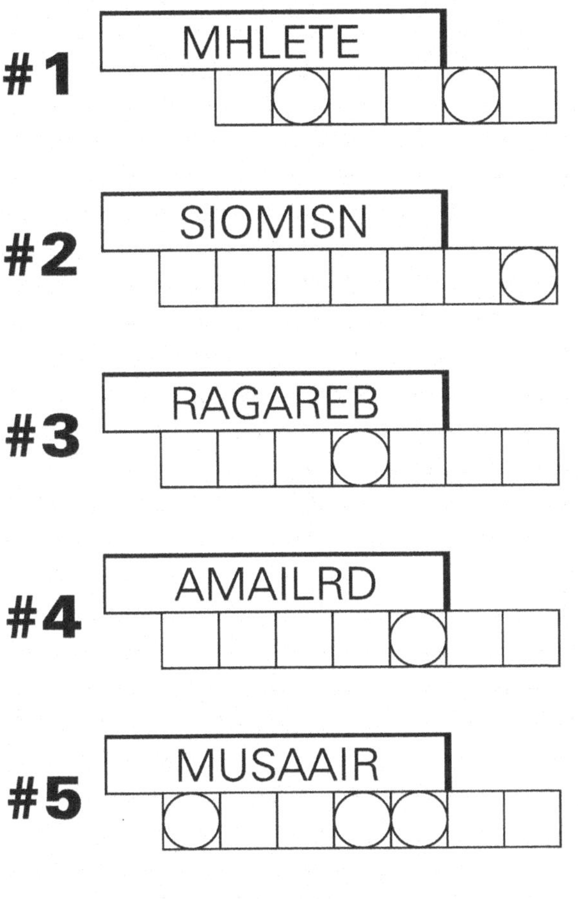

#1 MHLETE

#2 SIOMISN

#3 RAGAREB

#4 AMAILRD

#5 MUSAAIR

#6 MDOMNAC

Box of Clues

Stumped? Maybe you can find a clue below. (No clue for the mystery answer.)

- Heavy curtain of artillery fire
- The commander in chief of a fleet
- Protective headgear
- Order
- Assignment
- Japanese warrior

MYSTERY ANSWER

Arrange the circled letters to solve the mystery answer.

JUMBLE® JOKES

Unscramble the mixed up letters to reveal the punch lines as suggested by the jokes.

#1 What is drawn by everyone without pen or pencil?

TRBEHA

#2 What goes up and down but doesn't move?

TRASAISECA

#3 What has four legs and a back but no body?

ACIAHR

#4 What is the best day to go to the beach?

ANSUYD

#5 What insect runs away from everything?

AFAEL

#6 What kind of cup doesn't hold water?

AKCAUEPC

MYSTERY PERSON

JUMBLE BrainBusters

Unscramble the Jumbles, one letter to each square, to spell words that relate to the mystery person.

#1 LSRELSU

#2 NEDWUDO

#3 TRAJIYMO

#4 BOTOLALF

#5 CABRLINPUE

Box of Clues

Stumped? Maybe you can find a clue below.

-He played this sport in high school
-He was born in ______, Kansas
-He's a former ______ leader of the senate
-His political party affiliation
-He was severely ______ in WWII

Arrange the circled letters to solve the mystery person.

MYSTERY PERSON

PUZZLE 13

ALL ABOUT FOOD

JUMBLE BrainBusters

Unscramble the Jumbles, one letter to each square, to spell words related to food.

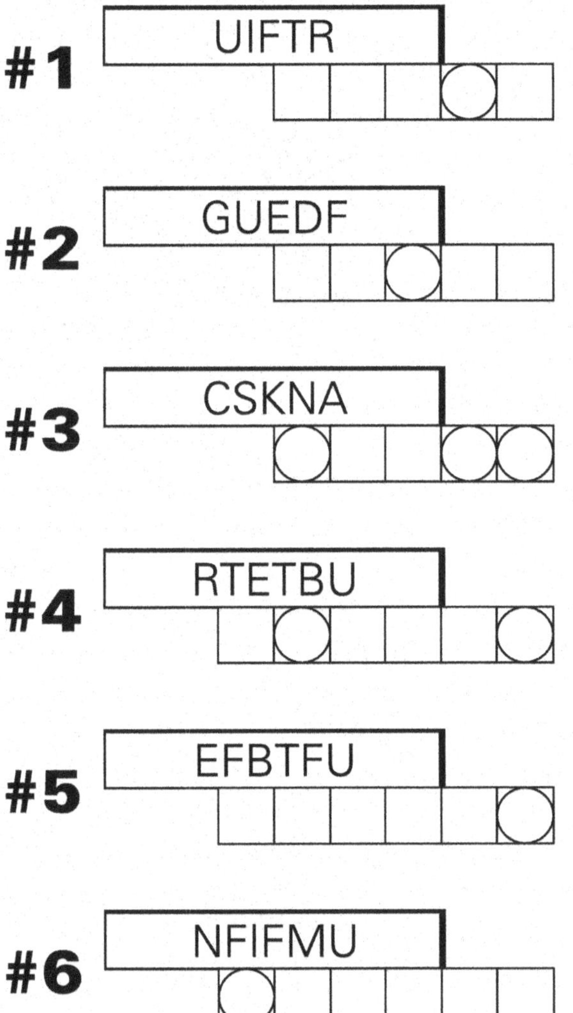

#1 UIFTR

#2 GUEDF

#3 CSKNA

#4 RTETBU

#5 EFBTFU

#6 NFIFMU

Interesting Food Facts

You have to eat about 10 pounds of potatoes to put on one pound of weight.

The darker the olive, the higher the oil content.

Arrange the circled letters to solve the mystery answer.

MYSTERY ANSWER

PUZZLE 14

MAGNUM, P.I.

JUMBLE BrainBusters

Unscramble the Jumbles, one letter to each square, to spell words related to the television show *Magnum, P.I.*.

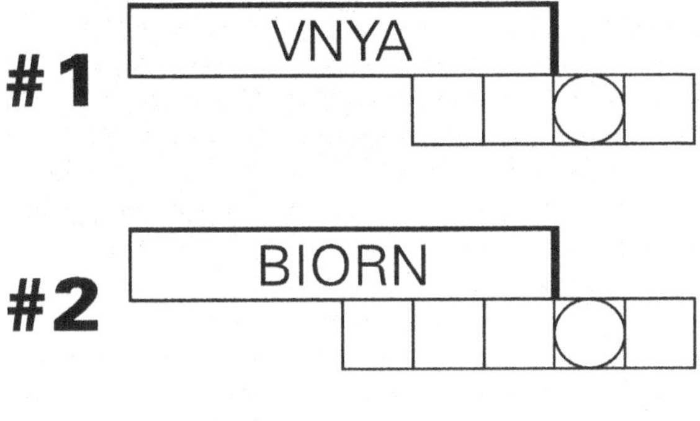

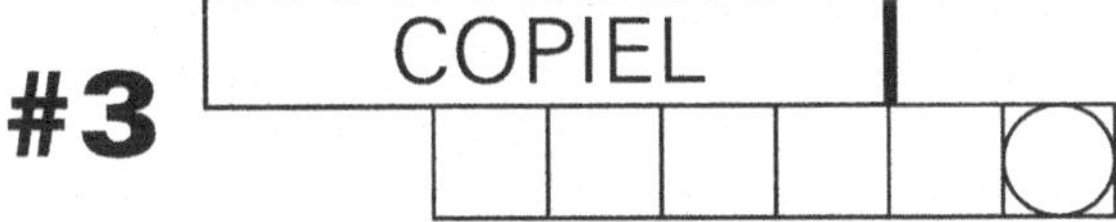

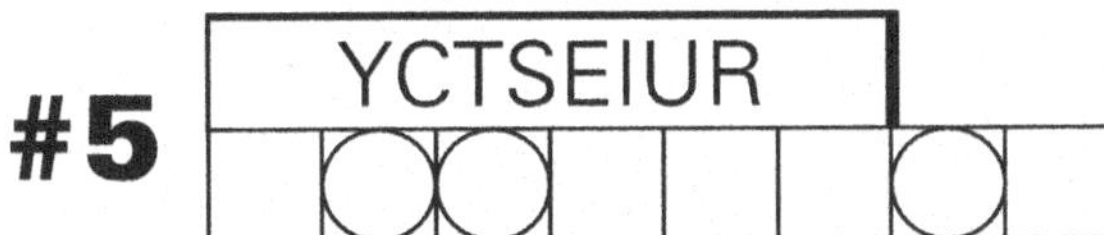

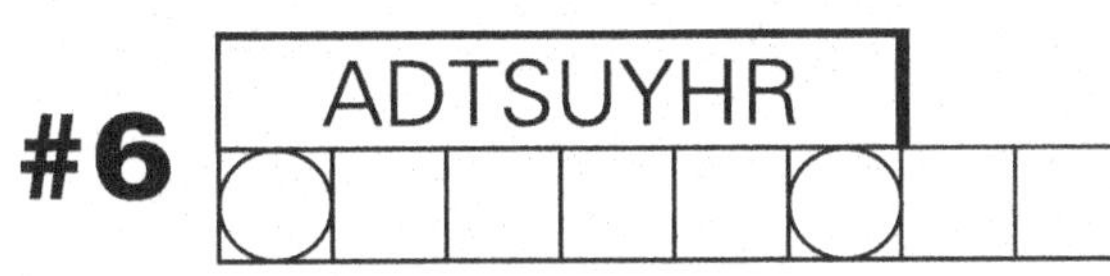

Box of Clues

Stumped? Maybe you can find a clue below. (No clue for the mystery answer.)

- -Lt. Tanaka's force
- -*Magnum, P.I.*'s night from 1981 to 1986
- -Service provided by Thomas to the Masters estate
- -This character was voiced by Orson Welles
- -Magnum's ride
- -Thomas served in this branch of the service

MYSTERY ANSWER

Arrange the circled letters to solve the mystery answer.

PUZZLE 15

UN-MIX AND MATCH
ACTRESSES

Section 1: Unscramble the mixed-up letters, one letter to each square, to spell names of actresses.

#1 LYSLA DILEF

#2 MLAAS EAKHY

#3 ADINE NEKOAT

#4 LHAYES DJDU

Arrange the circled letters to solve the mystery answer.

MYSTERY ANSWER

Section 2: Match the answers in the puzzle (including the mystery answer) to the following clues. (Write "MA." to represent the mystery answer.)

#____ This actress was born on April 19, 1968, in Granada Hills, California. Her mother and sister are musicians.

#____ This actress was born on January 5, 1946, in Los Angeles, California. In 1970, Woody Allen cast her in his Broadway play *Play It Again, Sam.*

#____ This actress was born on November 6, 1946, in Pasadena, California. She dated Burt Reynolds for a number of years.

#____ This actress was born on June 15, 1963, in Culver City, California. She made her TV acting debut at age eight.

#____ This actress was born on September 2, 1966, in Coatzacoalcos, Veracruz, Mexico. She began her career on Mexican TV soap operas in the late eighties.

PUZZLE 16

JUMBLE® TRIVIA

JUMBLE® BrainBusters

Unscramble the Jumbles, one letter to each square, to spell words as suggested by the trivia clues.

#1 ______ Randolph Hearst died in 1951.

#1 LIMAWIL

#2 ______ is a leading producer of blueberries.

#2 EIMAN

#3 Anthony ______ became a U.S. citizen in 2000, but is allowed to retain his British knighthood and the title of sir.

#3 KNPISOH

#4 ______ is the oldest continuously inhabited city in the world.

#4 SCADAUSM

#5 Noah ______ was referred to as "the walking question mark" while he was at Yale.

#5 TSWREEB

Arrange the circled letters to solve the mystery answer.

The ______ ______ was built in the 11th century.

MYSTERY ANSWER

PUZZLE 17

MEANS THE SAME

JUMBLE BrainBusters

Unscramble the Jumbles, one letter to each square, to spell pairs of words that have the same or similar meanings.

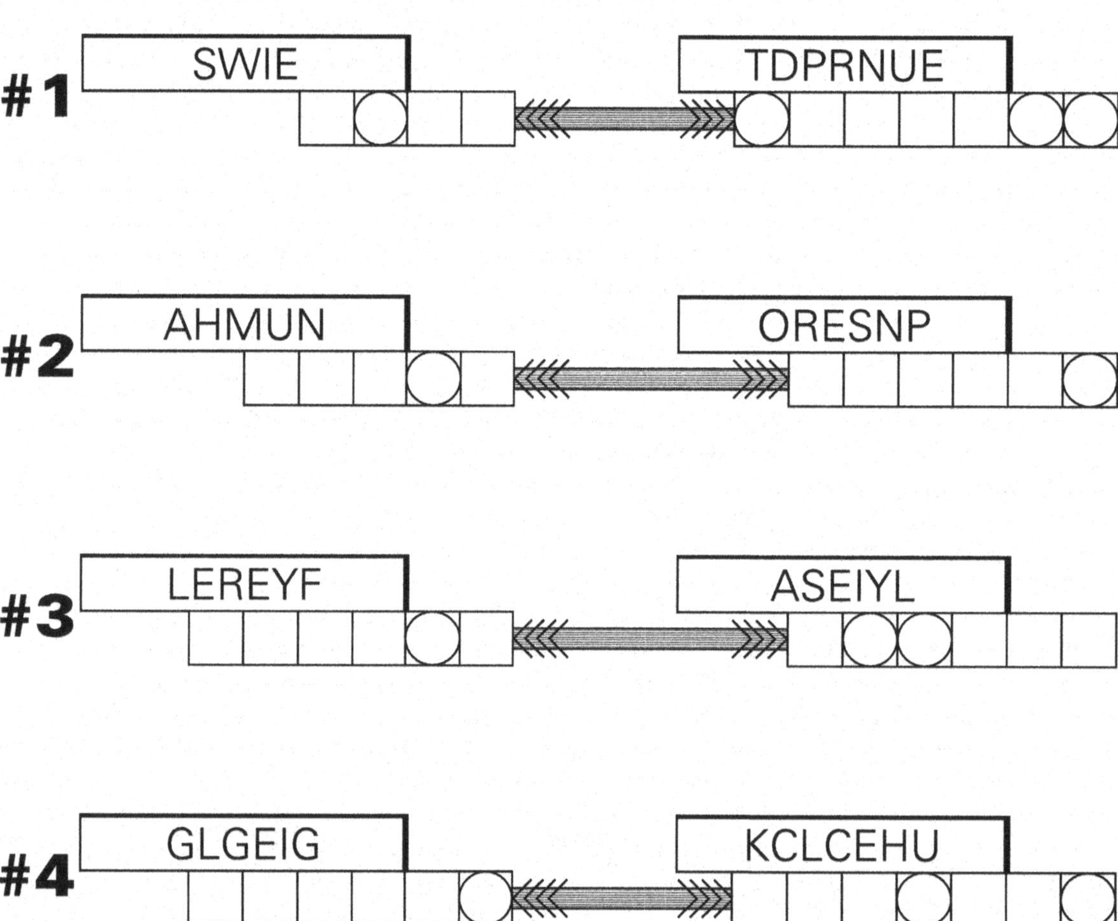

Arrange the circled letters to solve the mystery answer.
(Form two words that have the same or similar meanings.)

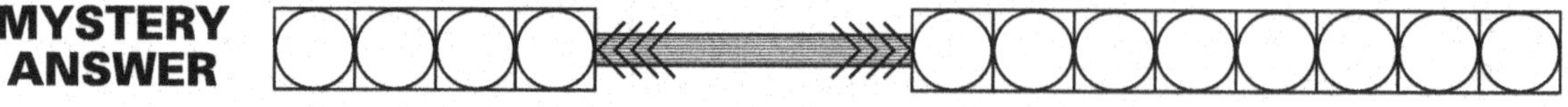

ALL ABOUT PLANTS

JUMBLE BrainBusters

Unscramble the Jumbles, one letter to each square, to spell words related to plants.

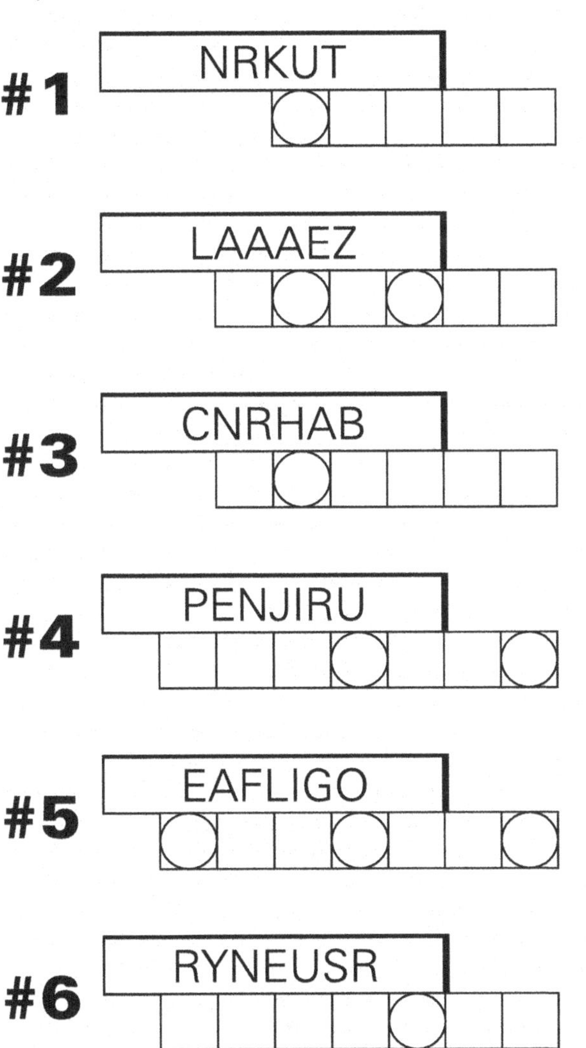

#1 NRKUT

#2 LAAAEZ

#3 CNRHAB

#4 PENJIRU

#5 EAFLIGO

#6 RYNEUSR

Box of Clues

Stumped? Maybe you can find a clue below. (No clue for the mystery answer.)

- Limb
- Leaves
- Main, woody stem of a tree
- Type of evergreen
- Plant growing area
- Flowering plant

MYSTERY ANSWER

Arrange the circled letters to solve the mystery answer.

PUZZLE 19

MEANS THE OPPOSITE

JUMBLE BrainBusters

Unscramble the Jumbles, one letter to each square, to spell pairs of words that have opposite or nearly opposite meanings.

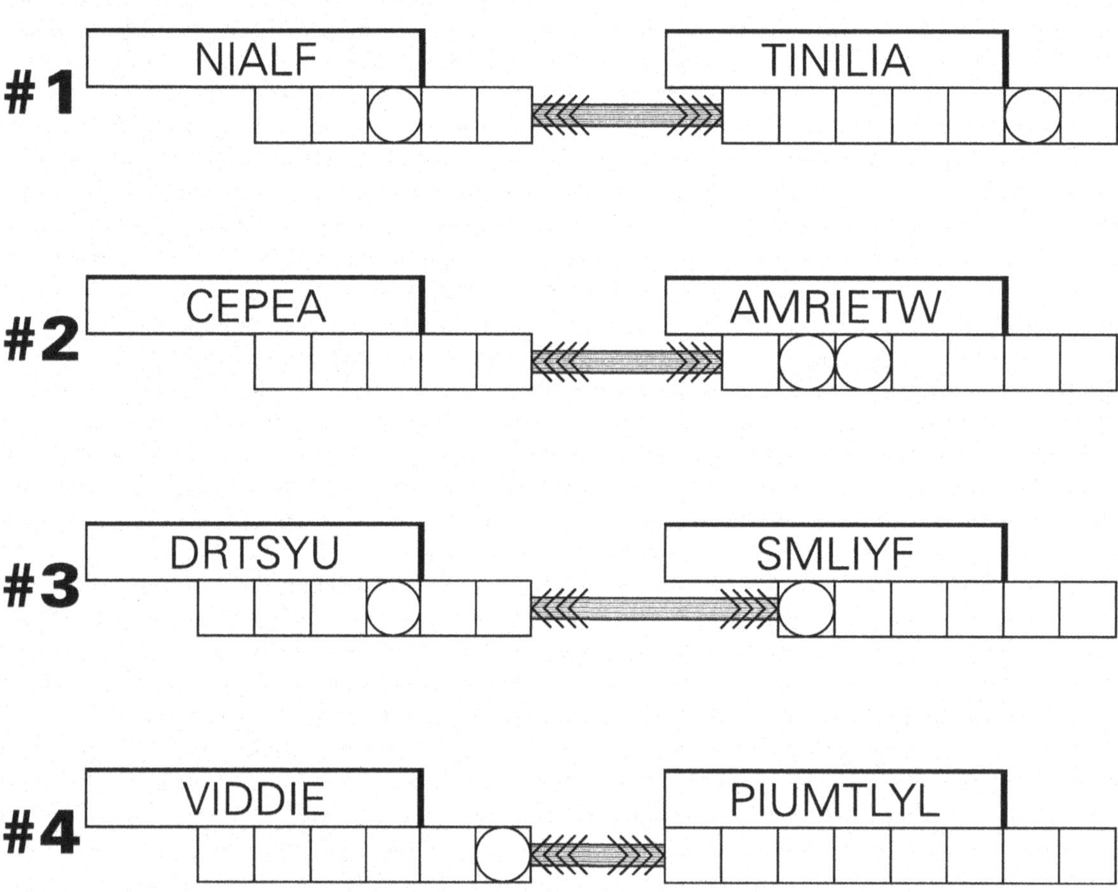

Arrange the circled letters to solve the mystery answer. (Form two words that have the opposite or nearly opposite meanings.)

MYSTERY ANSWER

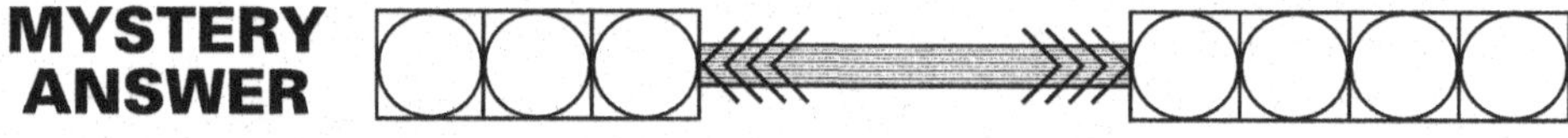

PUZZLE 20

IT'S GO TIME

JUMBLE BrainBusters

Unscramble the Jumbles, one letter to each square, to spell words that start with *GO*.

GOWN
GOBLET
GOSPEL
GOGGLES
GODDESS

#1

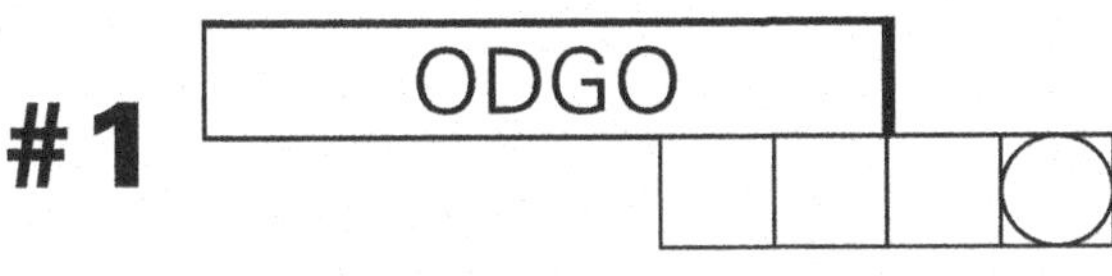

#2

#3

LOGINB

#4

#5

#6

Box of Clues

Stumped? Maybe you can find a clue below. (No clue for the mystery answer.)

-Nicklaus or Palmer
-Burrowing rodent
-Acceptable
-Received
-Pumpkin relative
-Elfin creature of folklore

Arrange the circled letters to solve the mystery answer.

MYSTERY ANSWER

ALL ABOUT DOGS

JUMBLE® BrainBusters

Unscramble the Jumbles, one letter to each square, to spell words related to dogs.

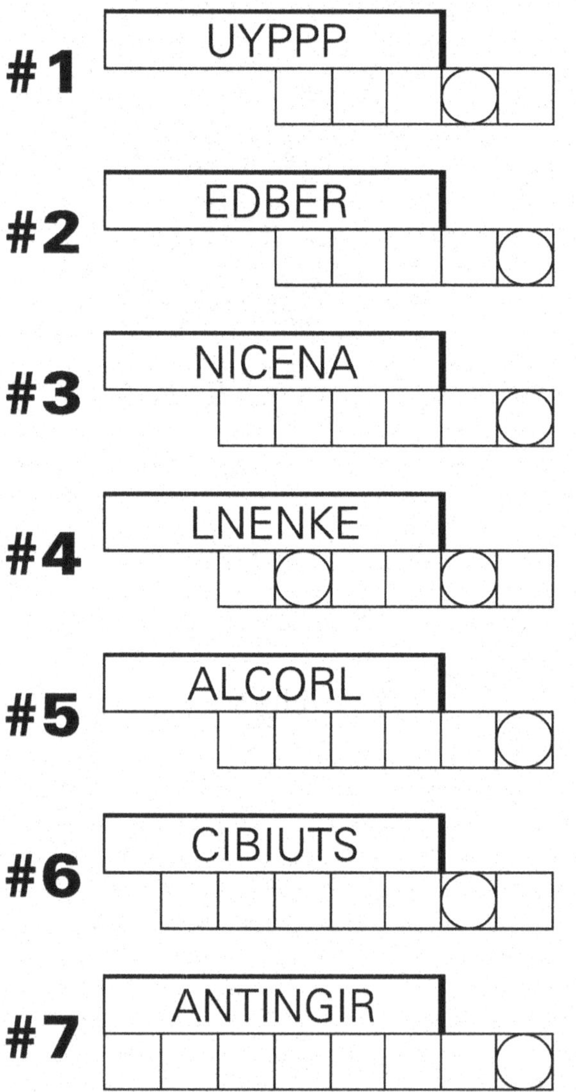

Box of Clues

Stumped? Maybe you can find a clue below.

-A group developed by artificial selection
-Dog family
-Dog's worn accessory
-Lineage
-Educational program for a dog
-Dog shelter
-Young dog
-Dog treat

MYSTERY ANSWER

Arrange the circled letters to solve the mystery answer.

PUZZLE 22

DOUBLE JUMBLE® BRAINBUSTERS

Unscramble the Jumbles, one letter to each square, to spell words.

#1 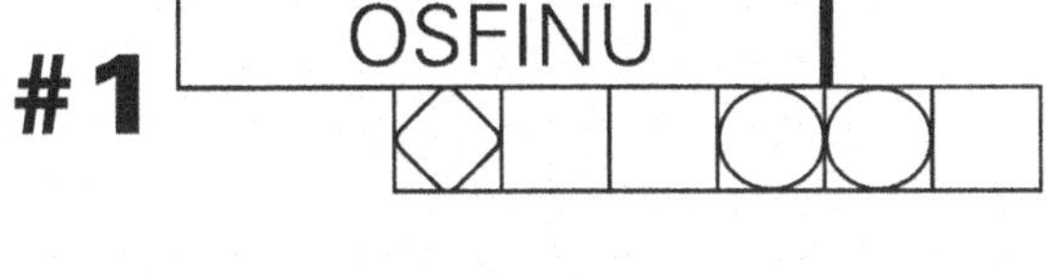

#2 

#3 

#4 

#5 

#6 

JUMBLE® BrainBusters

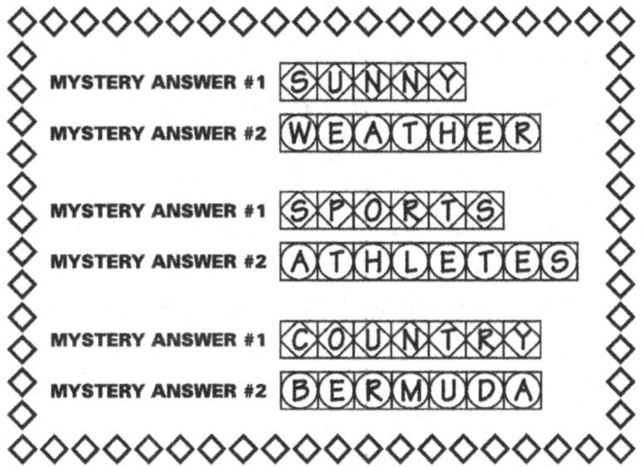

Box of Clues

Stumped? Maybe you can find a clue below. (No clues for the mystery answers.)

-______ practice
-Rigid device used to prevent motion
-Type of nuclear reaction
-Heritage
-Group of singers
-Performing

Arrange the diamonded letters to solve mystery answer #1. Arrange the circled letters to solve mystery answer #2.
(The mystery answers will relate to each other.)

MYSTERY ANSWER #1 

MYSTERY ANSWER #2

PUZZLE 23

COMPUTERS

JUMBLE BrainBusters

Unscramble the Jumbles, one letter to each square, to spell words related to computers.

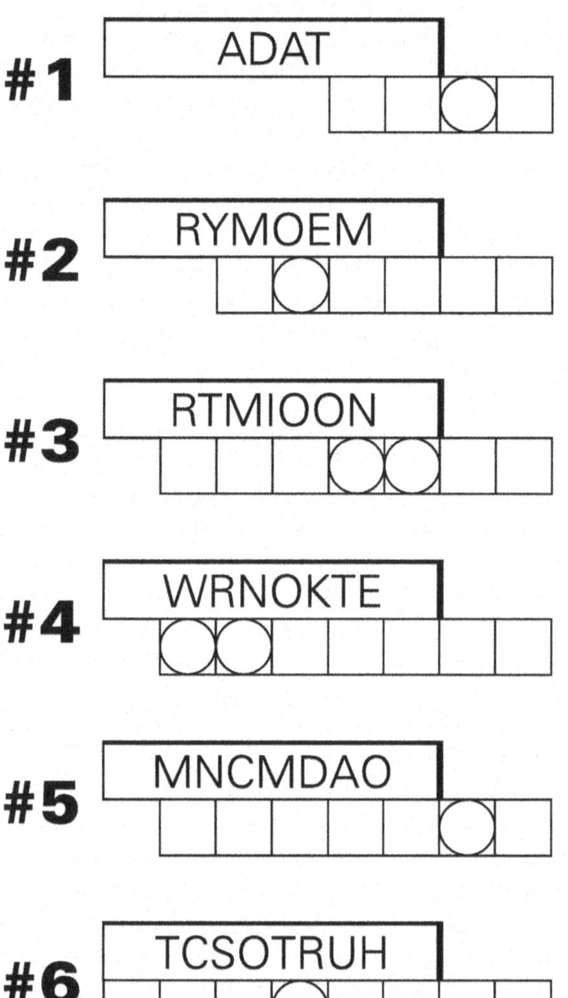

Box of Clues

Stumped? Maybe you can find a clue below. (No clue for the mystery answer.)

-Starts with *M*; ends with *Y*
-Starts with *N*; ends with *K*
-Starts with *M*; ends with *R*
-Starts with *S*; ends with *T*
-Starts with *C*; ends with *D*
-Starts with *D*; ends with *A*

Arrange the circled letters to solve the mystery answer.

MYSTERY ANSWER

PUZZLE 24

BIRDS

JUMBLE BrainBusters

Unscramble the Jumbles, one letter to each square, to spell varieties of birds.

#1 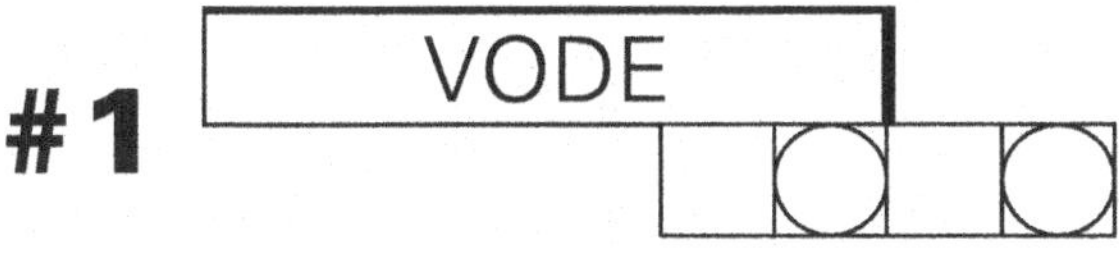

#2 

#3 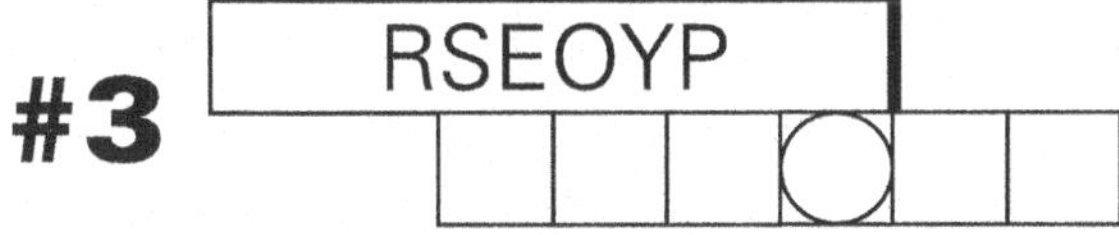

#4 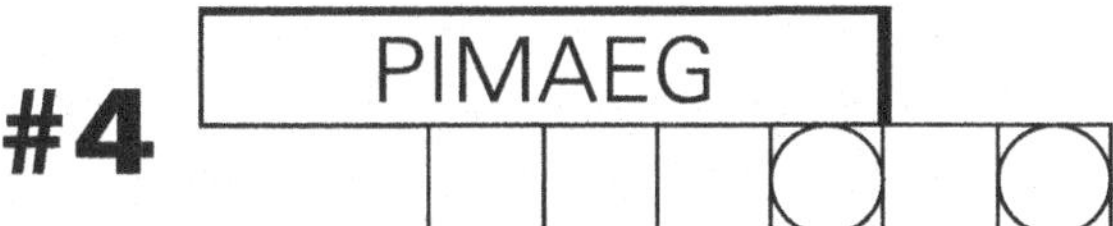

#5 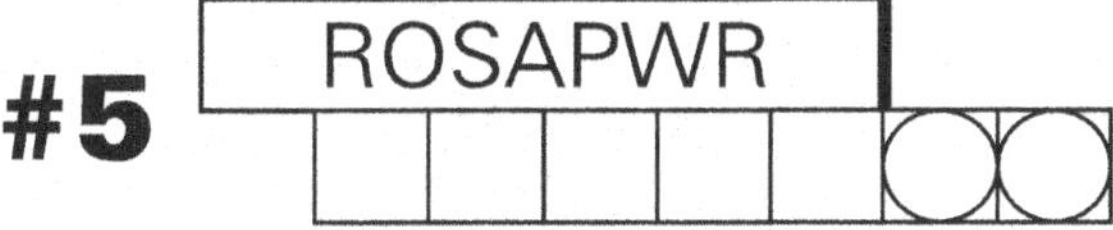

#6 

Box of Clues

Stumped? Maybe you can find a clue below. (No clue for the mystery answer.)

-Starts with *T*; ends with *Y*
-Starts with *M*; ends with *E*
-Starts with *C*; ends with *L*
-Starts with *D*; ends with *E*
-Starts with *O*; ends with *Y*
-Starts with *S*; ends with *W*

Arrange the circled letters to solve the mystery answer.

MYSTERY ANSWER

PUZZLE 25

TRIPLE JUMBLE® BRAINBUSTERS

Unscramble the Jumbles, one letter to each square, to spell words.

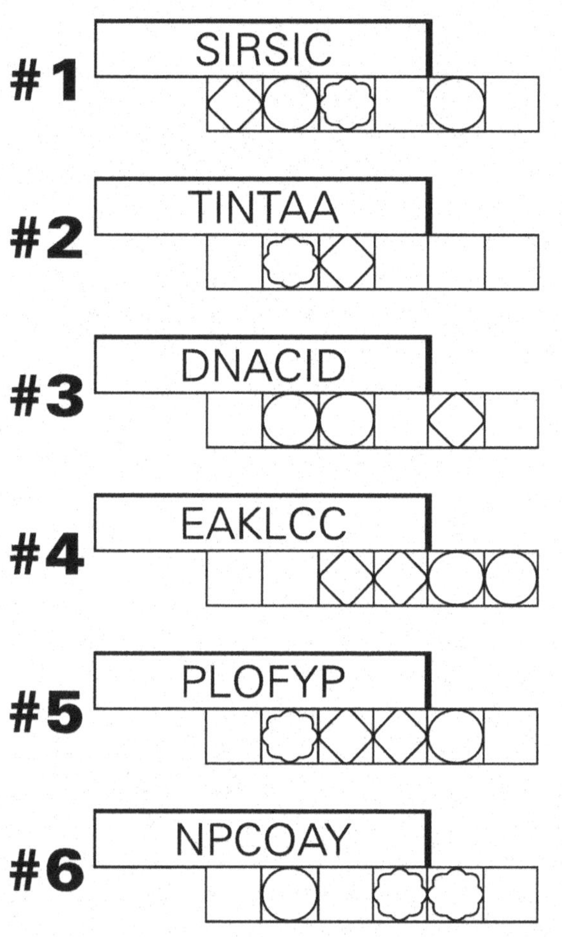

JUMBLE® BrainBusters

MYSTERY ANSWER #1 CHEF
MYSTERY ANSWER #2 BROIL
MYSTERY ANSWER #3 SEAFOOD

MYSTERY ANSWER #1 FISH
MYSTERY ANSWER #2 TROUT
MYSTERY ANSWER #3 UPSTREAM

Box of Clues

Stumped? Maybe you can find a clue below. (No clues for the mystery answers.)

- -Laugh
- -Rooflike cover
- -_______ disk
- -Frank
- -Gain, reach
- -Unstable condition or situation

Arrange the clouded letters to solve mystery answer #1. Arrange the diamonded letters to solve mystery answer #2. Arrange the circled letters to solve mystery answer #3. (The mystery answers will relate to each other.)

MYSTERY ANSWER #1

MYSTERY ANSWER #2

MYSTERY ANSWER #3

PUZZLE 26

UN-MIX AND MATCH

U.S. STATE CAPITALS

JUMBLE BrainBusters

Section 1: Unscramble the mixed-up letters, one letter to each square, to spell U.S. state capitals.

#1 SILANGN

#2 PLYIOAM

#3 NORIMHDC

#4 MCOULUSB

Arrange the circled letters to solve the mystery answer.

MYSTERY ANSWER

Section 2: Match the answers in the puzzle (including the mystery answer) to the following clues. (Write "M.A." to represent the mystery answer.)

#____ Capital of the "Buckeye State."

#____ Capital of the "Wolverine State."

#____ Capital of the "Hoosier State."

#____ Capital of the "Evergreen State."

#____ Capital of the "Old Dominion."

PUZZLE 27

GO FOR IT

JUMBLE BrainBusters

Unscramble the Jumbles, one letter to each square, to spell words that contain *GO*.

WAGON
ANGOLA
LAGOON
ONGOING
HANGOVER

#1

GBOIN

#2
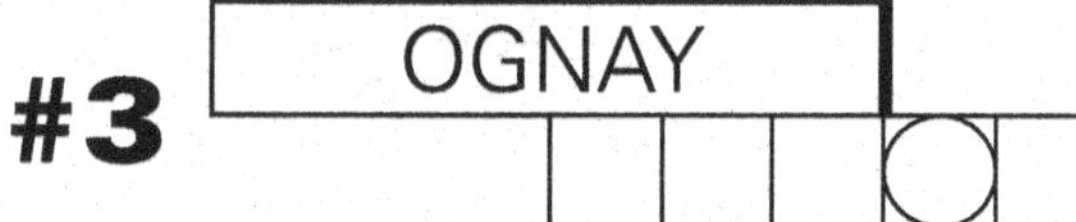
RGAOC

#3
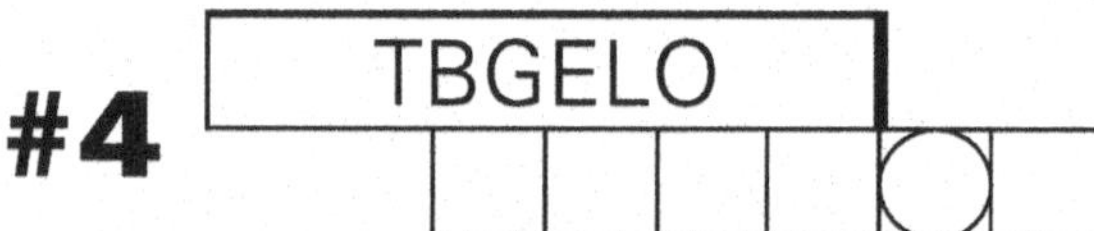
OGNAY

#4
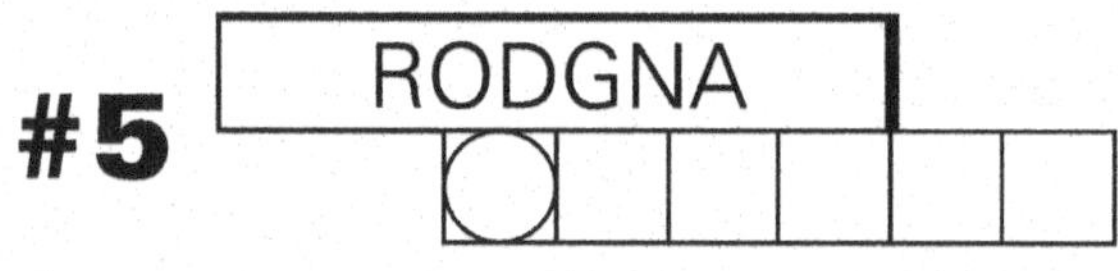
TBGELO

#5
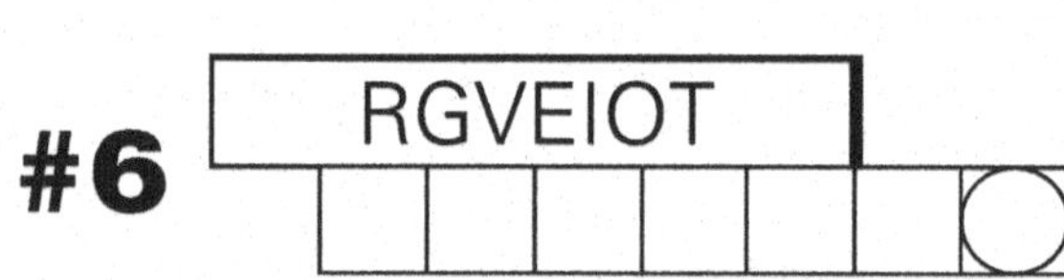
RODGNA

#6

RGVEIOT

Box of Clues

Stumped? Maybe you can find a clue below. (No clue for the mystery answer.)

- -Mythical monster
- -Type of game
- -Dizzy sensation
- -Freight
- -Suffering of intense physical or mental pain
- -Drinking vessel

Arrange the circled letters to solve the mystery answer.

MYSTERY ANSWER

PUZZLE 28

FIND THE JUMBLES®

JUMBLE® BrainBusters

Unscramble the Jumbles, one letter to each square, to spell words.

#1 SDKE

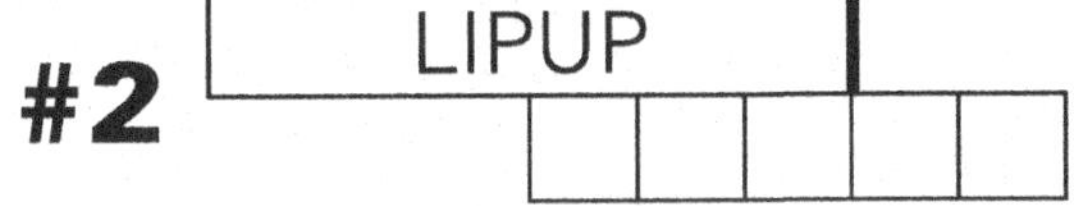

#2 LIPUP

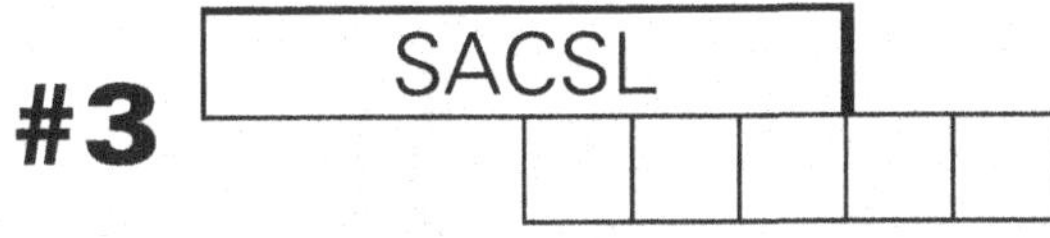

#3 SACSL

#4 COSOLH

#5 TCEUEAD

#6 TBSJEUC

#7 GLOELEC

#8 RNNLEIGA

Find and circle the answers (from above) in the grid of letters below.

A E D J D Z G K T B L I T D L B
O P U P I L S I G S V E C R A S
G H S P W E G N U F G M E H F S
J E O C D P I E H E W R J E C A
B O C X H N X F L Z C L B P R L
F A H G R O H L X Y B E U Y E C
I B F A J M O Z P A M N S O I G
J I E H F C I L M I G I N F A J
C L O B F E D U C A T E J B E N

PUZZLE 29

JUMBLE® JOKES

Unscramble the mixed up letters to reveal the punch lines as suggested by the jokes.

#1 What people travel the most?

NARSOM

#2 Who never gets his hair wet in the shower?

MADNLABA

#3 What belongs to you, but is used more by others?

ARYEOMUN

#4 What goes to sleep with its shoes on?

RSHEOA

#5 What piece of wood is like a king?

ELAURR

#6 What turns everything around but doesn't move?

RMRIROA

PUZZLE 30

JUMBLE® TRIVIA

Unscramble the Jumbles, one letter to each square, to spell words as suggested by the trivia clues.

#1 The ______ Dam was built in less than five years.

#1 VOHROE

#2 This animal, which is sometimes called a "sand rat," is native to Africa and Asia.

#2 EBGLIR

#3 This U.S. city was named for the U.S. vice president under James Polk.

#3 ALLDSA

#4 The average life span of a ______ is about 20 years.

#4 OSMEO

#5 On March 18, 1925, a tornado tore through Illinois, Indiana, and ______, killing 695 people.

#5 SIUMSOIR

Arrange the circled letters to solve the mystery answer.

Private automobiles were not allowed in ______ until 1948.

MYSTERY ANSWER

PUZZLE 31

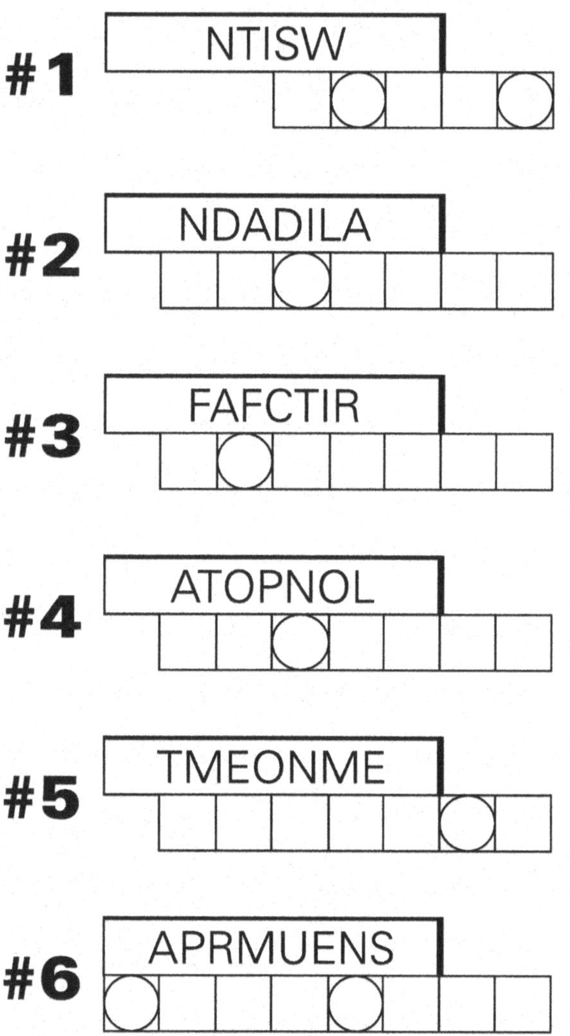

MOVIES

Unscramble the mixed-up letters, one letter to each square, to spell movie titles.

#1 NTISW

#2 NDADILA

#3 FAFCTIR

#4 ATOPNOL

#5 TMEONME

#6 APRMUENS

Box of Clues

Stumped? Maybe you can find a clue below.

-2000 movie starring Michael Douglas and Benicio Del Toro
-1988 movie starring Danny DeVito and Arnold Schwarzenegger
-1977 blockbuster
-1978 movie about a comic book hero
-1986 Best Picture
-1992 movie featuring the voice of Robin Williams
-2000 Guy Pearce movie

Arrange the circled letters to solve the mystery answer.

MYSTERY ANSWER

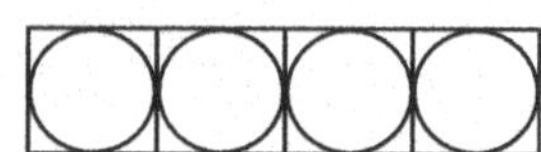

PUZZLE 32

MATH

JUMBLE BrainBusters

Unscramble the Jumbles, one letter to each square, so that each equation is correct.

For example: NONTEOEOW
ONE + ONE = TWO

#1 WORTOWTOUF

☐☐☐☐ ÷ ☐☐☐ = ☐☐☐

#2 FTORRNUEOEHE

☐☐☐ + ☐☐☐☐☐ = ☐☐☐☐

#3 ZZROEROEZROE

☐☐☐☐ × ☐☐☐☐ = ☐☐☐☐

#4 RWFETEEVHTIO

☐☐☐☐ − ☐☐☐ = ☐☐☐☐☐

#5 RRZFOEORUFUO

☐☐☐☐ + ☐☐☐☐ = ☐☐☐☐

Arrange the circled letters to solve the mystery equation.

MYSTERY EQUATION

☐☐☐☐ − ☐☐☐☐☐ = ☐☐☐

PUZZLE 33

NEIGHBORS

JUMBLE BrainBusters

Unscramble the Jumbles, one letter to each square, to spell pairs of U.S. states that border each other.

IOWA	MINNESOTA
UTAH	ARIZONA
OREGON	CALIFORNIA
TEXAS	LOUISIANA

#1 AHUT — ROCODAOL

#2 NINIAAD — HAIGMINC

#3 NIVIGAIR — LNAYDMRA

#4 HOMLAAKO — ARANSASK

Arrange the circled letters to solve the mystery answer.

MYSTERY ANSWER

PUZZLE 34

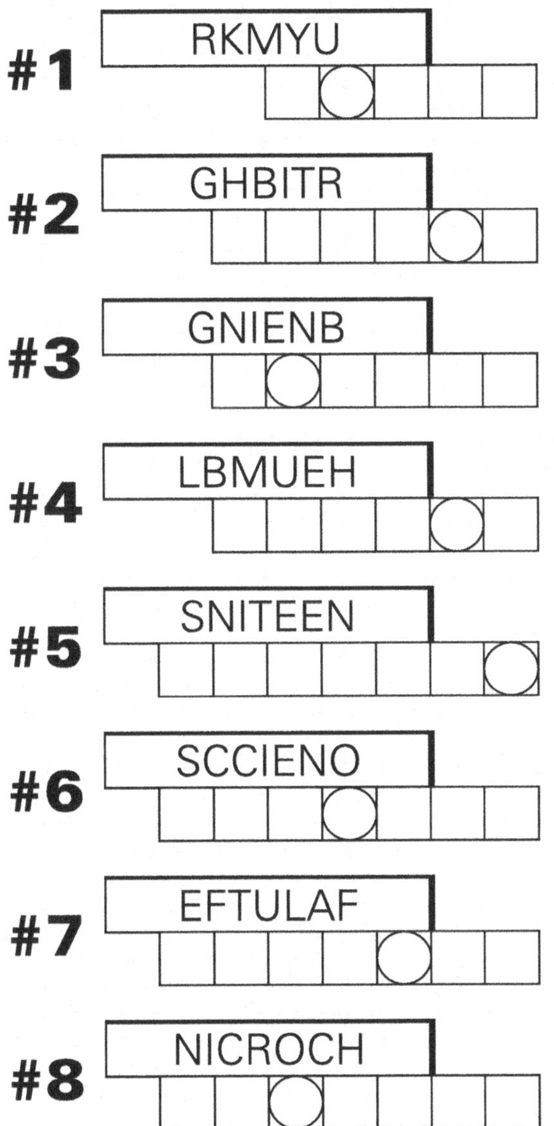

JUMBLE BrainBusters

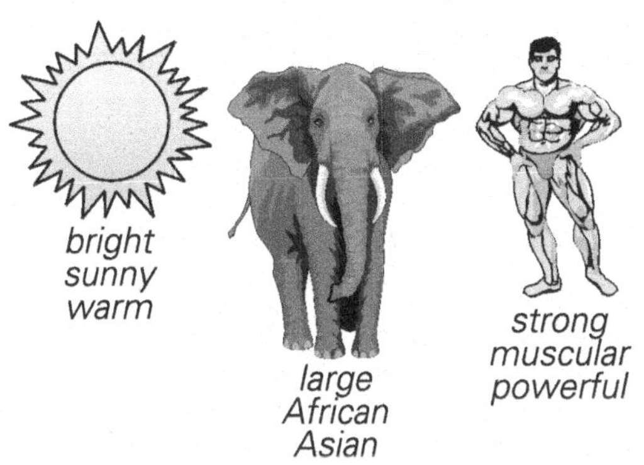

Box of Clues

Stumped? Maybe you can find a clue below.

- -Portending future disaster
- -Lingering, persistent
- -Lacking vividness in color
- -Smart
- -Chipper
- -Not life threatening
- -Deep, strong
- -Modest
- -Succinct

Arrange the circled letters to solve the mystery answer.

MYSTERY ANSWER

PUZZLE 35

JUMBLE® JOKES

Unscramble the mixed up letters to reveal the punch lines as suggested by the jokes.

#1 What fly has laryngitis?

FEAOYSRLH

#2 Who has friends for lunch?

NACNALAIB

#3 What can stay hot in the refrigerator?

ATSUDRM

#4 What is an ant dictator?

NRATYTA

#5 What is the most valuable fish?

FDAOISLHG

#6 What do liars do after they die?

LSLITILE

PUZZLE 36

UN-MIX AND MATCH ACTORS

JUMBLE BrainBusters

Section 1: Unscramble the mixed-up letters, one letter to each square, to spell names of actors.

#1 LIBL RAUYRM

#2 ECAL NDAILBW

#3 NEKIV NAOCB

#4 LNITC DWOATESO

Arrange the circled letters to solve the mystery answer. **MYSTERY ANSWER**

Section 2: Match the answers in the puzzle (including the mystery answer) to the following clues. (Write " M.A." to represent the mystery answer.)

#____ This actor was born on July 8, 1958, in Philadelphia, Pennsylvania. He is married to actress Kyra Sedgwick.

#____ This actor was born on April 3, 1958, in Massapequa, New York. He has brothers who are also actors.

#____ This actor was born on May 31, 1930, in San Francisco, California. He received an "American Film Institute Life Achievement Award" in 1996.

#____ This actor was born on March 19, 1955, in Idar-Oberstein, West Germany. He was married to a well-known actress for 13 years.

#____ This actor was born on September 21, 1950, in Wilmette, Illinois. He was a regular on *Saturday Night Live*.

PUZZLE 37

BEWITCHED

JUMBLE BrainBusters

Unscramble the Jumbles, one letter to each square, to spell words related to the television show *Bewitched.*

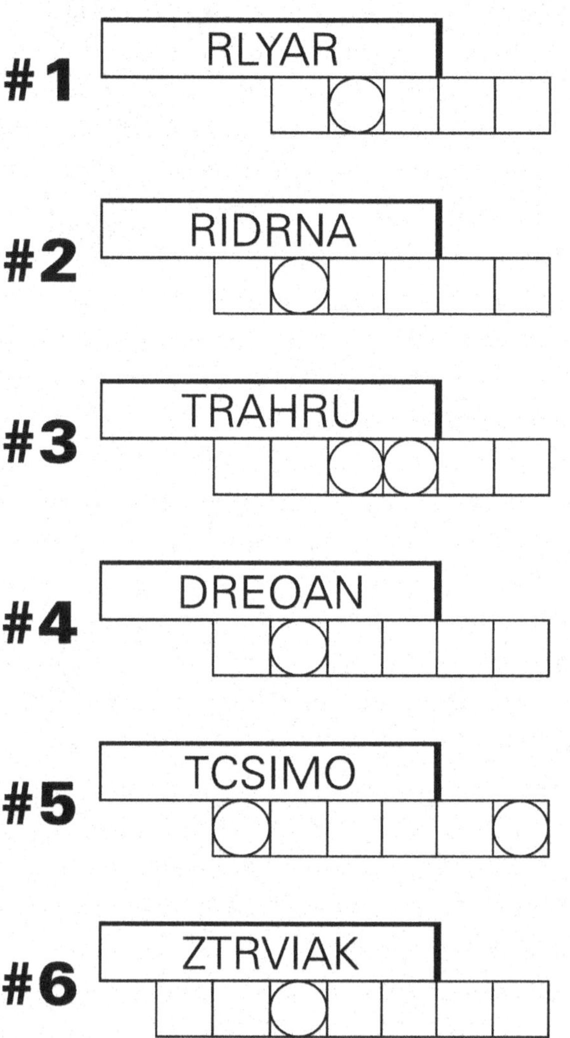

Box of Clues

Stumped? Maybe you can find a clue below. (No clue for the mystery answer.)

- -Samantha's uncle
- -______ Tate
- -Type of show
- -Role played by Dick York and Dick Sargent
- -Samantha's mother
- -Abner and Gladys ______

Arrange the circled letters to solve the mystery answer.

MYSTERY ANSWER

MAMMALS

JUMBLE BrainBusters

Unscramble the Jumbles, one letter to each square, to spell names of mammals.

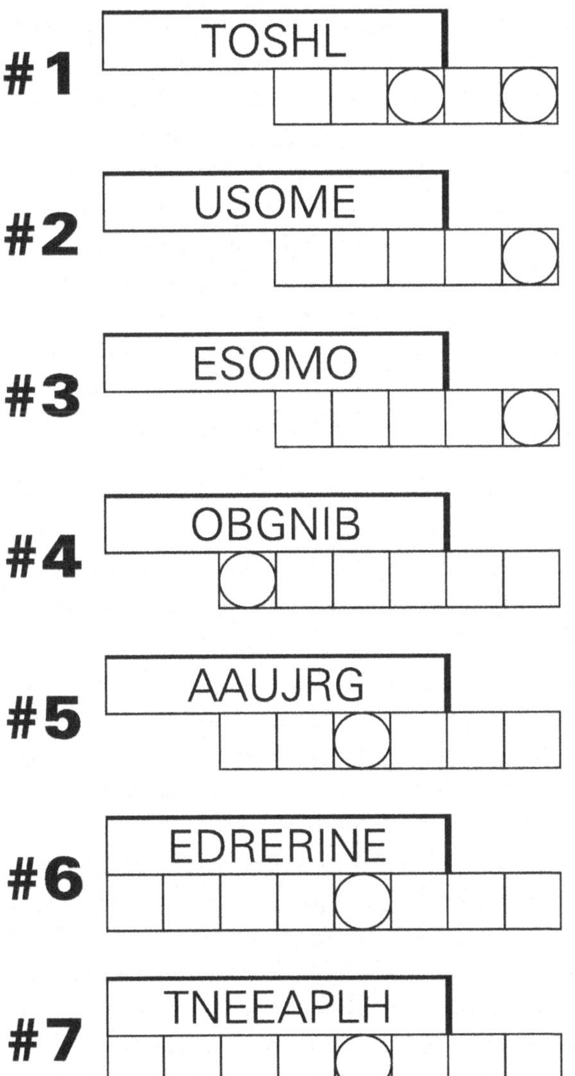

#1 TOSHL

#2 USOME

#3 ESOMO

#4 OBGNIB

#5 AAUJRG

#6 EDRERINE

#7 TNEEAPLH

Box of Clues

Stumped? Maybe you can find a clue below. (No clue for the mystery answer.)

- -Starts with *G*; ends with *N*
- -Starts with *M*; ends with *E*
- -Starts with *E*; ends with *T*
- -Starts with *M*; ends with *E*
- -Starts with *S*; ends with *H*
- -Starts with *R*; ends with *R*
- -Starts with *J*; ends with *R*

Arrange the circled letters to solve the mystery answer.

MYSTERY ANSWER

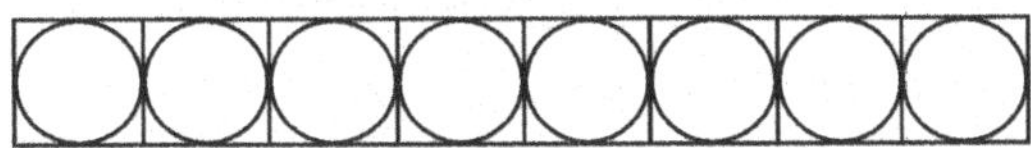

PUZZLE 39

JUMBLE BrainBusters

WEATHER

Unscramble the Jumbles, one letter to each square, to spell words related to weather.

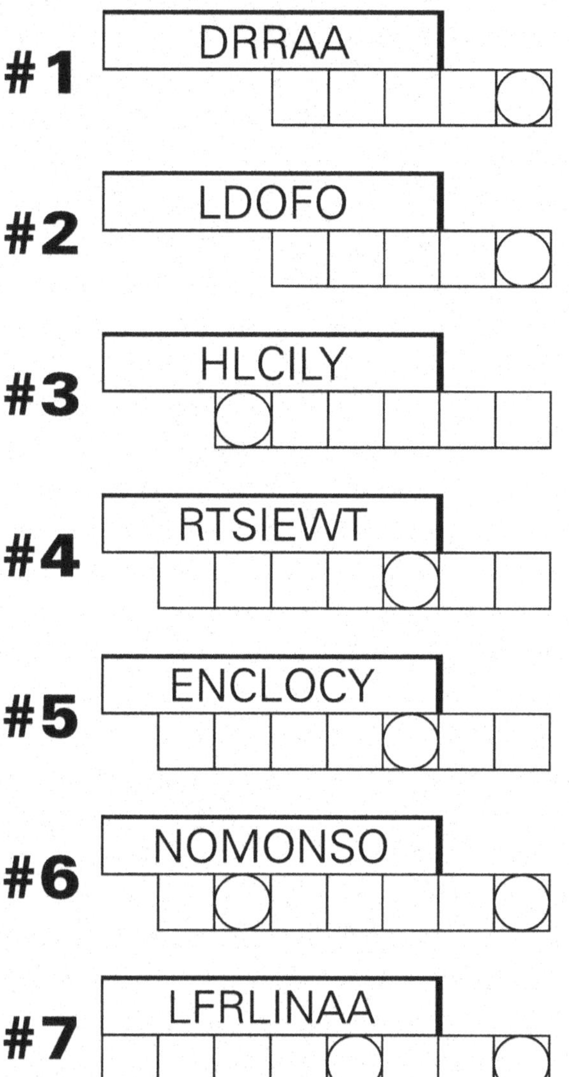

Box of Clues

Stumped? Maybe you can find a clue below. (No clue for the mystery answer.)

-Starts with *C*; ends with *E*
-Starts with *C*; ends with *Y*
-Starts with *R*; ends with *R*
-Starts with *T*; ends with *R*
-Starts with *M*; ends with *N*
-Starts with *R*; ends with *L*
-Starts with *F*; ends with *D*

Arrange the circled letters to solve the mystery answer.

MYSTERY ANSWER

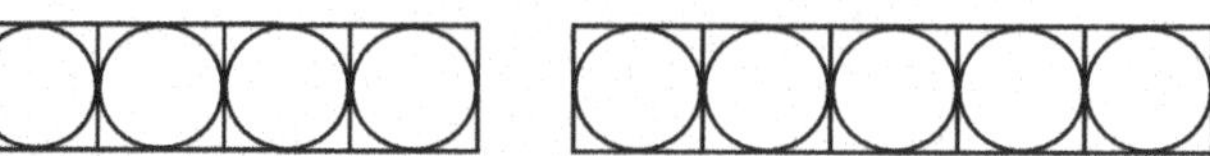

PUZZLE 40

HUMAN BODY

JUMBLE® BrainBusters

Unscramble the Jumbles, one letter to each square, to spell words related to the human body.

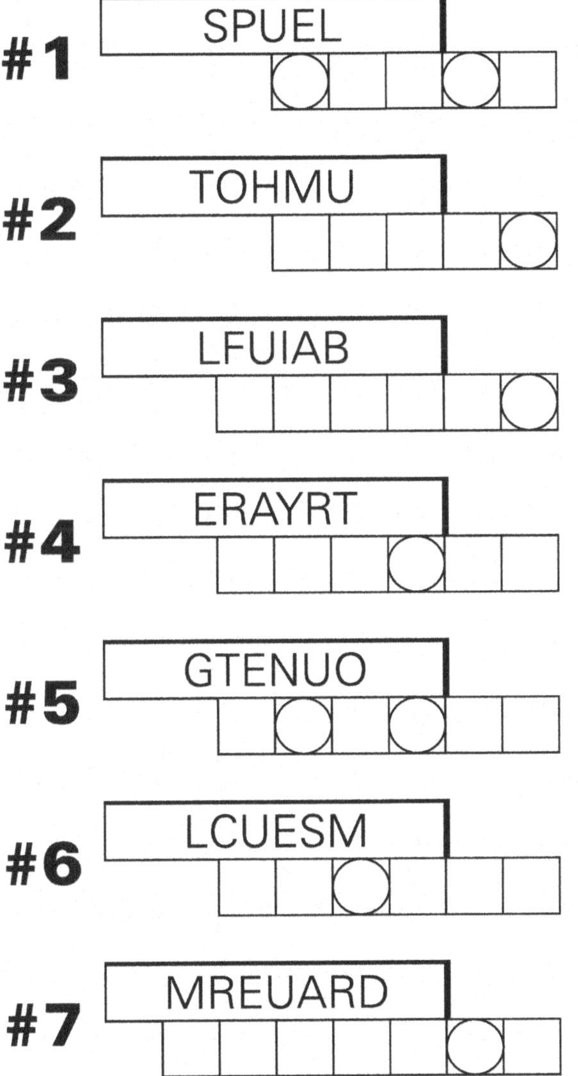

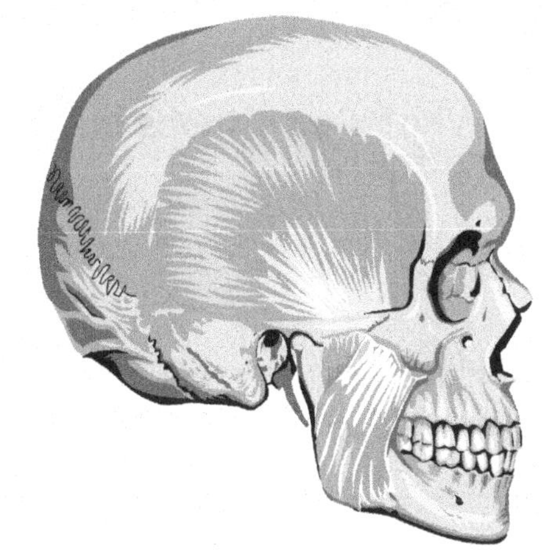

Box of Clues

Stumped? Maybe you can find a clue below.

-Starts with *M*; ends with *E*
-Starts with *E*; ends with *S*
-Starts with *T*; ends with *E*
-Starts with *F*; ends with *A*
-Starts with *M*; ends with *H*
-Starts with *E*; ends with *M*
-Starts with *A*; ends with *Y*
-Starts with *P*; ends with *E*

Arrange the circled letters to solve the mystery answer.

MYSTERY ANSWER

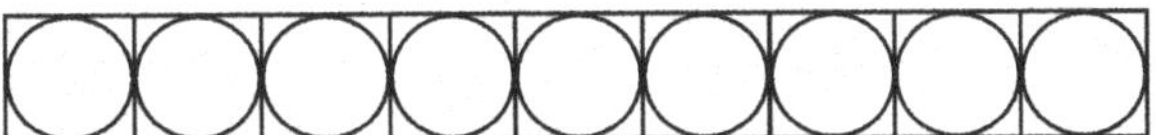

PUZZLE 41

JUMBLE® JOKES

Unscramble the mixed up letters to reveal the punch lines as suggested by the jokes.

#1 What wears shoes but has no feet?

AESDALKIW

#2 How did the clock feel when no one wound it up?

WNUODNR

#3 What is a ghost's favorite rock?

SNMAOTOETB

#4 Where do sick steamships go?

KCTOEOTDH

#5 How does a hot dog speak?

LKFNRYA

#6 What do you call nervous insects?

TBJIRESTGU

PUZZLE 42

MYSTERY PERSON

JUMBLE BrainBusters

Unscramble the Jumbles, one letter to each square, to spell words that relate to the mystery person.

#1
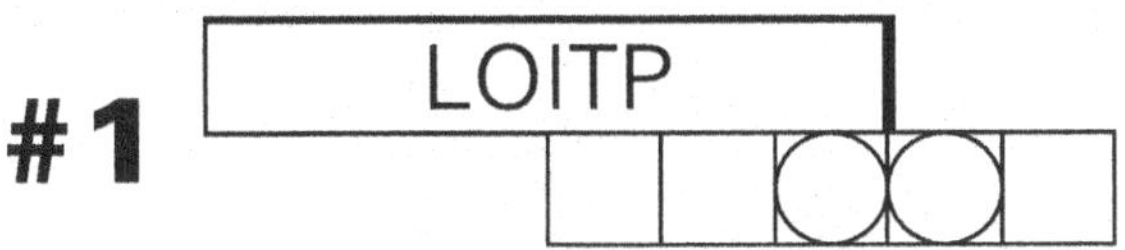

#2

#3

#4
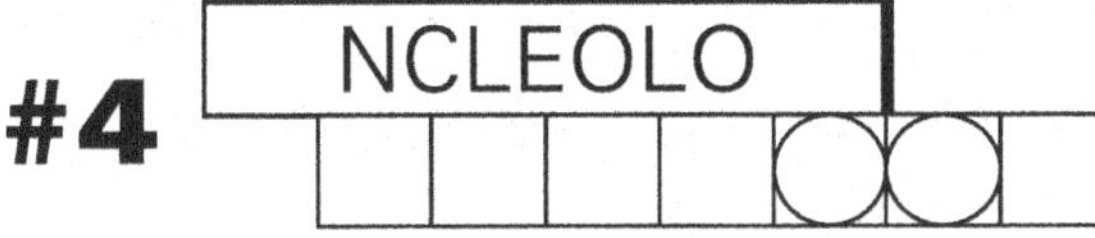

#5
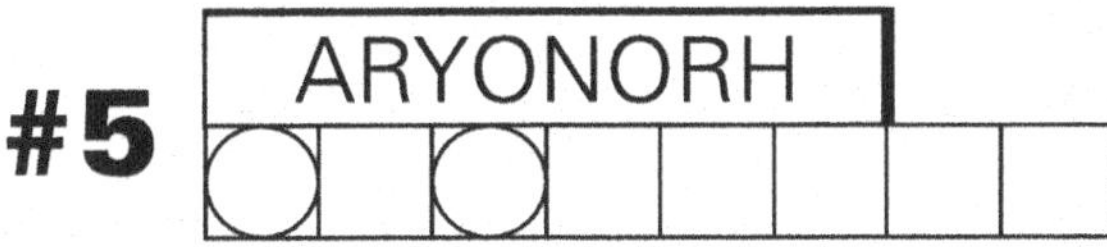

Box of Clues

Stumped? Maybe you can find a clue below.

-He ______ Marine Fighter Squadron 155 and spent a year flying F-4U fighters
-He has an ______ doctor of science degree in engineering
-He achieved this rank in the military
-After Korea he attended test ______ school
-He received a bachelor of science ______ in engineering

Arrange the circled letters to solve the mystery person.

MYSTERY PERSON

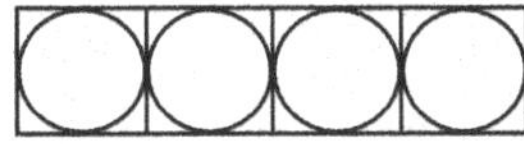

PUZZLE
43

FRASIER

JUMBLE BrainBusters

Unscramble the Jumbles, one letter to each square, to spell words related to the television show *Frasier*.

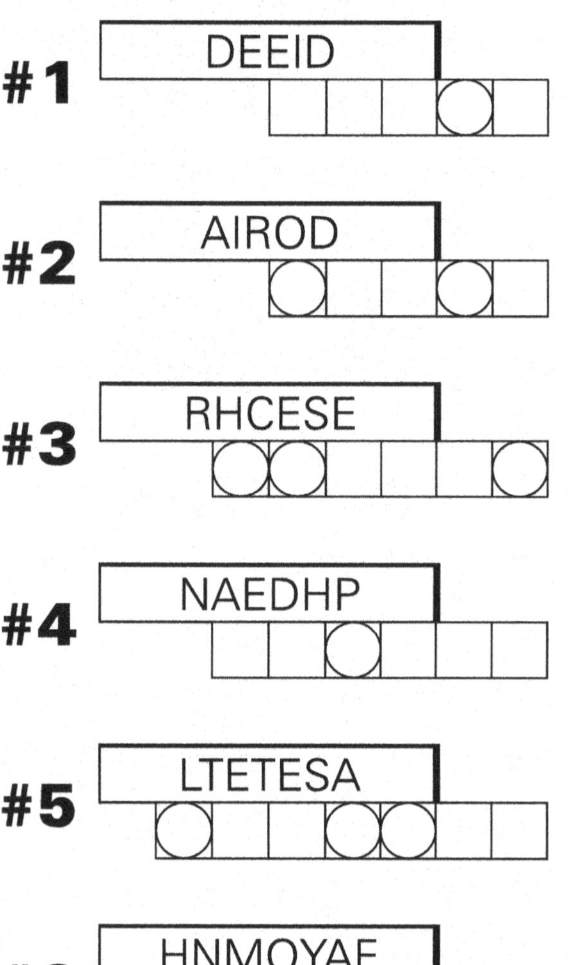

#1 DEEID

#2 AIROD

#3 RHCESE

#4 NAEDHP

#5 LTETESA

#6 HNMOYAE

Box of Clues

Stumped? Maybe you can find a clue below. (No clue for the mystery answer.)

-KACL's type of station
-*Frasier* setting
-*Frasier*'s origination
-John ______
-______ Moon
-Character played by "Moose"

Arrange the circled letters to solve the mystery answer.

MYSTERY ANSWER

MOVIES

JUMBLE BrainBusters

Unscramble the mixed-up letters, one letter to each square, to spell movie titles.

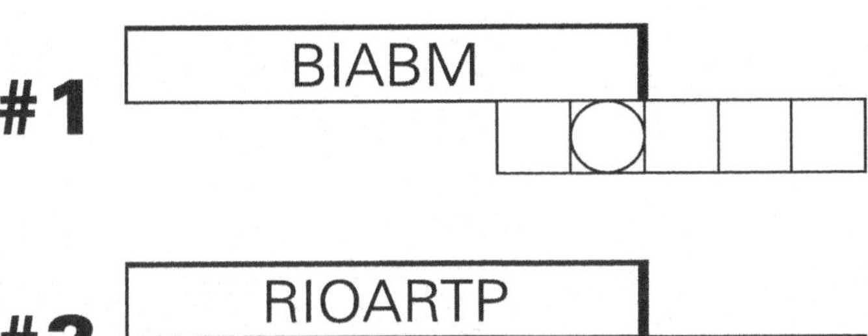

#1 BIABM

#2 RIOARTP

#3 CTCNTOA

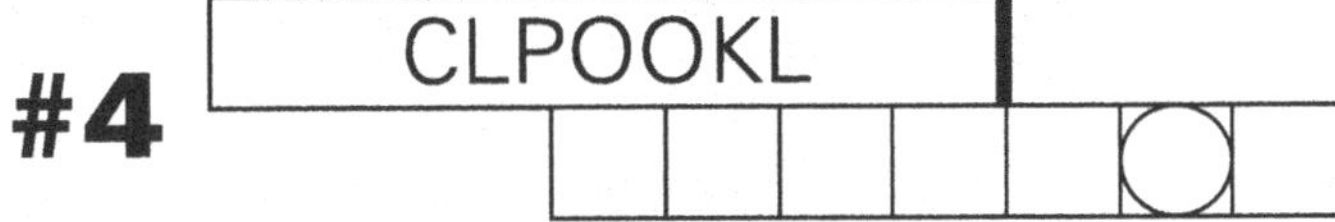

#4 CLPOOKL

#5 GTE THOYSR

#6 HTE OIATPRT

Box of Clues

Stumped? Maybe you can find a clue below.

- -1997 Jodie Foster movie
- -1942 Disney movie
- -1970 movie featuring George Kennedy as Joe Patroni
- -2000 Mel Gibson movie
- -2000 Ed Harris movie about a famous painter
- -1995 Disney movie
- -1995 movie starring John Travolta, Gene Hackman, Rene Russo, and Danny DeVito

Arrange the circled letters to solve the mystery answer.

MYSTERY ANSWER

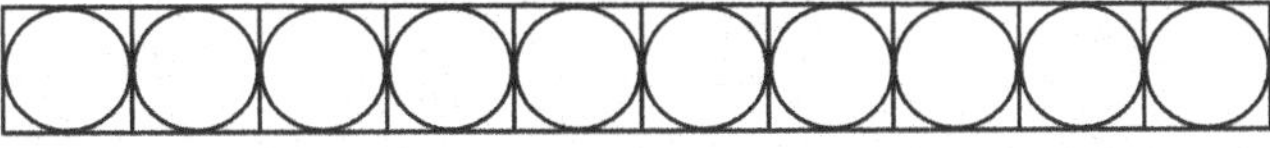

PUZZLE 45

MYSTERY PERSON

JUMBLE BrainBusters

Unscramble the Jumbles, one letter to each square, to spell words that relate to the mystery person.

#1 CIAVED

#2 MANINECK

#3 THDEURAG

#4 SAMLNETA

#5 TSMCONILU

Box of Clues

Stumped? Maybe you can find a clue below.

- -Her real _____ _____ is Friedman
- -She was this type of writer
- -Her ______ was "Eppie"
- -She had one named Margo
- -What she offered on a regular basis

Arrange the circled letters to solve the mystery person.

MYSTERY PERSON

PUZZLE 46

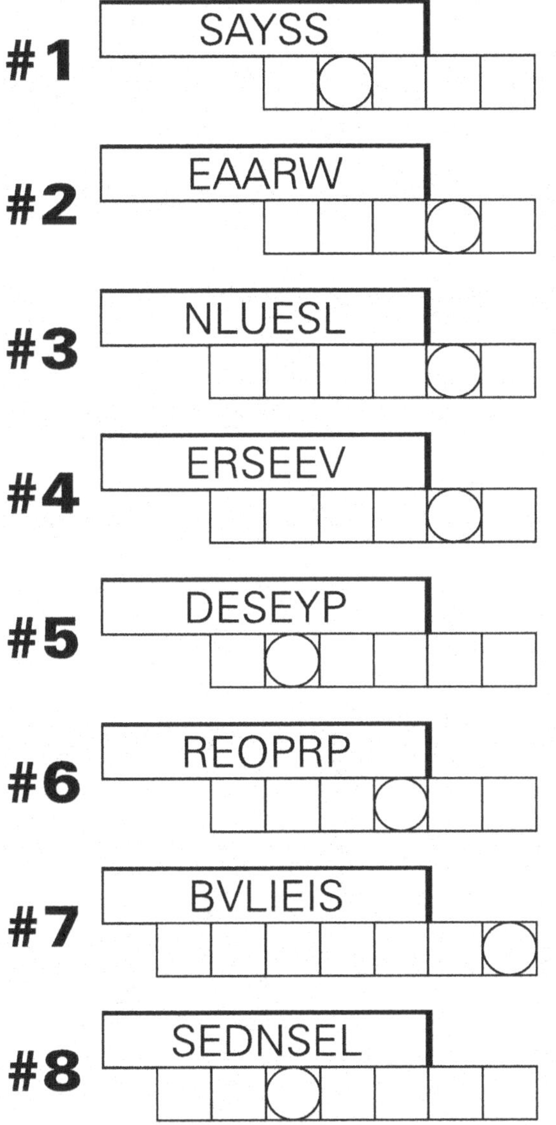

JUMBLE BrainBusters

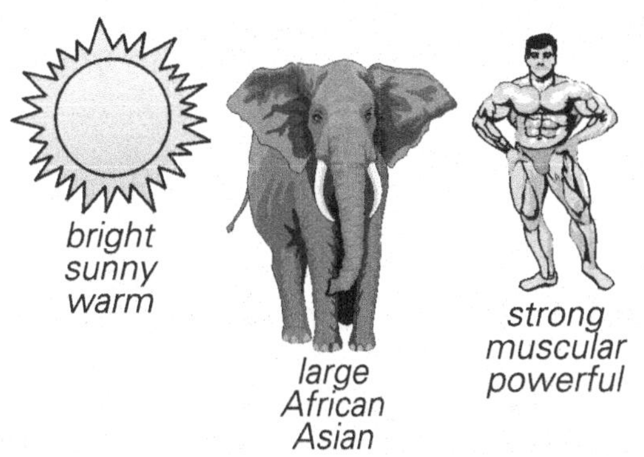

Box of Clues

Stumped? Maybe you can find a clue below.

- Cognizant
- Gloomy
- Appropriate
- Harsh
- Quick
- Ongoing
- Ready
- Rude and disrespectful
- In sight

Arrange the circled letters to solve the mystery answer.

MYSTERY ANSWER

PUZZLE 47

JUMBLE® JOKES

JUMBLE® BrainBusters

Unscramble the mixed up letters to reveal the punch lines as suggested by the jokes.

#1 What is bought by the yard and worn by the foot?

ECARTAP

#2 What is the healthiest kind of water?

LTWELEARW

#3 What is the perfect cure for dandruff?

NSDABLES

#4 What happened when the horse swallowed a dollar bill?

KUHBCEDE

#5 What is a foreign ant?

RMATIONTP

#6 What is the dirtiest word in the world?

OTPLUINOL

PUZZLE 48

JUMBLE BrainBusters

WARS AND THE MILITARY

Unscramble the Jumbles, one letter to each square, to spell words related to wars and the military.

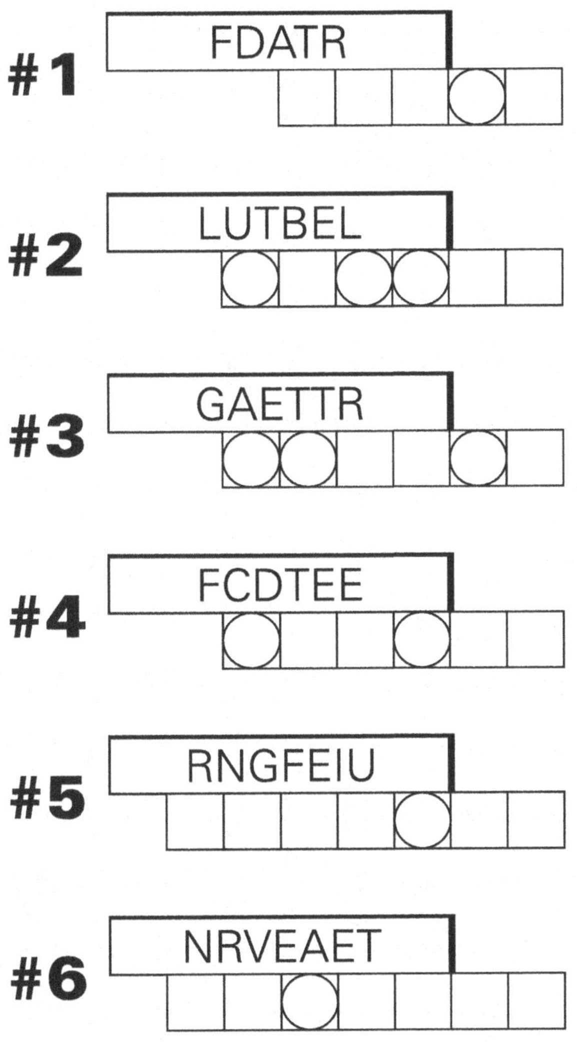

#1 FDATR

#2 LUTBEL

#3 GAETTR

#4 FCDTEE

#5 RNGFEIU

#6 NRVEAET

Box of Clues

Stumped? Maybe you can find a clue below.

-Starts with *G*; ends with *E*
-Starts with *D*; ends with *T*
-Starts with *T*; ends with *T*
-Starts with *D*; ends with *T*
-Starts with *V*; ends with *N*
-Starts with *B*; ends with *D*
-Starts with *B*; ends with *T*

Arrange the circled letters to solve the mystery answer.

MYSTERY ANSWER

PUZZLE 49

MEANS THE OPPOSITE

JUMBLE BrainBusters

Unscramble the Jumbles, one letter to each square, to spell pairs of words that have opposite or nearly opposite meanings.

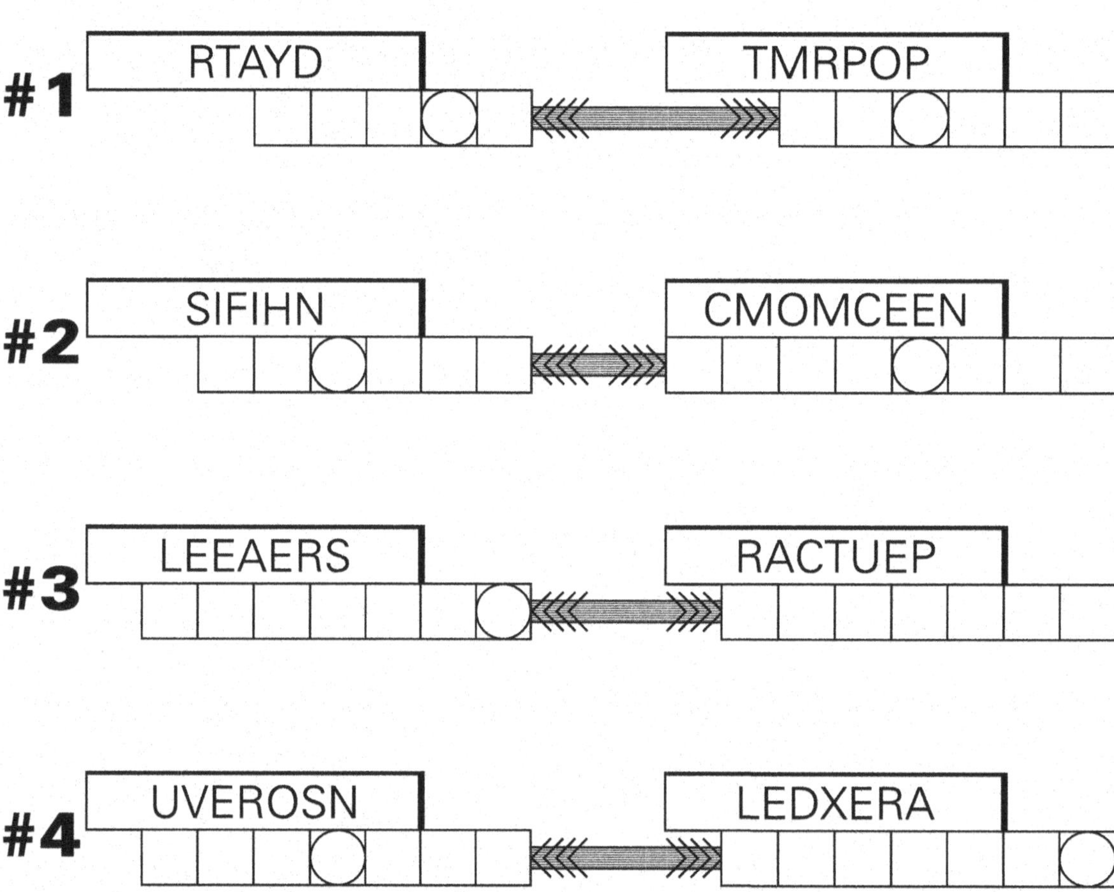

Arrange the circled letters to solve the mystery answer. (Form two words that have the opposite or nearly opposite meanings.)

MYSTERY ANSWER

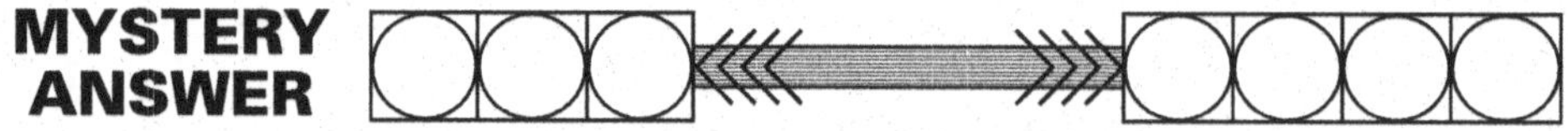

PUZZLE 50

MATH

JUMBLE BrainBusters

Unscramble the Jumbles, one letter to each square, so that each equation is correct.

For example: NOTLSWOEOPNEU

ONE PLUS ONE = TWO

#1 STXMSOIEXSINIE

#2 SPLFOUSWOIXRTU

#3 VPISFELIFEEUNTV

#4 EMNTNETISTUNETNWY

#5 TFTVNPLESEFEFIEINU

Then arrange the circled letters to solve the mystery equation.

MYSTERY EQUATION

PUZZLE 51

ANIMALS

Unscramble the Jumbles, one letter to each square, to spell names of animals.

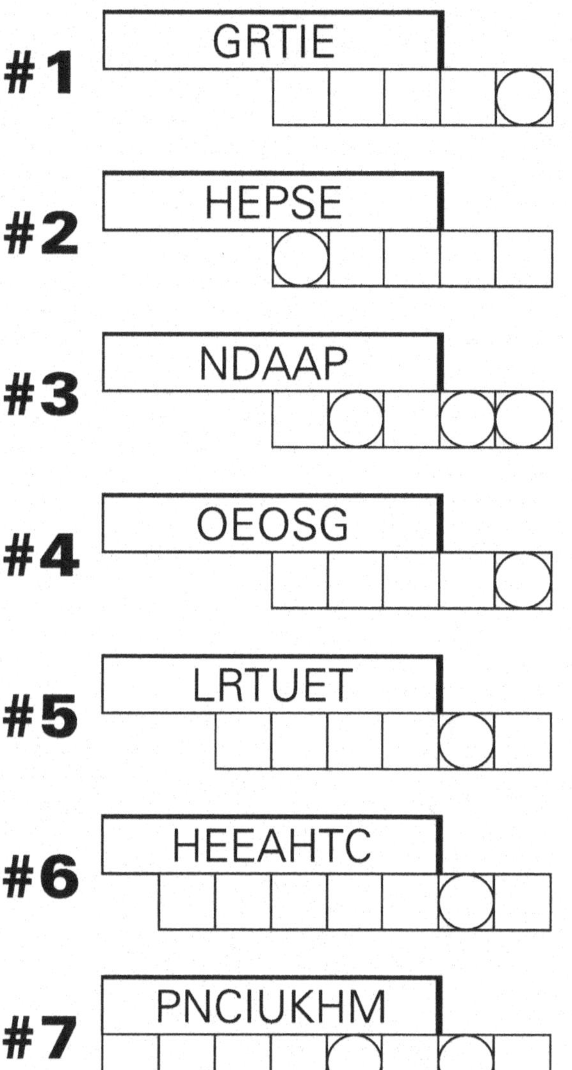

JUMBLE BrainBusters

Interesting Animal Facts

The Mojave ground squirrel hibernates for about half of every year.

A striped skunk can fire its musk stream accurately for up to 12 feet.

Arrange the circled letters to solve the mystery answer.

MYSTERY ANSWER

SPORTS

JUMBLE® BrainBusters

Unscramble the Jumbles, one letter to each square, to spell words related to sports.

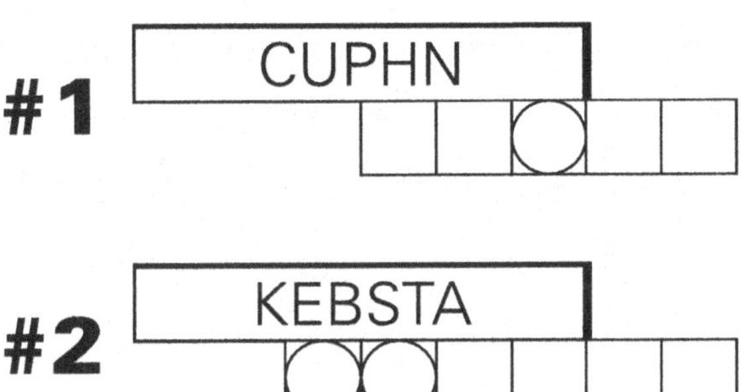

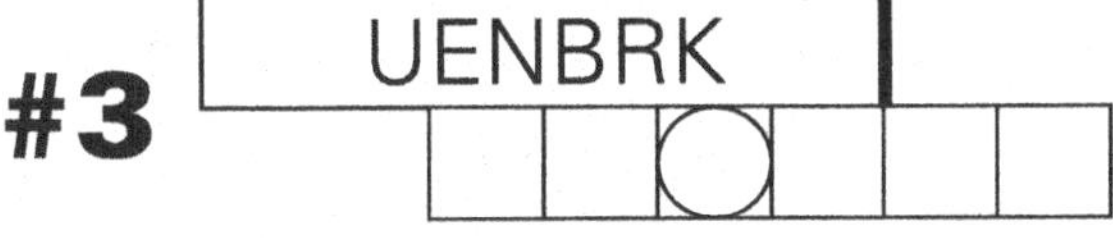

Box of Clues

Stumped? Maybe you can find a clue below. (No clue for the mystery answer.)

- -Protective headgear
- -Fast-paced sport
- -Boxing blow
- -Arena
- -Basketball score
- -Trap

MYSTERY ANSWER

Arrange the circled letters to solve the mystery answer.

PUZZLE 53

PLANET EARTH

JUMBLE® BrainBusters

Unscramble the Jumbles, one letter to each square, to spell words related to planet Earth.

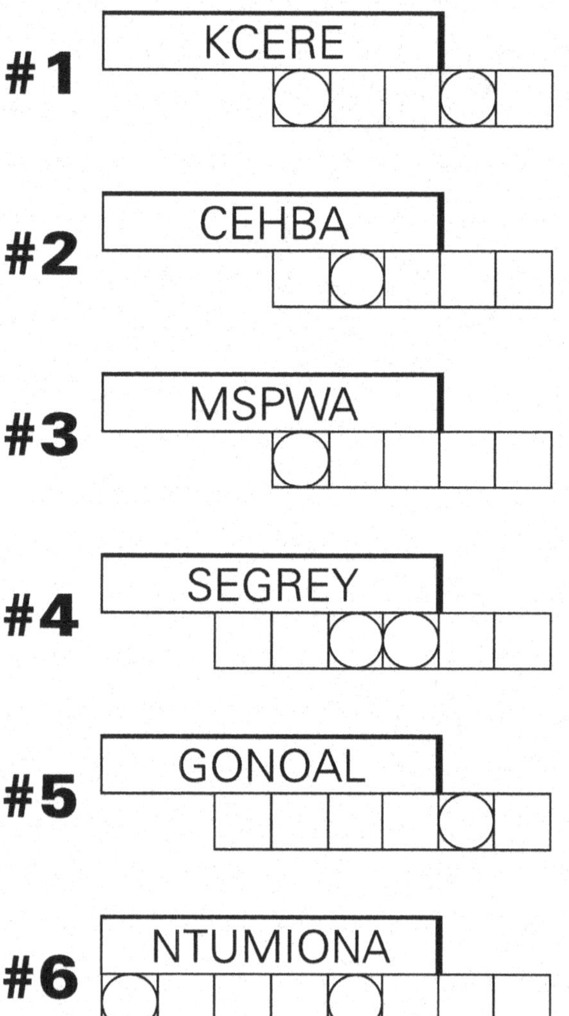

Box of Clues

Stumped? Maybe you can find a clue below.

- -Starts with *L*; ends with *N*
- -Starts with *M*; ends with *N*
- -Starts with *S*; ends with *P*
- -Starts with *C*; ends with *K*
- -Starts with *G*; ends with *R*
- -Starts with *E*; ends with *M*
- -Starts with *B*; ends with *H*

MYSTERY ANSWER

Arrange the circled letters to solve the mystery answer.

ABBREVIATIONS

JUMBLE BrainBusters

Unscramble the Jumbles, one letter to each square, to spell words that are often abbreviated.

#1 CONEU

#2 UNAEEV

#3 ADSUYN

#4 GIDBINUL

#5 NAITSEDC

#6 RMEDEBEC

MYSTERY ANSWER

Arrange the circled letters to solve the mystery answer.

PUZZLE 55

MEANS THE SAME

JUMBLE BrainBusters

Unscramble the Jumbles, one letter to each square, to spell pairs of words that have the same or similar meanings.

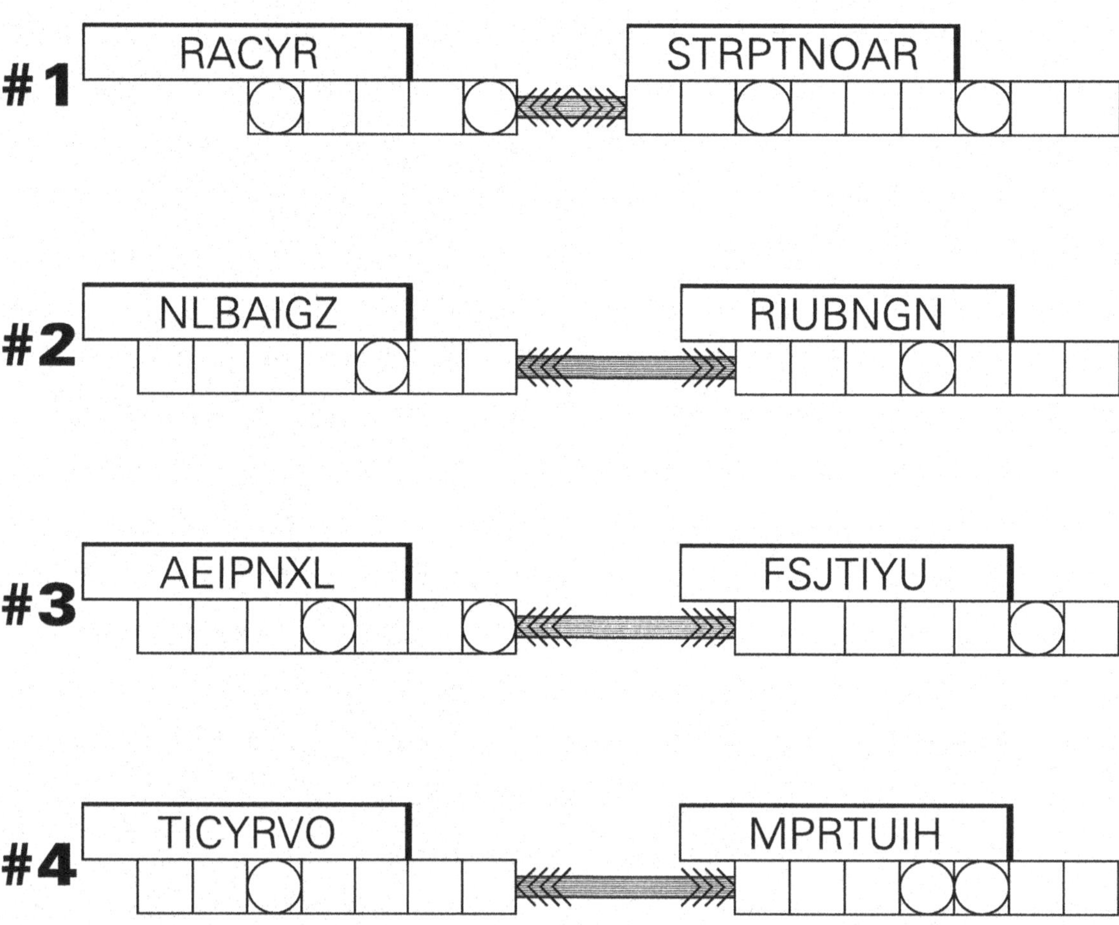

Arrange the circled letters to solve the mystery answer. (Form two words that have the same or similar meanings.)

MYSTERY ANSWER

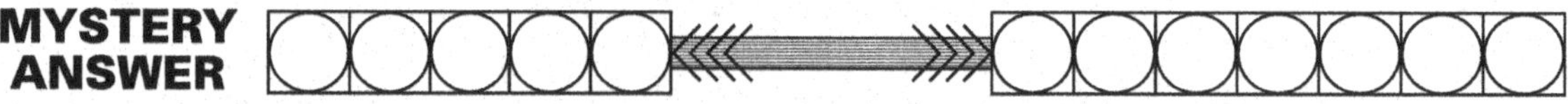

PUZZLE 56

AROUND THE HOME

JUMBLE® BrainBusters

Unscramble the Jumbles, one letter to each square, to spell words related to the home.

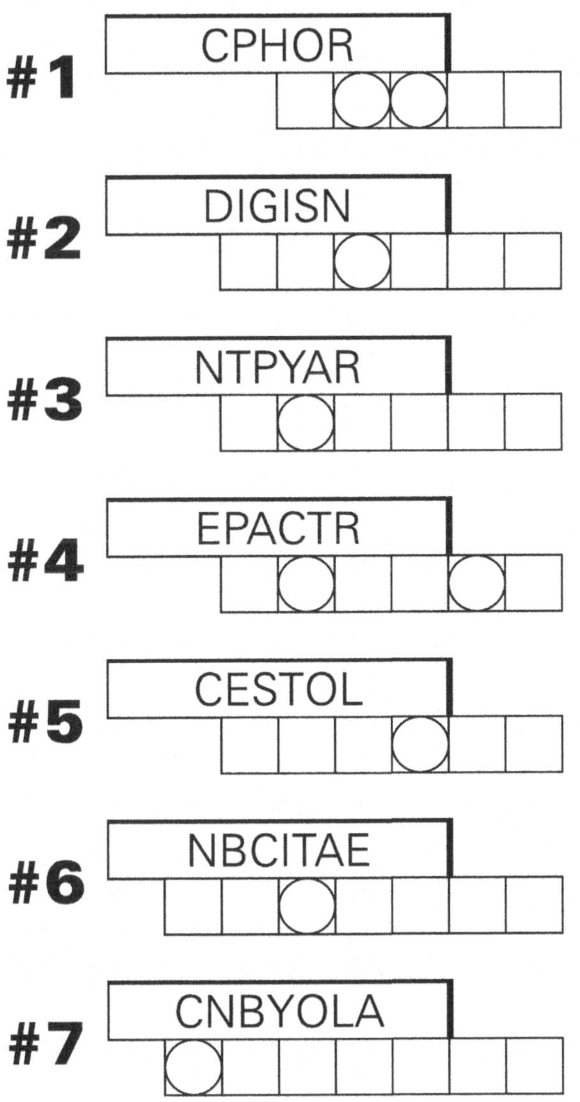

#1 CPHOR

#2 DIGISN

#3 NTPYAR

#4 EPACTR

#5 CESTOL

#6 NBCITAE

#7 CNBYOLA

Box of Clues

Stumped? Maybe you can find a clue below. (No clue for the mystery answer.)

-Starts with *C*; ends with *T*
-Starts with *P*; ends with *H*
-Starts with *B*; ends with *Y*
-Starts with *P*; ends with *Y*
-Starts with *C*; ends with *T*
-Starts with *S*; ends with *G*
-Starts with *C*; ends with *T*

Arrange the circled letters to solve the mystery answer.

MYSTERY ANSWER

PUZZLE 57

RHYMING WORDS

JUMBLE BrainBusters

Unscramble the Jumbles, one letter to each square, to spell pairs of words that rhyme.

#1

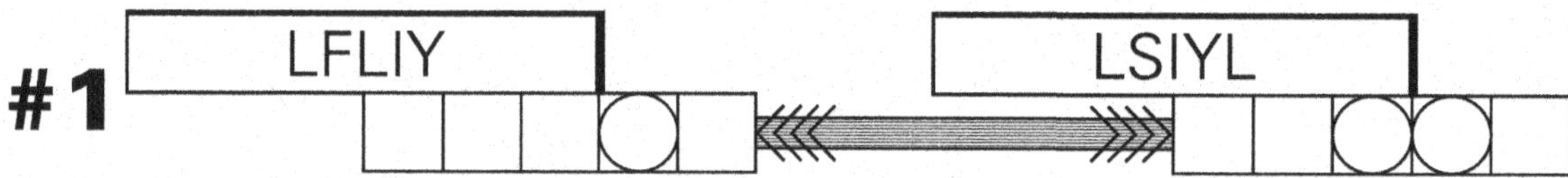

#2

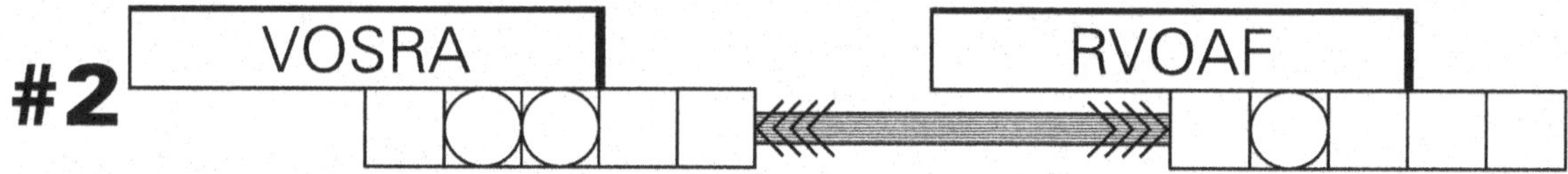

#3

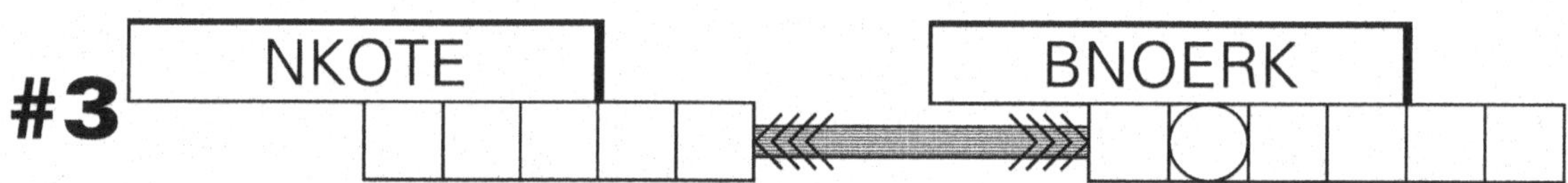

#4

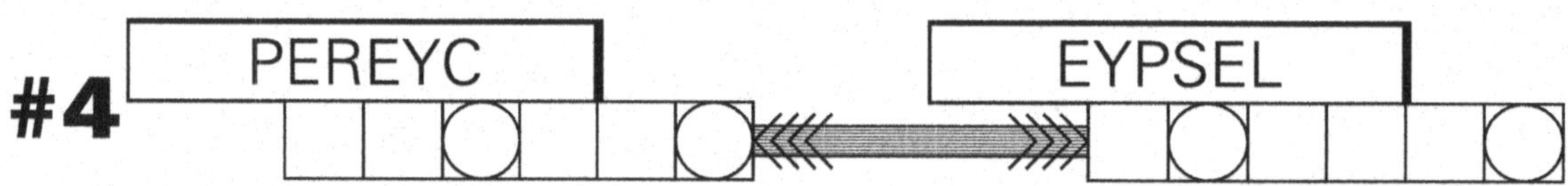

Arrange the circled letters to solve the mystery answer.
(Form two words that rhyme.)

MYSTERY ANSWER

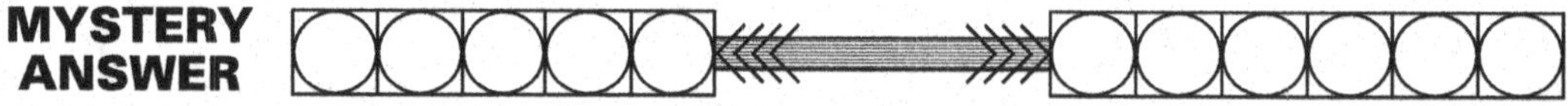

PUZZLE 58

EGYPT

JUMBLE BrainBusters

Unscramble the Jumbles, one letter to each square, to spell words related to Egypt.

#1 YLAIB

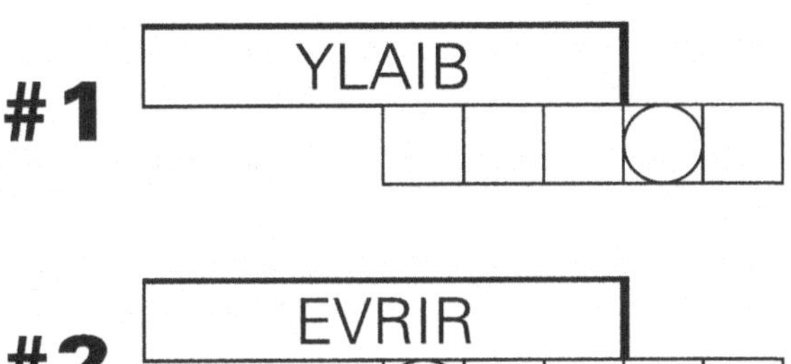

#2 EVRIR

#3 RCIOA

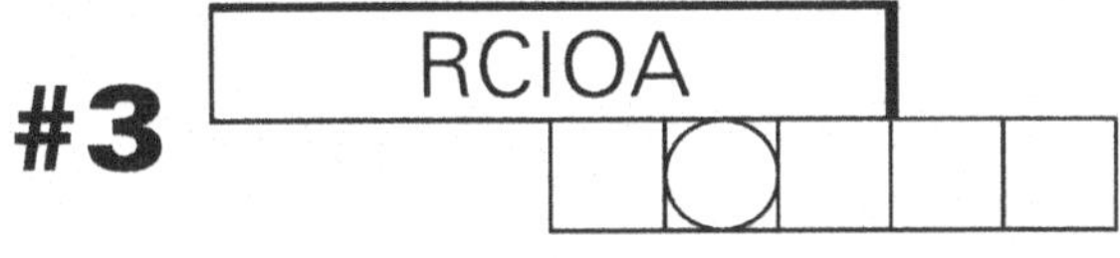

#4 ARAICF

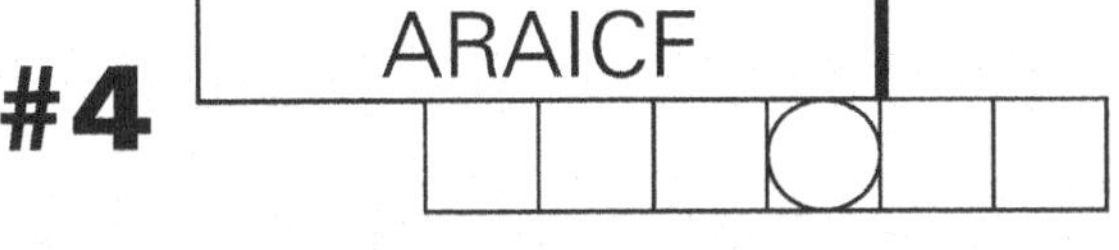

#5 HNSIXP

#6 NOKIMGD

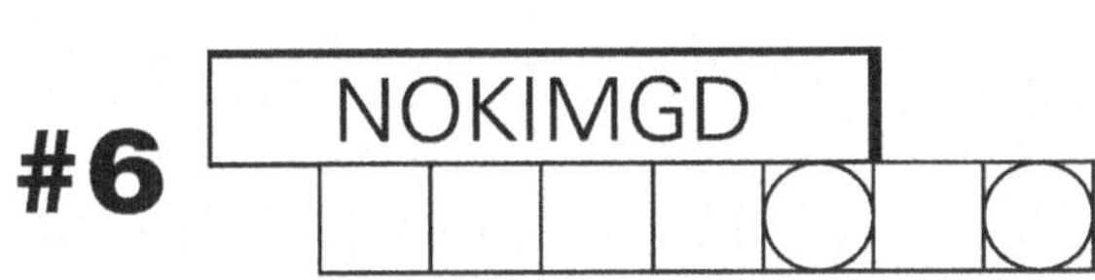

Box of Clues

Stumped? Maybe you can find a clue below. (No clue for the mystery answer.)

- -Where most of Egypt lies
- -The Nile ______
- -Egypt's ancient territorial unit
- -The capital of Egypt
- -Egypt's neighbor to the west
- -Figure from Egyptian mythology

Arrange the circled letters to solve the mystery answer.

MYSTERY ANSWER

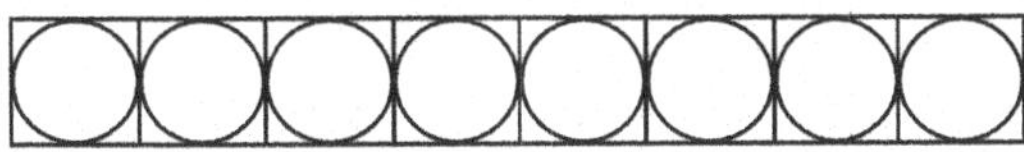

REPTILES

Unscramble the Jumbles, one letter to each square, to spell names of reptiles.

#1

#2
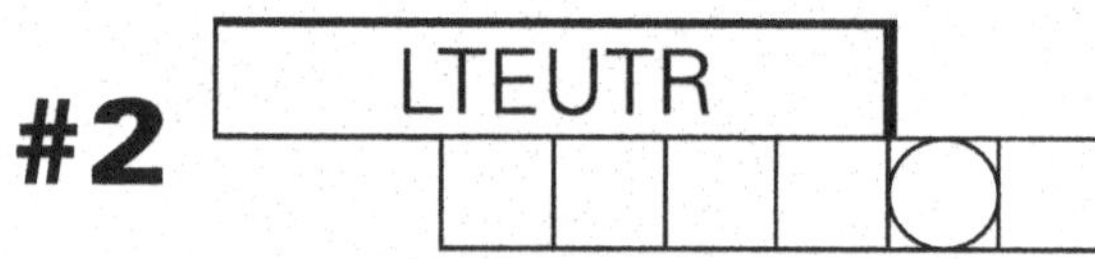

#3

Box of Clues

Stumped? Maybe you can find a clue below. (No clue for the mystery answer.)

- -Type of poisonous snake
- -Small lizard
- -Turtle with a high-domed shell
- -Sea or box ______
- -Extinct reptile

#4
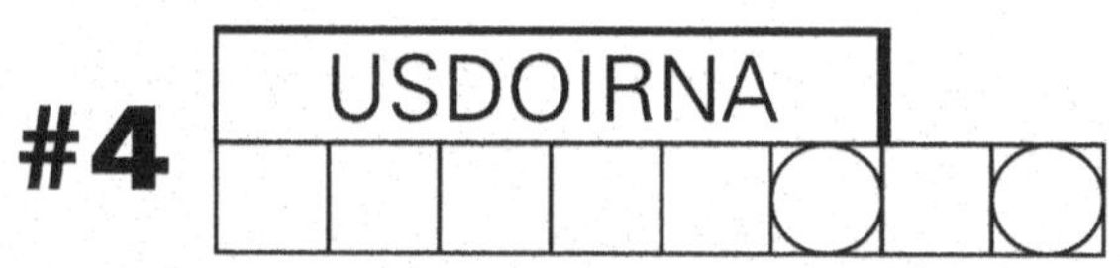

#5
STOOITER

Arrange the circled letters to solve the mystery answer.

MYSTERY ANSWER

JUMBLE®

BrainBusters™

Intermediate Puzzles

PUZZLE 60

MATH

JUMBLE BrainBusters

Unscramble the Jumbles, one letter to each square, so that each equation is correct.

For example: NONTEOEOW

ONE + ONE = TWO

#1 ETRWOTOZOW

☐☐☐ – ☐☐◯☐ = ☐☐☐

#2 WEISRTETXOH

☐☐☐ ÷ ☐◯☐ = ☐☐☐☐◯

#3 EFTFEIFIYVTN

◯☐◯ × ☐☐☐◯ = ☐☐☐◯☐

#4 ETRHINHETENERE

◯◯☐☐ ÷ ☐☐☐☐◯ = ☐◯☐☐☐

#5 VEEVENTLEWLOEEN

☐☐◯ + ☐◯☐◯☐☐ = ☐☐☐☐☐◯

Arrange the circled letters to solve the mystery equation.

MYSTERY EQUATION

◯◯◯◯◯◯ – ◯◯◯◯◯ = ◯◯◯◯

PUZZLE 61

DOUBLE JUMBLE® BRAINBUSTERS

Unscramble the Jumbles, one letter to each square, to spell words.

#1 

#2 

#3 

#4 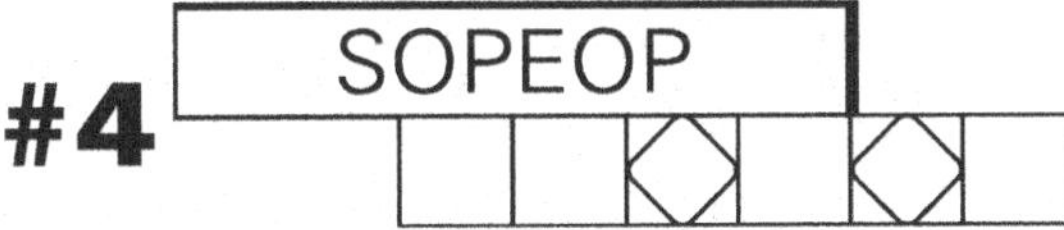

#5 

#6 

JUMBLE® BrainBusters

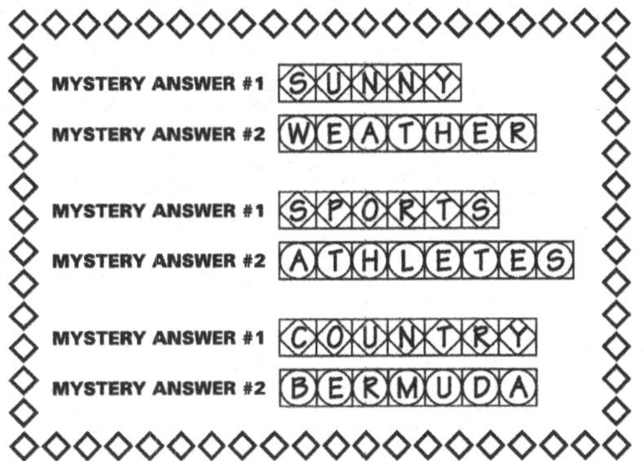

Box of Clues

Stumped? Maybe you can find a clue below. (No clues for the mystery answers.)

- -Pierce with a sharp point
- -A kind of blue
- -Development
- -Except
- -To be resistant to
- -Stoop, especially with the knees bent

Arrange the diamonded letters to solve mystery answer #1. Arrange the circled letters to solve mystery answer #2. (The mystery answers will relate to each other.)

MYSTERY ANSWER #1

MYSTERY ANSWER #2

PUZZLE 62

JUMBLE BrainBusters

POETRY

Unscramble the Jumbles, one letter to each square, to spell words found in the poem.

#1 YOSLLW

#2 CNIETO

#3 RRVFEEO

#4 ZRAIEEL

#5 VELECR

#6 OBSCEEM

TIME by Kim Nolan

Minutes tick so ______ #1
Yet hours slip away
Before you even ______ #2
It's a whole new day

Weeks drag on ______ #3
Yet months just disappear
Then you stop and ______ #4
It's a brand new year

Time is very ______ #5
First slow then fast
It only takes a second
Then present ______ #6 past

Arrange the circled letters to solve the mystery answer. (The mystery answer is not in the poem.)

MYSTERY ANSWER

PUZZLE 63

JUMBLE® TRIVIA

JUMBLE® BrainBusters

Unscramble the Jumbles, one letter to each square, to spell words as suggested by the trivia clues.

#1 Scientists believe that ______ comprises at least 90 percent of all the matter in the universe.

#1 REGHONDY

#2 The size of the first ______ on the moon was about 13 inches long.

#2 NORFPITOT

#3 In ancient Rome, ______ tongues were considered a delicacy.

#3 LGMFIOAN

#4 In ______, eggs are a very popular topping for pizza.

#4 SIAUARLAT

#5 Before hitting it big, Kevin ______ worked at Disneyland.

#5 RTCNEOS

Arrange the circled letters to solve the mystery answer.

Before becoming an actor, ______ ______ was a seminary student.

MYSTERY ANSWER

PUZZLE 64

TRIPLE JUMBLE® BRAINBUSTERS

Unscramble the Jumbles, one letter to each square, to spell words.

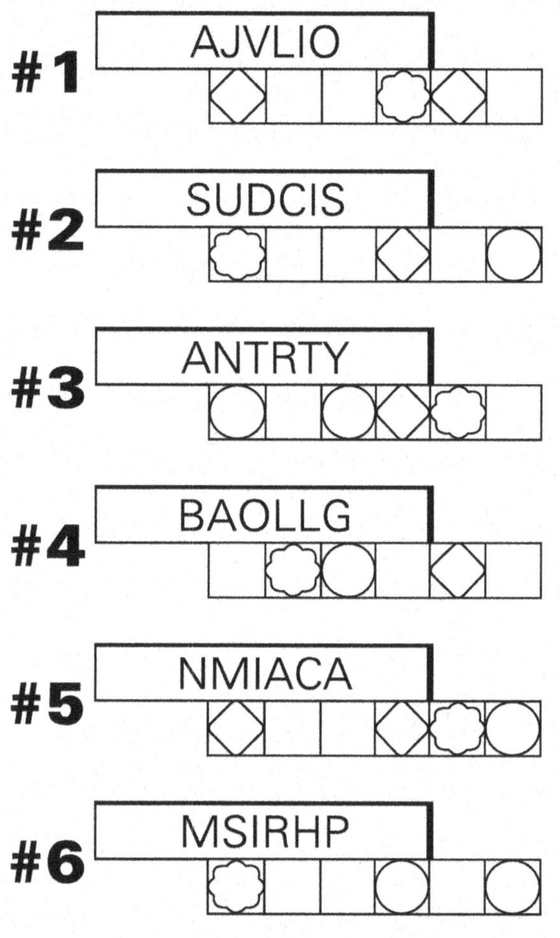

JUMBLE® BrainBusters

MYSTERY ANSWER #1 CHEF
MYSTERY ANSWER #2 BROIL
MYSTERY ANSWER #3 SEAFOOD

MYSTERY ANSWER #1 FISH
MYSTERY ANSWER #2 TROUT
MYSTERY ANSWER #3 UPSTREAM

Box of Clues

Stumped? Maybe you can find a clue below. (No clues for the mystery answers.)

- Fried ______
- Oppressive person
- Insane person
- Worldwide
- Marked by good cheer
- Circular plate

Arrange the clouded letters to solve mystery answer #1. Arrange the diamonded letters to solve mystery answer #2. Arrange the circled letters to solve mystery answer #3. (The mystery answers will relate to each other.)

MYSTERY ANSWER #1

MYSTERY ANSWER #2

MYSTERY ANSWER #3

PUZZLE 65

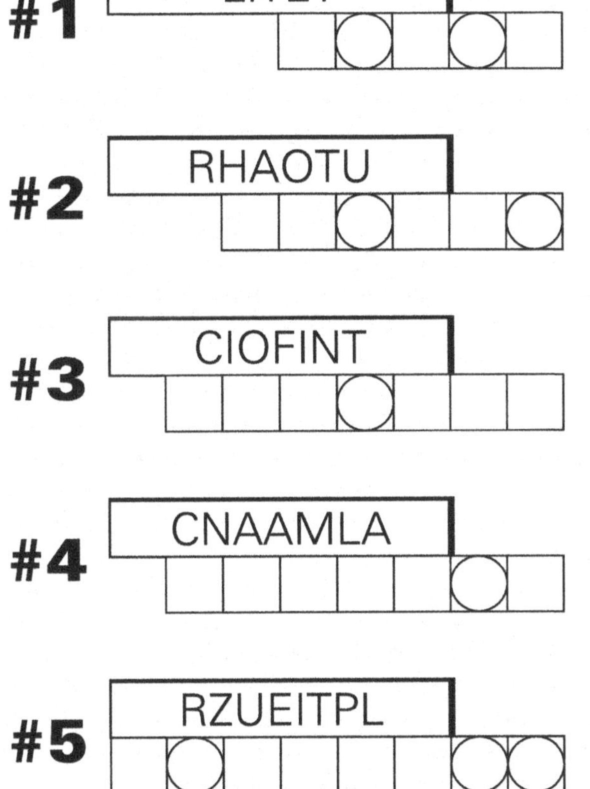

Box of Clues

Stumped? Maybe you can find a clue below.

- -Science ______
- -Annual reference book
- -Writer
- -Body of written works of a language
- -Name
- -Publications used in schools
- -______ Prize

MYSTERY ANSWER

Arrange the circled letters to solve the mystery answer.

PUZZLE 66

STARTS AND ENDS WITH THE SAME LETTER

JUMBLE BrainBusters

Unscramble the Jumbles, one letter to each square, to spell words that start and end with the same letter.

RADAR
ARENA
POP
GOING
RIVER
HIGH
DICED
CRYPTIC

#1 MEEUHX

#2 CAOCGN

#3 LOWIWL

#4 RUTIOTS

#5 DTDOEEV

#6 NNANAET

Box of Clues

Stumped? Maybe you can find a clue below.

- -Loyal
- -Weeping ______
- -Comprehensive
- -Dig up
- -Type of brandy
- -Traveler
- -TV ______

Arrange the circled letters to solve the mystery answer.

MYSTERY ANSWER

TREES

JUMBLE BrainBusters

Unscramble the Jumbles, one letter to each square, to spell varieties of trees.

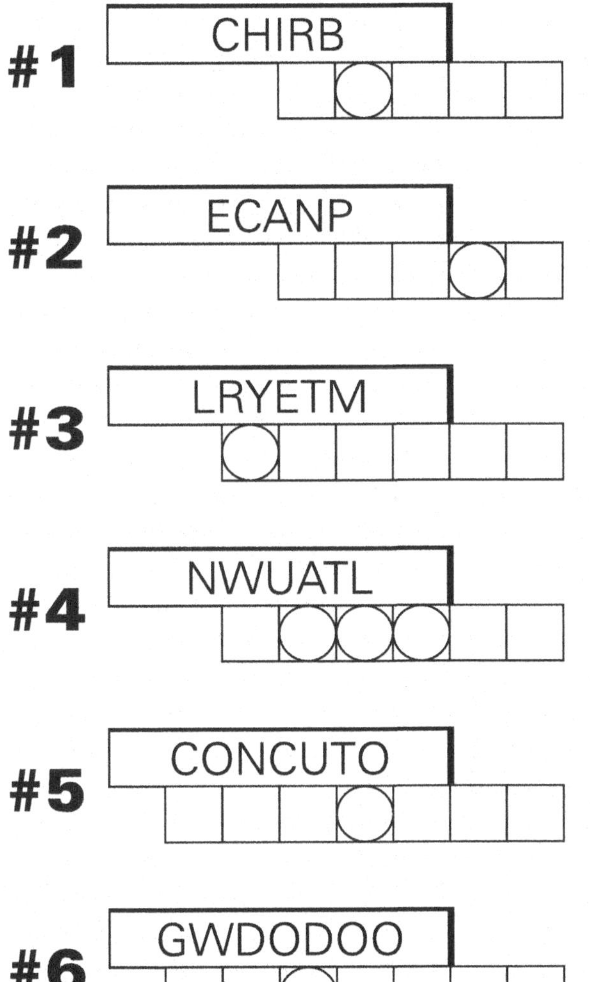

Box of Clues

Stumped? Maybe you can find a clue below. (No clue for the mystery answer.)

- -Wax or crape ______
- -White or river ______
- -______ palm
- -Tree found in southern U.S. with edible nuts
- -Black or English ______
- -White or pink ______

MYSTERY ANSWER

Arrange the circled letters to solve the mystery answer.

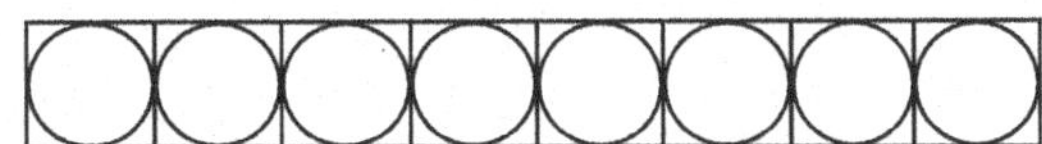

PUZZLE 68

ALL ABOUT FOOD

JUMBLE® BrainBusters

Unscramble the Jumbles, one letter to each square, to spell words related to food.

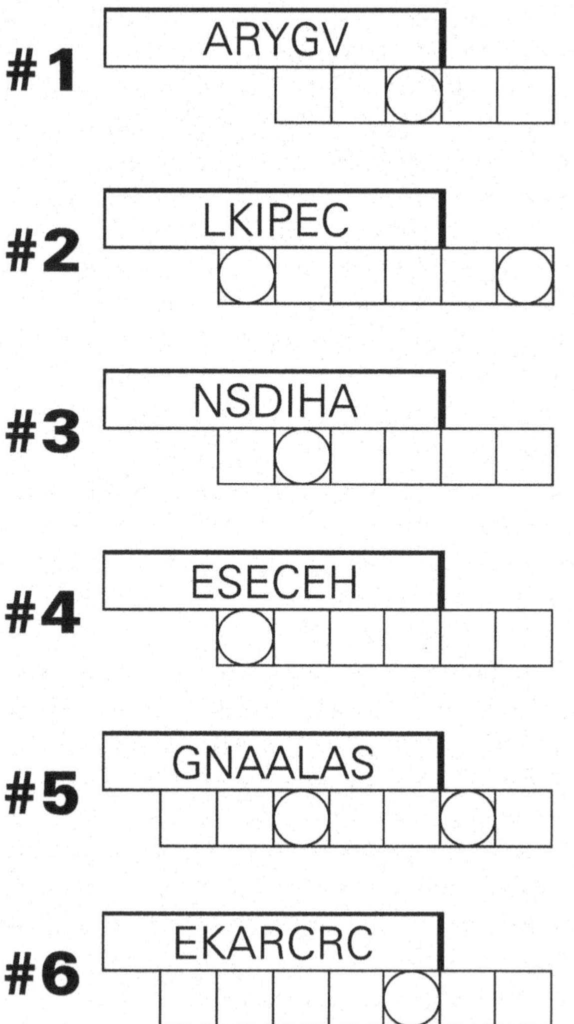

Box of Clues

Stumped? Maybe you can find a clue below. (No clue for the mystery answer.)

-Dill ______
-Italian dish
-Jack ______
-Biscuits and ______
-Animal ______
-Type of pastry

Arrange the circled letters to solve the mystery answer.

MYSTERY ANSWER

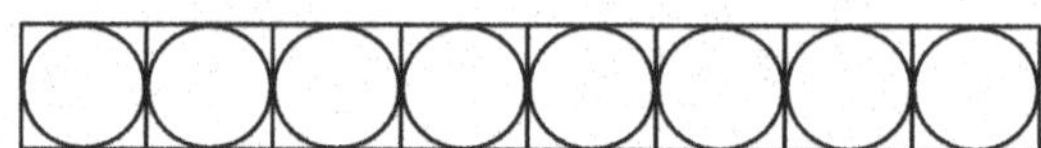

PUZZLE 69

SUPER JUMBLE® CHALLENGE

JUMBLE® BrainBusters

Unscramble the Jumbles, one letter to each square, to spell words.

#1 WNI

#2 VCEA

#3 URGPO

#4 ECOTKP

#5 UDHETIO

#6 RDWRAAEH

#7 EOLSURNWF

#8 TSBALHEPIT

#9 RTNAOTIOCNP

Box of Clues

Stumped? Maybe you can find a clue below.

- -Natural, hollow chamber
- -Gizmo
- -Triumph
- -______ billiards
- -Place of concealment
- -______ piece
- -Type of war vessel
- -______ seed
- -______ store
- -Congregation

Arrange the circled letters to solve the mystery answer.

MYSTERY ANSWER

PUZZLE 70

THE ANDY GRIFFITH SHOW

JUMBLE BrainBusters

Unscramble the Jumbles, one letter to each square, to spell words related to the television show *The Andy Griffith Show.*

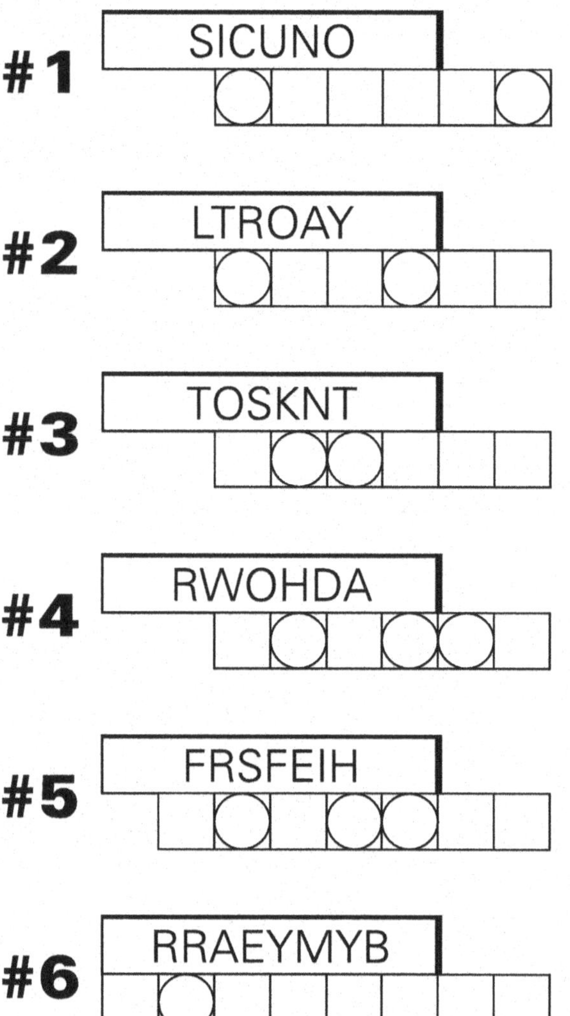

Box of Clues

Stumped? Maybe you can find a clue below. (No clue for the mystery answer.)

-Ron ______
-Show setting
-Andy's position
-Don ______
-Andy, to Barney
-Name shared by Andy and Opie

Arrange the circled letters to solve the mystery answer.

MYSTERY ANSWER

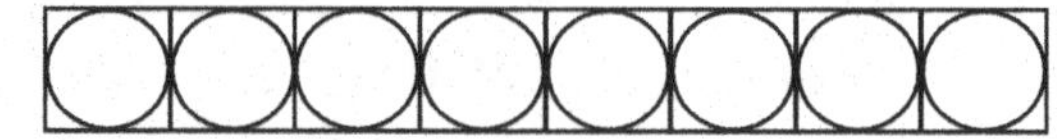

UN-MIX AND MATCH

U.S. STATES

Section 1: Unscramble the mixed-up letters, one letter to each square, to spell names of U.S. states.

#1 NMVRTOE

#2 HGICINMA

#3 NKAARSAS

#4 WREAEDLA

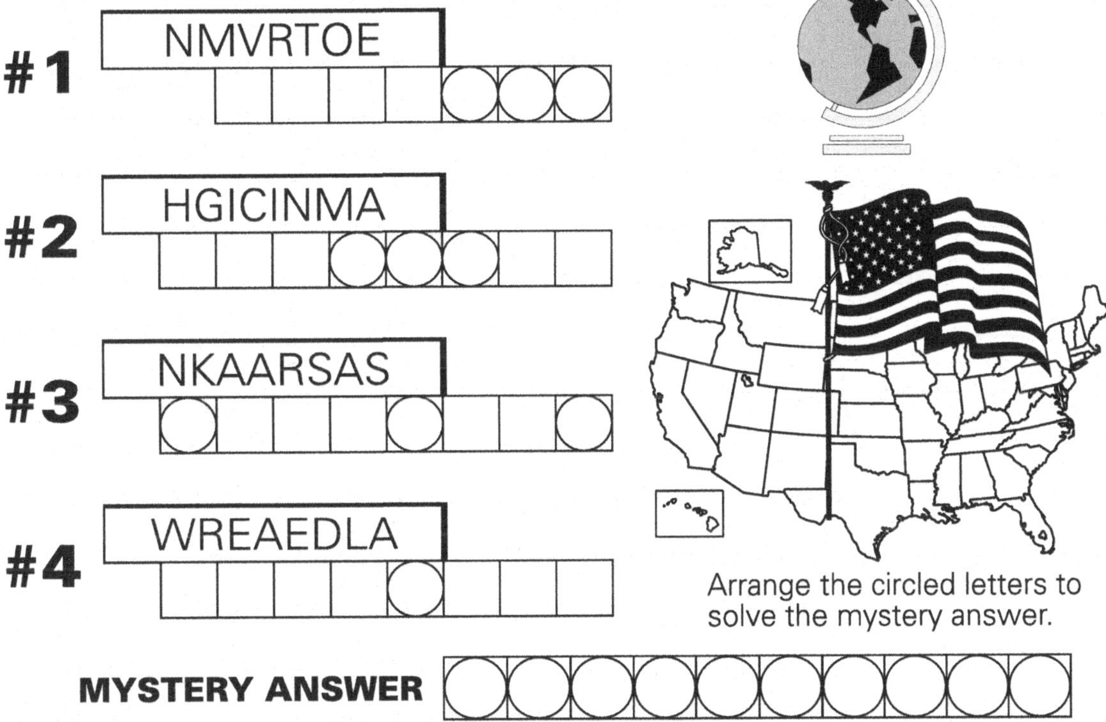

Arrange the circled letters to solve the mystery answer.

MYSTERY ANSWER

Section 2: Match the answers in the puzzle (including the mystery answer) to the following clues. (Write "MA." to represent the mystery answer.)

#____ U.S. state consisting of two peninsulas.

#____ The "Green Mountain State."

#____ U.S. state that achieved statehood in 1889 and whose state flower is the rhododendron.

#____ U.S. state that achieved statehood in 1836 and home to Hot Springs.

#____ The second-smallest U.S. state.

PUZZLE 72

UN-MIX AND MATCH
U.S. PRESIDENTS

Section 1: Unscramble the mixed-up letters, one letter to each square, to spell last names of U.S. presidents.

#1 VOREOH

#2 GDHINRA

#3 AKJCNSO

#4 LMRILEOF

Arrange the circled letters to solve the mystery answer.

MYSTERY ANSWER

Section 2: Match the answers in the puzzle (including the mystery answer) to the following clues. (Write "MA." to represent the mystery answer.)

#____ Before becoming U.S. president, this man was a general in the War of 1812 who defeated the British at New Orleans in 1815.

#____ This vice president became U.S. president after the death of Zachary Taylor in 1850.

#____ Before becoming U.S. president, this man served as the mayor of Buffalo and the governor of New York.

#____ Before becoming U.S. president, this man served as secretary of commerce from 1921-29 under presidents Harding and Coolidge.

#____ This U.S. president died in office in 1923.

PUZZLE 73

GET UP AND GO

JUMBLE BrainBusters

Unscramble the Jumbles, one letter to each square, to spell words that start with *UP*.

UPSET
UPPER
UPRIGHT
UPSTREAM
UPCOMING

#1 PYIUPT

#2 BUETAP

#3 APUTDE

#4 HUSPOT

#5 AURORP
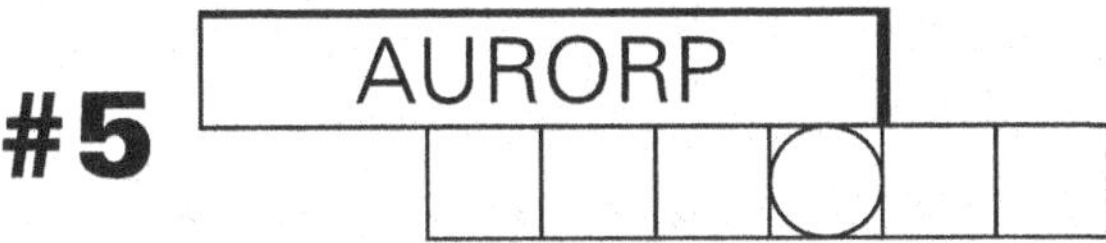

#6 AURGEPD
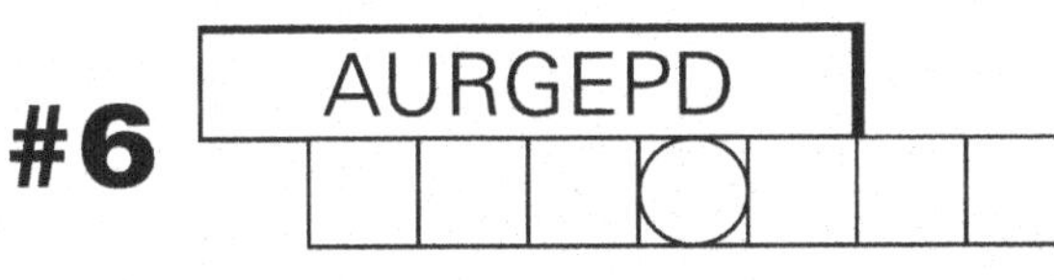

#7 NIUSPGW

Box of Clues

Stumped? Maybe you can find a clue below. (No clue for the mystery answer.)

-Final result
-Modernize
-Optimistic
-Improve
-Commotion
-An increase
-Snobby

Arrange the circled letters to solve the mystery answer.

MYSTERY ANSWER

PUZZLE 74

JUMBLE BrainBusters

FISH

Unscramble the Jumbles, one letter to each square, to spell types of fish.

#1 #2
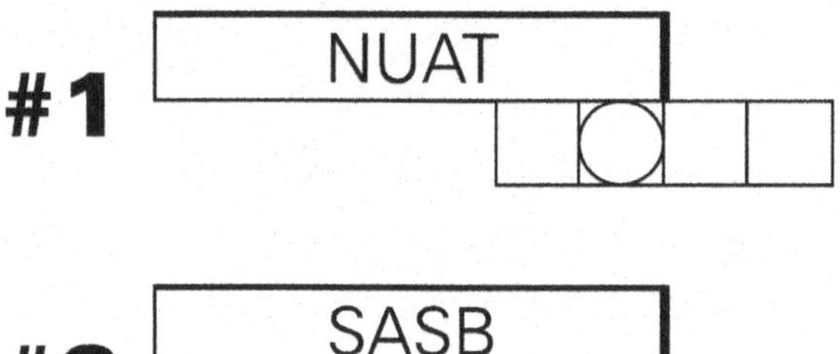

#3
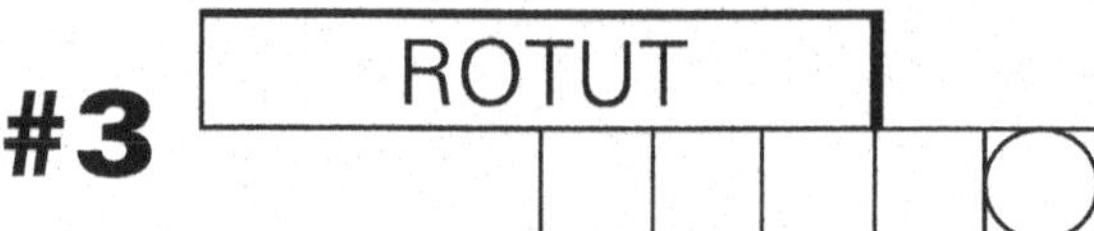

#4
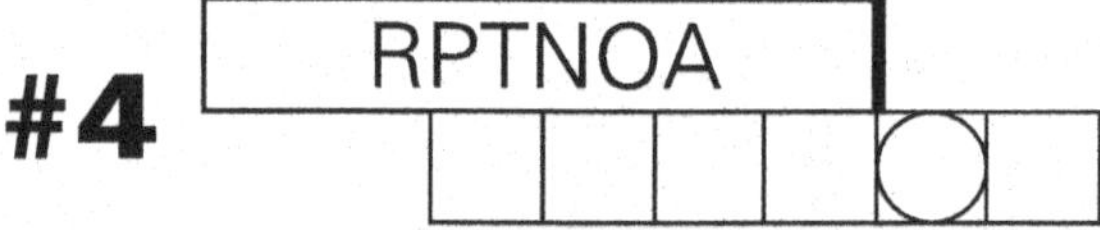

#5
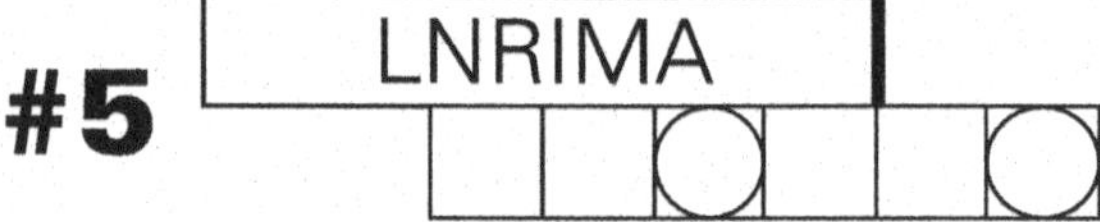

#6

Box of Clues

Stumped? Maybe you can find a clue below.

-Starts with *H*; ends with *G*
-Starts with *T*; ends with *T*
-Starts with *T*; ends with *A*
-Starts with *B*; ends with *S*
-Starts with *S*; ends with *N*
-Starts with *M*; ends with *N*
-Starts with *T*; ends with *N*

Arrange the circled letters to solve the mystery answer.

MYSTERY ANSWER

FIND THE JUMBLES®

JUMBLE® BrainBusters

Unscramble the Jumbles, one letter to each square, to spell words.

#5 PENWHE

#6 RTOEHM

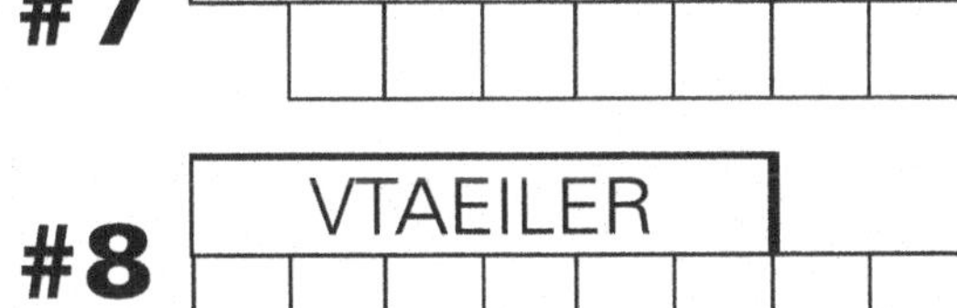

Find and circle the answers (from above) in the grid of letters below.

```
B A S N K E M I A C B E P A J B
I E C J M O T H E R X Y W O A P
M A O U W F R P K A G Z E B F R
D L B F Z N A G B D C O H L Z E
A E L C I Y J T R R E E P U L H
T B W S K A F O H C W K E C R T
J T U Z D C U P E E R R N F Z O
U O R E L A T I V E R U Z A D R
C I Y A I M N P A U B A E G U B
```

PUZZLE 76

GO FOR IT

JUMBLE BrainBusters

Unscramble the Jumbles, one letter to each square, to spell words that contain *GO*.

WAGON
ANGOLA
LAGOON
ONGOING
HANGOVER

#1 GORIR

#2 OFYGO

#3 NOGJRA

#4 EGOFOR

#5 NGEOOR

#6 GCIOHAC

Box of Clues

Stumped? Maybe you can find a clue below. (No clue for the mystery answer.)

- -Speech or writing having unusual or pretentious vocabulary
- -Harsh or trying circumstance
- -A U.S. state
- -Foolish
- -Lakeside U.S. city
- -Relinquish the enjoyment or advantage of

Arrange the circled letters to solve the mystery answer.

MYSTERY ANSWER

PUZZLE 77

MOVIES

JUMBLE BrainBusters

Unscramble the mixed-up letters, one letter to each square, to spell movie titles.

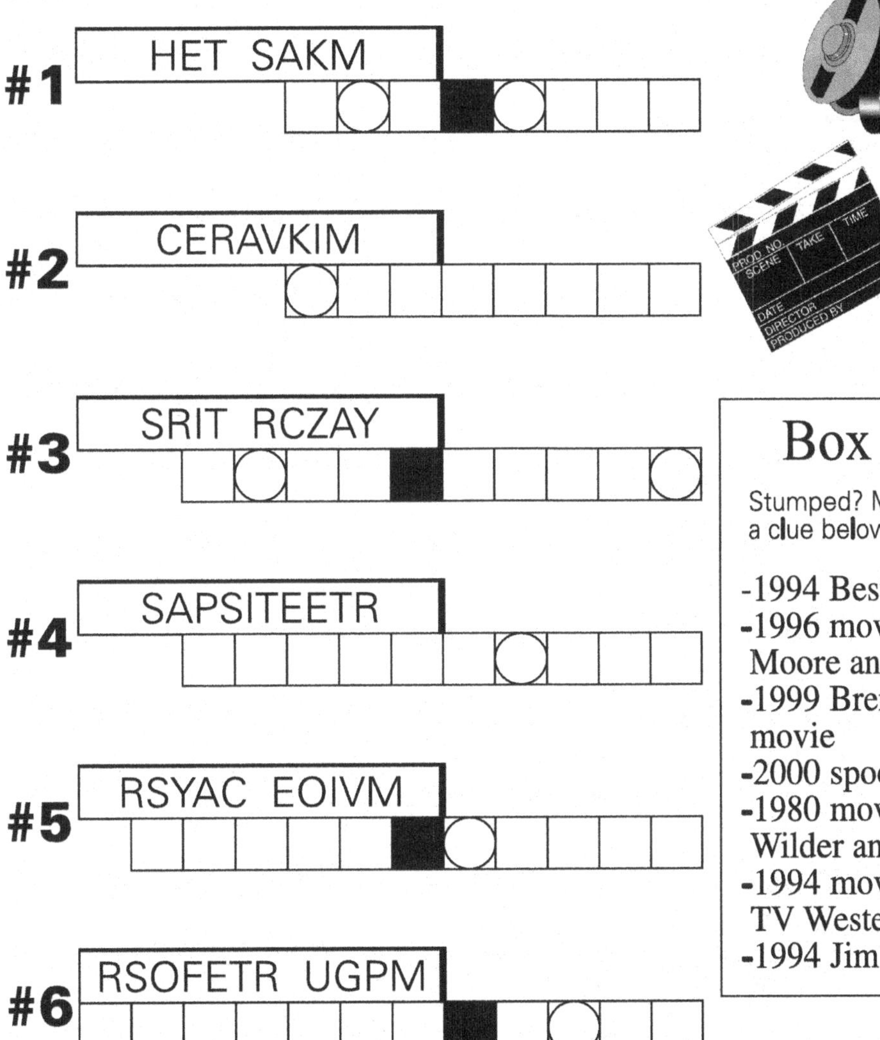

Box of Clues

Stumped? Maybe you can find a clue below.

- 1994 Best Picture
- 1996 movie starring Demi Moore and Burt Reynolds
- 1999 Brendan Fraser movie
- 2000 spoof
- 1980 movie starring Gene Wilder and Richard Pryor
- 1994 movie based on a TV Western
- 1994 Jim Carrey movie

MYSTERY ANSWER

Arrange the circled letters to solve the mystery answer.

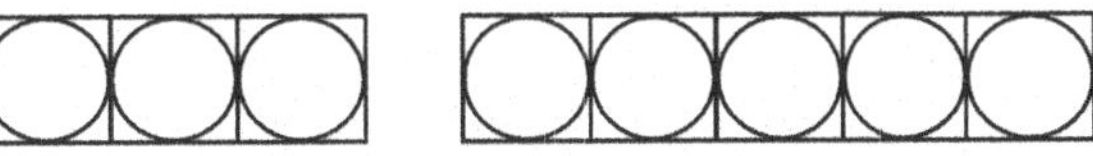

PUZZLE 78

MATH

JUMBLE BrainBusters

Unscramble the Jumbles, one letter to each square, so that each equation is correct.

For example: NONTEOEOW

ONE + ONE = TWO

#1 OTOSIFXUWR

☐◯☐ − ☐☐◯☐ = ◯☐☐

#2 NUFOFRUROOE

◯☐☐☐ ÷ ☐☐☐ = ☐◯☐☐

#3 EIYFNFOYTFTIF

☐☐☐☐☐ × ◯☐☐ = ☐☐☐◯☐

#4 OEEOZRGZITHER

☐☐◯☐☐ × ☐☐☐☐ = ☐☐◯☐

#5 TEETNYWTTIYHNRT

☐◯☐☐☐☐ + ☐◯☐ = ☐◯☐☐☐☐

Arrange the circled letters to solve the mystery equation.

MYSTERY EQUATION

◯◯◯◯◯ ÷ ◯◯◯ = ◯◯◯◯

PUZZLE 79

JUMBLE® TRIVIA

JUMBLE® BrainBusters

Unscramble the Jumbles, one letter to each square, to spell words as suggested by the trivia clues.

#1 There are about 40,000 characters in ______ script.

#1 SIHEECN

#2 Standard ______ cards are 3.5 inches wide by 2 inches long.

#2 NESUISBS

#3 Ben ______ invented the glass harmonica in 1761.

#3 LNKFNIRA

#4 The ______ swallowtail is the official state insect of ______.

#4 NGOOER

#5 The world's largest ______ is the leatherback (it can weigh over 1,000 pounds).

#5 LRUTET

Arrange the circled letters to solve the mystery answer.

Arnold Schwarzenegger paid $772,500 for President John F. Kennedy's ______ ______ at a 1996 auction.

MYSTERY ANSWER

PUZZLE 80

JUMBLE BrainBusters

RADAR
ARENA POP GOING
RIVER HIGH
DICED CRYPTIC

STARTS AND ENDS WITH THE SAME LETTER

Unscramble the Jumbles, one letter to each square, to spell words that start and end with the same letter.

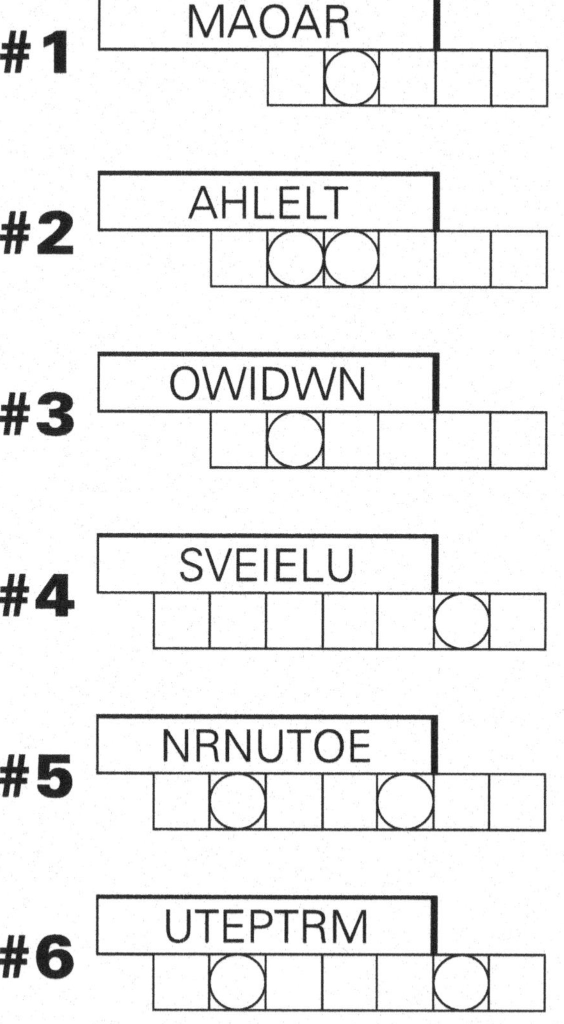

Box of Clues

Stumped? Maybe you can find a clue below.

-A subatomic particle
-Bay ______
-Deadly
-Smell
-A dog designation
-A musical instrument
-Difficult to define or describe

Arrange the circled letters to solve the mystery answer.

MYSTERY ANSWER

PUZZLE 81

JUMBLE BrainBusters

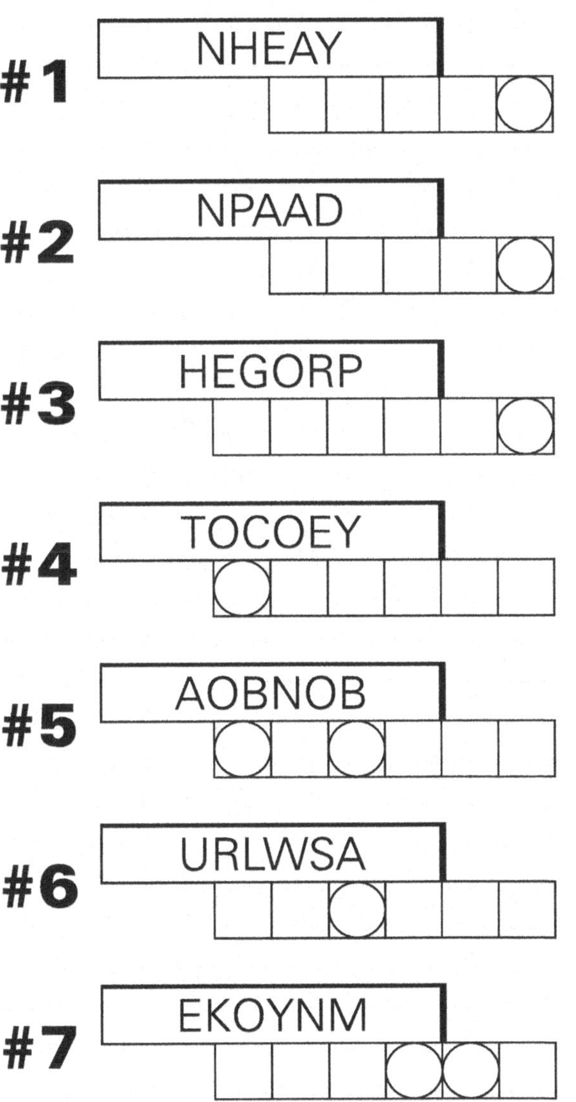

Interesting Mammal Facts

There is a debate about whether the hippopotamus or the white rhino is the second-heaviest land mammal (behind the elephant).

The killer whale, or orca, is the fastest sea mammal, capable of reaching speeds in excess of 30 miles per hour.

Arrange the circled letters to solve the mystery answer.

MYSTERY ANSWER

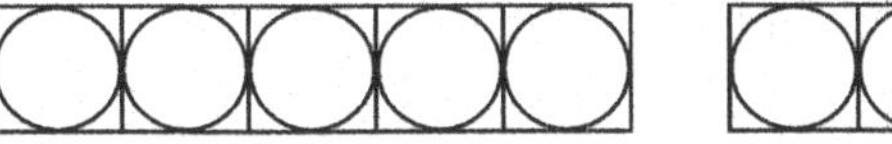

PUZZLE 82

JUMBLE® JOKES

Unscramble the mixed up letters to reveal the punch lines as suggested by the jokes.

#1 What has a head but no brain?

BGCAAEAB

#2 What lands as often on its tail as it does on its head?

NEYANP

#3 How should you treat a baby goat?

KALIDEIK

#4 What room can you bounce around in?

ORABLOMAL

#5 What kind of pliers do you use in arithmetic?

SIPMLLERIUT

#6 On what kind of ships do students study?

PHSCSORAHISL

PUZZLE 83

SUPER JUMBLE® CHALLENGE

JUMBLE® BrainBusters

#1 UGB

#2 OCBM

#3 RIFTU

#4 EMROEV

#5 PUCEKCH

#6 DLILALNF

#7 NESYORUTG

#8 KEICOPCTKP

#9 NFSICAITGIN

Unscramble the Jumbles, one letter to each square, to spell words.

Box of Clues

Stumped? Maybe you can find a clue below.

- -Important
- -Dump
- -Kid
- -An orange, for example
- -Type of thief
- -Bother
- -Fine-toothed ______
- -Despicable
- -Take away
- -Inspection

Arrange the circled letters to solve the mystery answer.

MYSTERY ANSWER

PUZZLE 84

UN-MIX AND MATCH
ELEMENTS

Section 1: Unscramble the mixed-up letters, one letter to each square, to spell names of elements.

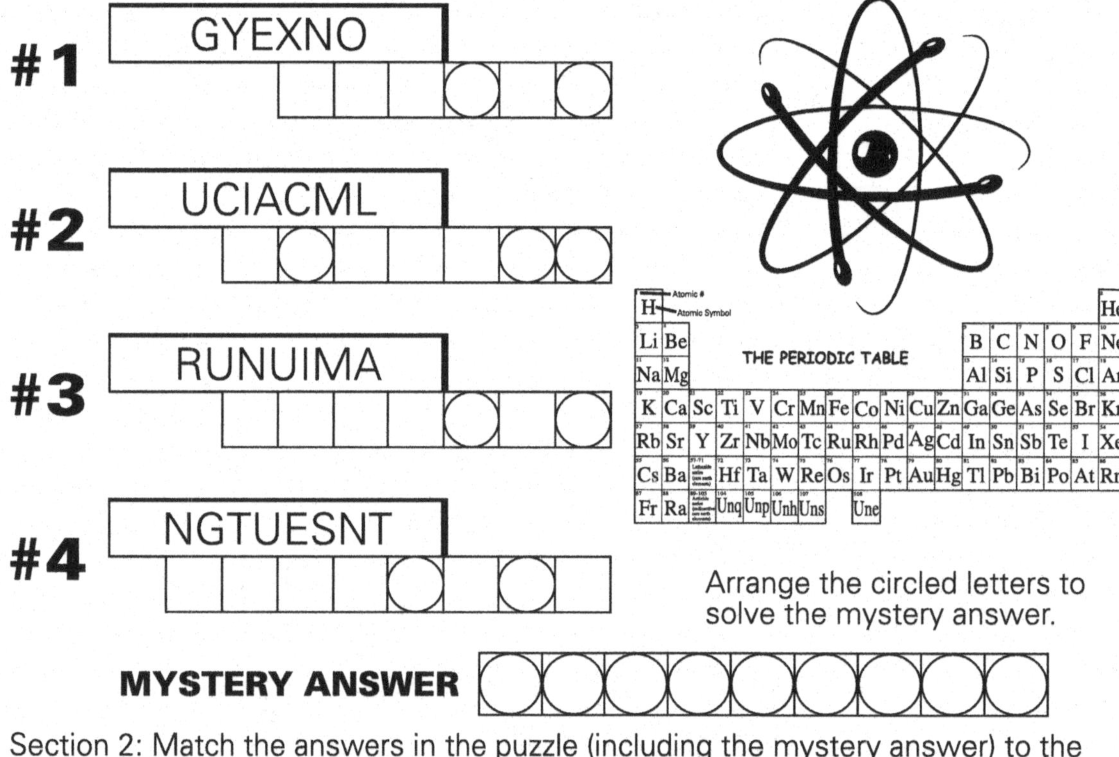

Arrange the circled letters to solve the mystery answer.

MYSTERY ANSWER

Section 2: Match the answers in the puzzle (including the mystery answer) to the following clues. (Write " MA." to represent the mystery answer.)

#____ A silvery, metallic element that makes up about three percent of the Earth's crust and is a basic component of most animals and plants.

#____ A gaseous element that makes up about 20 percent of the Earth's atmosphere.

#____ In powder form, this light, silvery-white metallic element burns with a brilliant white flame.

#____ This element and its alloys are commonly used in high-temperature structural materials and electrical elements, notably lamp filaments.

#____ A radioactive and toxic metallic element.

PUZZLE 85

OUTER SPACE

JUMBLE BrainBusters

Unscramble the Jumbles, one letter to each square, to spell words related to outer space.

#1 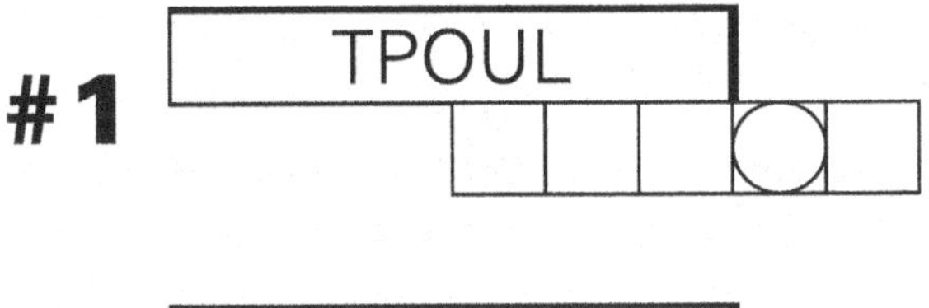

#2 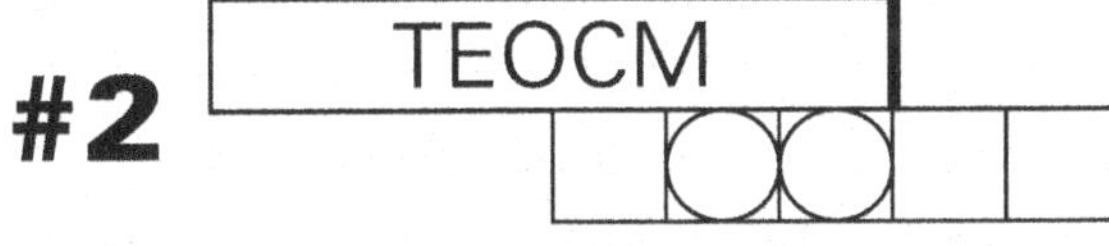

#3 

#4 

#5 

#6 

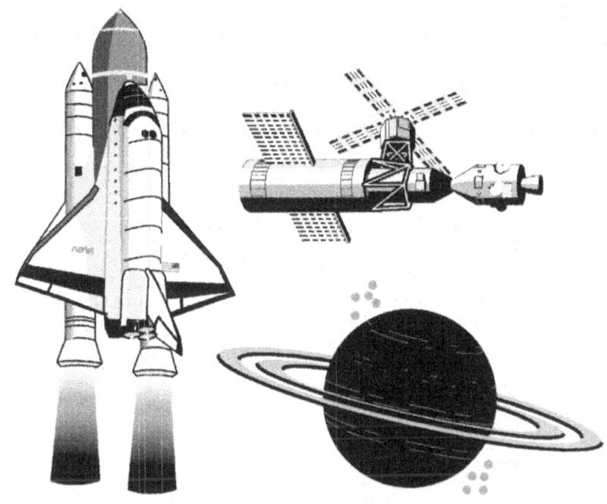

Box of Clues

Stumped? Maybe you can find a clue below. (No clue for the mystery answer.)

-Starts with *C*; ends with *T*
-Starts with *J*; ends with *R*
-Starts with *U*; ends with *S*
-Starts with *N*; ends with *E*
-Starts with *M*; ends with *E*
-Starts with *U*; ends with *E*
-Starts with *P*; ends with *O*

MYSTERY ANSWER

Arrange the circled letters to solve the mystery answer.

PUZZLE 86

JUMBLE® JOKES

Unscramble the mixed up letters to reveal the punch lines as suggested by the jokes.

#1 What has a big mouth but doesn't say a word?

RRIEAV

#2 What is the best thing to put into a pie?

HRYUOETET

#3 How did the 800-pound man feel when he lost 25 pounds?

TEHDIGDLE

#4 What has a head, can't think, but drives?

MAAHRME

#5 What happens when you throw a green rock in the Red Sea?

WSIGTETET

#6 What do you get if you cross an insect and a rabbit?

NSBUYUBNG

PUZZLE 87

ER

JUMBLE BrainBusters

Unscramble the Jumbles, one letter to each square, to spell words related to the television show *ER*.

#1

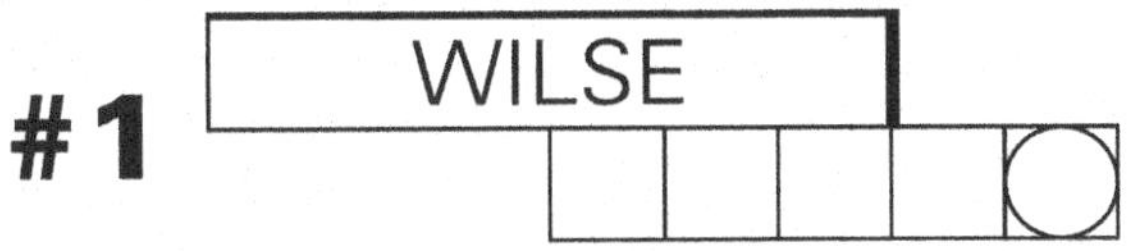

#2

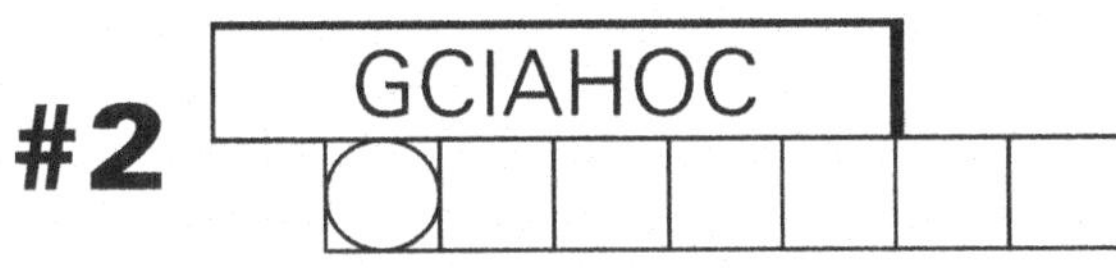

#3

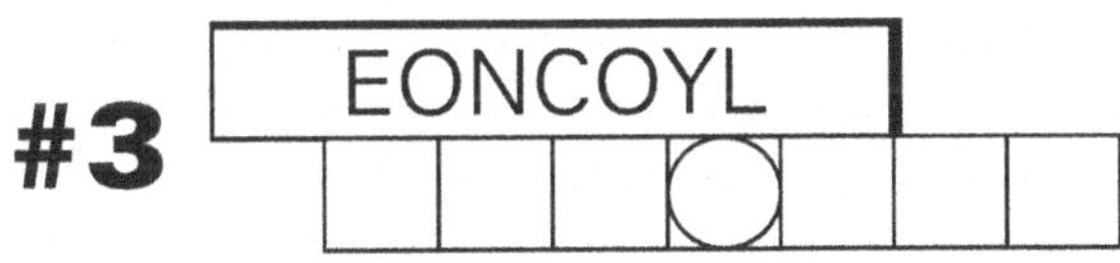

#4

#5

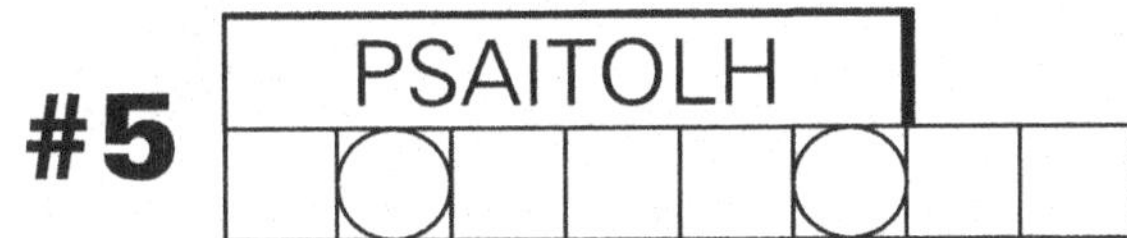

Box of Clues

Stumped? Maybe you can find a clue below. (No clue for the mystery answer.)

-Anthony ______
-Dr. Susan ______
-*ER* workplace
-Actor who played Dr. Ross
-*ER* setting

Arrange the circled letters to solve the mystery answer.

MYSTERY ANSWER

PUZZLE 88

JUMBLE® TRIVIA

Unscramble the Jumbles, one letter to each square, to spell words as suggested by the trivia clues.

#1 This company was bought by Ford for about $2.6 billion.

#1 UJGARA

#2 This classic female got her first car in 1962 (an Austin Healy).

#2 RBBEIA

#3 Andrew Jackson was appointed military governor of this state in 1821.

#3 RDFOIAL

#4 The world uses more than one billion gallons of this each day.

#4 MLPEOEURT

#5 This fish-eating bird is found everywhere throughout the world, except in Antarctica.

#5 PSEOYR

Arrange the circled letters to solve the mystery answer.

In 1869, Charles Alfred ______ started the company that shares his name.

MYSTERY ANSWER

PUZZLE 89

JUMBLE® CONNECTIONS

JUMBLE® BrainBusters

Unscramble the Jumbles, one letter to each square, to spell words that fit into the puzzle below.

ACROSS		DOWN	
#1	PORSUTP	#1	PSLEIC
#5	ZBEURZ	#2	DRUGEP
#7	MGIEA	#3	ETFTH
#8	TRTATCA	#4	ZACTE
#10	EEDY	#5	BAODR
#12	TOAAIRV	#6	ENRHRAC
#13	HSEREA	#8	DSAIVE
		#9	HTICTW
		#11	TCYAH

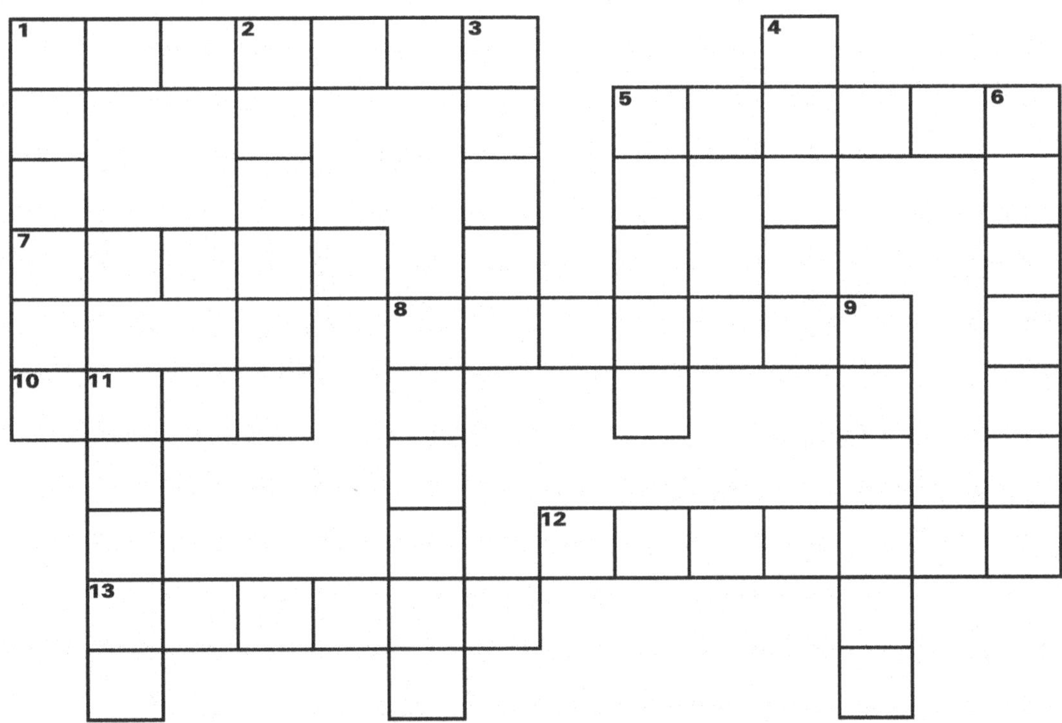

PUZZLE 90

ALL ABOUT WEDDINGS

JUMBLE BrainBusters

Unscramble the Jumbles, one letter to each square, to spell words related to weddings.

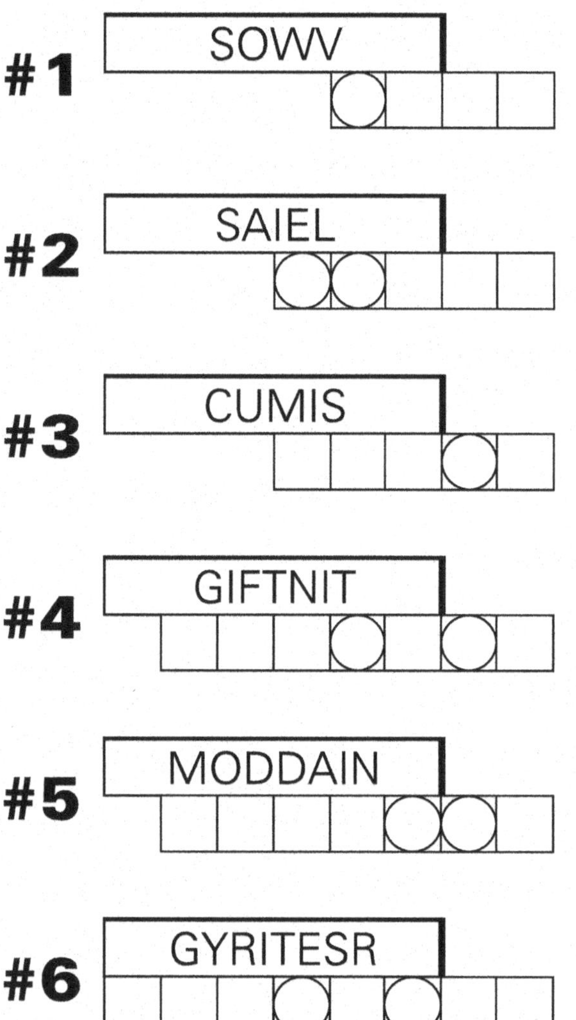

Interesting Wedding Facts

The custom of passing out sugared almonds wrapped in tulle as wedding favors dates back to early European history.

In ancient times, the traditional color of a bride's gown was red.

MYSTERY ANSWER

Arrange the circled letters to solve the mystery answer.

SPORTS

JUMBLE BrainBusters

Unscramble the Jumbles, one letter to each square, to spell words related to sports.

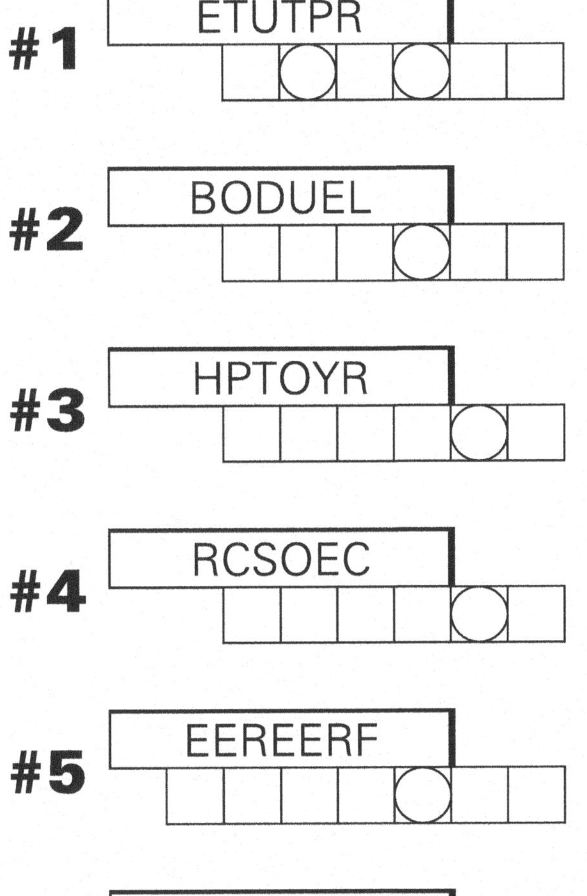

#1 ETUTPR

#2 BODUEL

#3 HPTOYR

#4 RCSOEC

#5 EEREERF

#6 OLBFTALO

Box of Clues

Stumped? Maybe you can find a clue below.

-Game played on a rectangular field with a round ball
-Type of award
-Game played by two teams of 11 players each
-Remarkable baseball player
-Golf club used to hit a ball a short distance
-Judge
-A baseball hit

MYSTERY ANSWER

Arrange the circled letters to solve the mystery answer.

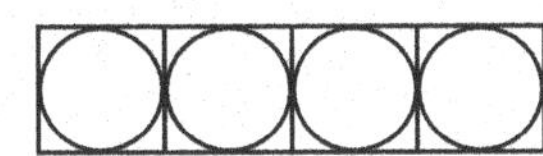

PUZZLE 92

ALL ABOUT PLANTS

JUMBLE BrainBusters

Unscramble the Jumbles, one letter to each square, to spell words related to plants.

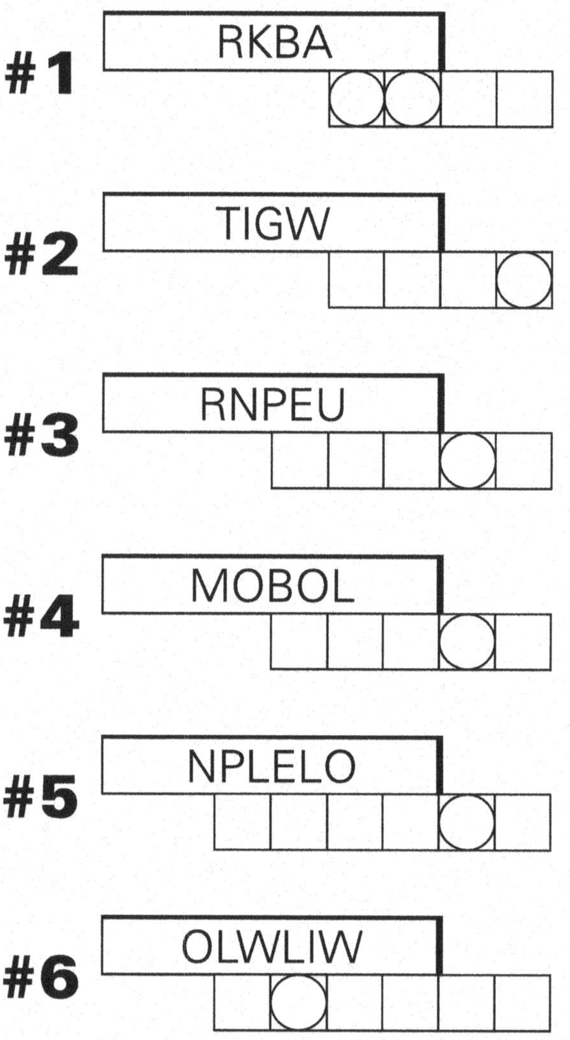

#1 RKBA

#2 TIGW

#3 RNPEU

#4 MOBOL

#5 NPLELO

#6 OLWLIW

Interesting Plant Facts

A mature oak tree can shed more than 500,000 leaves.

Oil of wintergreen comes from the bark of the sweet birch.

Arrange the circled letters to solve the mystery answer.

MYSTERY ANSWER

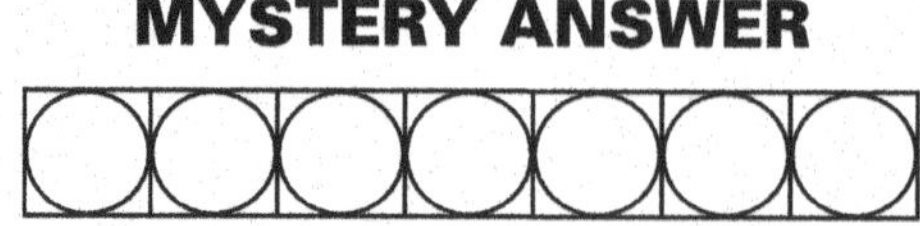

PUZZLE 93

JUMBLE® JOKES

JUMBLE® BrainBusters

Unscramble the mixed up letters to reveal the punch lines as suggested by the jokes.

#1 What kind of dance do buns do?

CUABADNEN

#2 What kind of pool can't you swim in?

OCLAPOAR

#3 What has four fingers and a thumb but is not a hand?

GAOVEL

#4 What is always coming but never arrives?

ROORTWMO

#5 What has a foot on each end and one in the middle?

RCYDKATIAS

#6 What is dark but made by light?

SAAODWH

PUZZLE 94

GUNSMOKE

JUMBLE BrainBusters

Unscramble the Jumbles, one letter to each square, to spell words related to the television show *Gunsmoke*.

#1
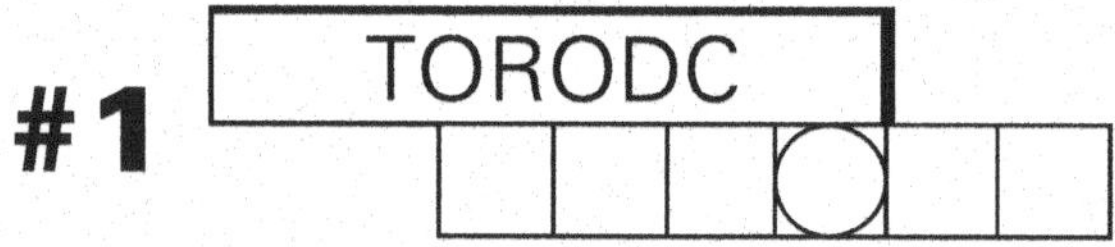

#2

#3

#4
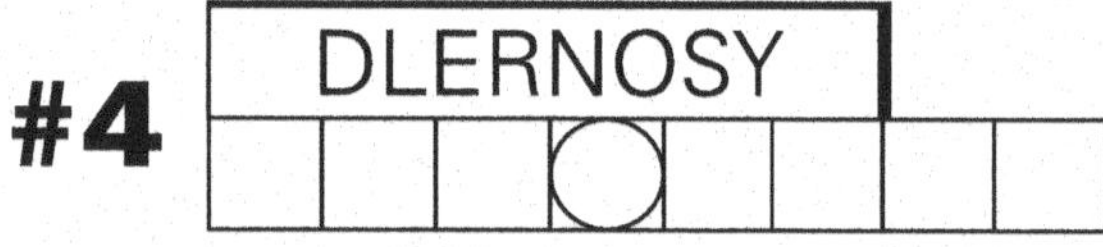

#5
TCDEOIYDG

Box of Clues

Stumped? Maybe you can find a clue below. (No clue for the mystery answer.)

-______ Matt Dillon
-Galen Adams' profession
-Dennis ______
-*Gunsmoke* setting
-Actor who played Quint Asper from 1962 to 1965

Arrange the circled letters to solve the mystery answer.

MYSTERY ANSWER

PUZZLE 95

IT'S TIME TO GET *UP*

JUMBLE BrainBusters

Unscramble the Jumbles, one letter to each square, to spell words that contain *UP*.

#1 PICDU

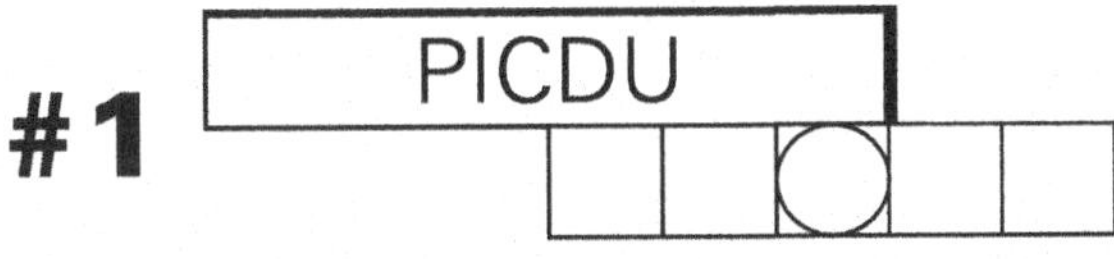

#2 PAUTBR

#3 PCUEOL

#4 NPOUOC

#5 ETJIRPU

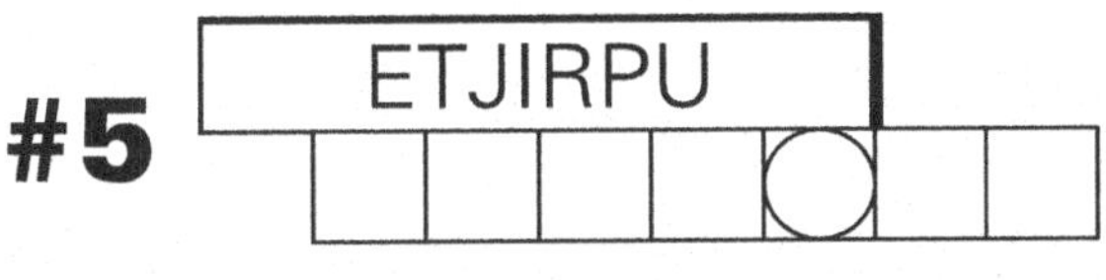

#6 PRUTOSP

SOUP
SUPER
GROUP
CUPFUL
ERUPTED

Box of Clues

Stumped? Maybe you can find a clue below. (No clue for the mystery answer.)

- -Discount certificate
- -The son of Venus
- -Planet or Roman god
- -Brace
- -Pair
- -Sudden

Arrange the circled letters to solve the mystery answer.

MYSTERY ANSWER

ADJECTIVES

JUMBLE BrainBusters

Unscramble the Jumbles, one letter to each square, to spell adjectives.

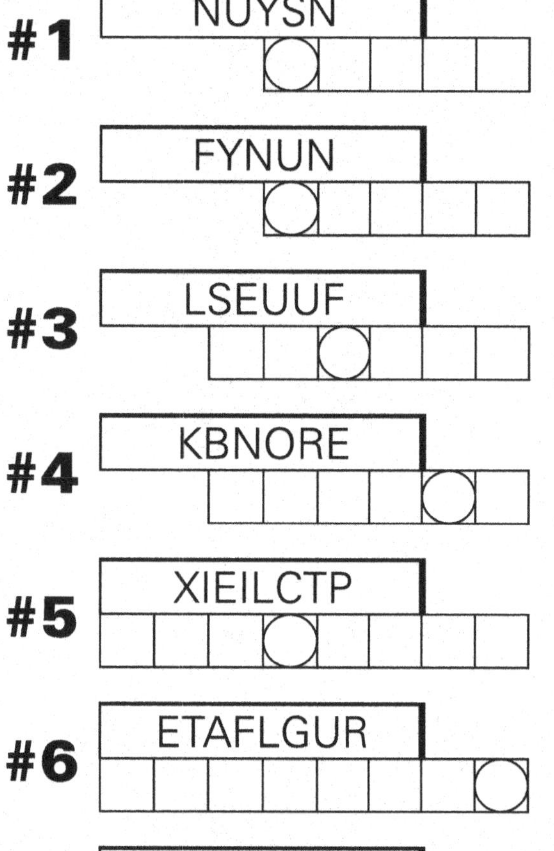

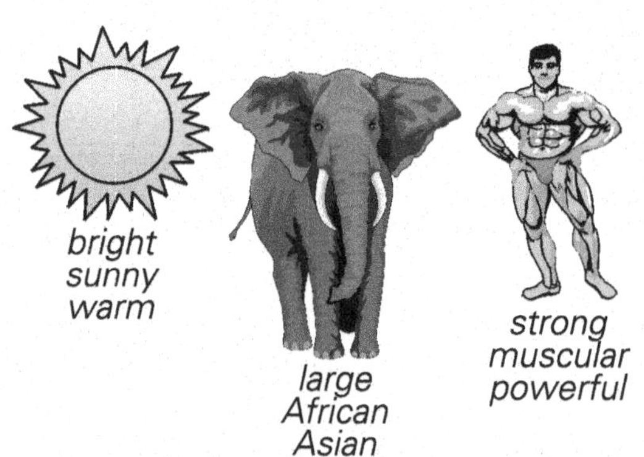

Box of Clues

Stumped? Maybe you can find a clue below.

- Clearly expressed
- Cracked
- Altruistic
- Humorous
- Attractive
- Bright, clear
- Advantageous
- Thankful
- Notorious

Arrange the circled letters to solve the mystery answer.

MYSTERY ANSWER

PUZZLE 97

DOUBLE JUMBLE® BRAINBUSTERS

Unscramble the Jumbles, one letter to each square, to spell words.

#1
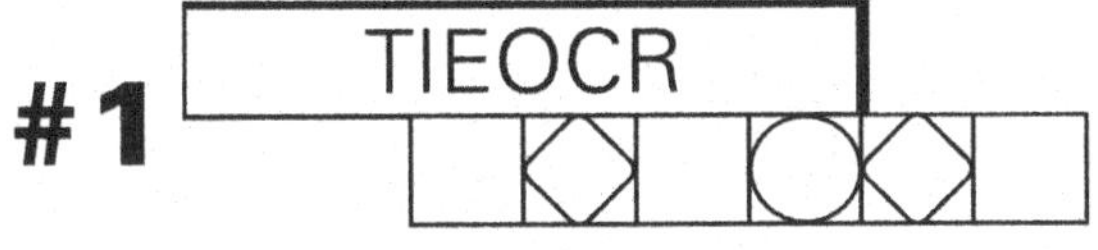

#2

#3

#4

#5

#6
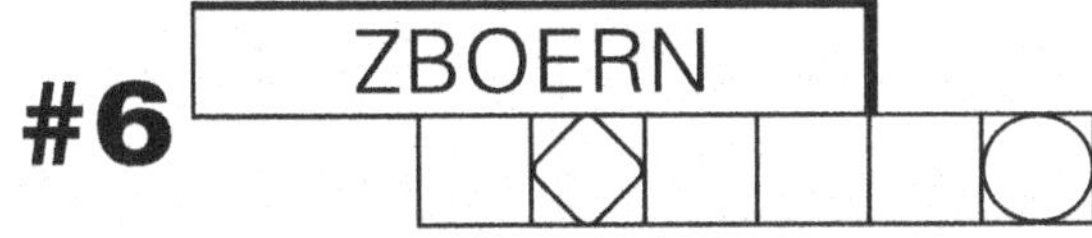

JUMBLE® BrainBusters

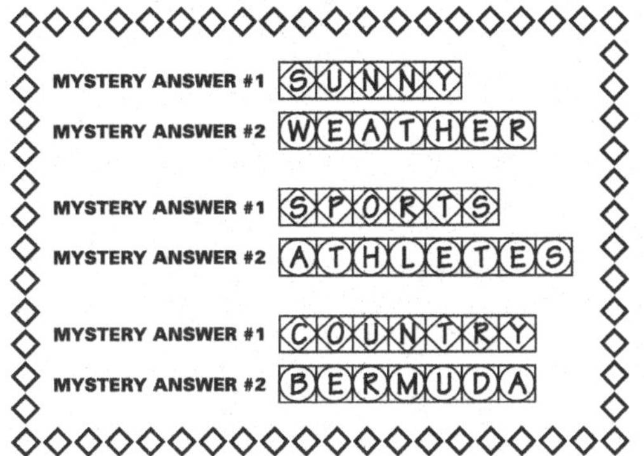

Box of Clues

Stumped? Maybe you can find a clue below. (No clues for the mystery answers.)

- -Sexual
- -Small bed
- -Daily occurrence
- -Grumpy
- -Grasp and hold tightly
- -An alloy

Arrange the diamonded letters to solve mystery answer #1. Arrange the circled letters to solve mystery answer #2. (The mystery answers will relate to each other.)

MYSTERY ANSWER #1

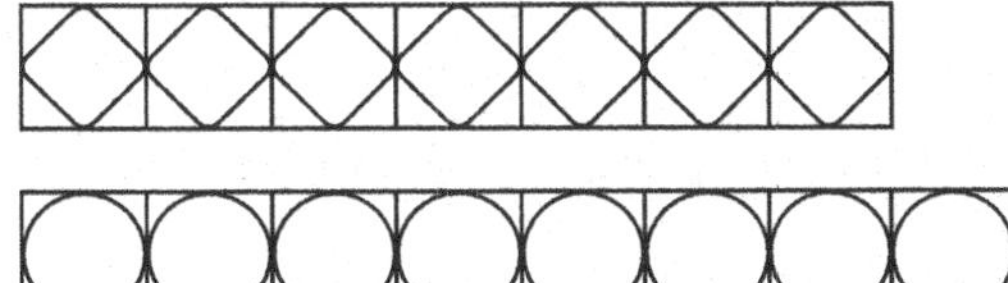

MYSTERY ANSWER #2

PUZZLE 98

JUMBLE® CONNECTIONS

JUMBLE® BrainBusters

Unscramble the Jumbles, one letter to each square, to spell words that fit into the puzzle below.

ACROSS		DOWN	
#1	DEFMREO	#1	NCIHLF
#5	NBOAOB	#2	BEKMRA
#7	ANLAV	#3	EIMVO
#8	UCBEEAS	#4	BEOSO
#10	HOKO	#5	NGBAE
#12	TAUCCON	#6	LNCEEGT
#13	RNYELA	#8	EDILBR
		#9	UGNOHE
		#11	NOZOE

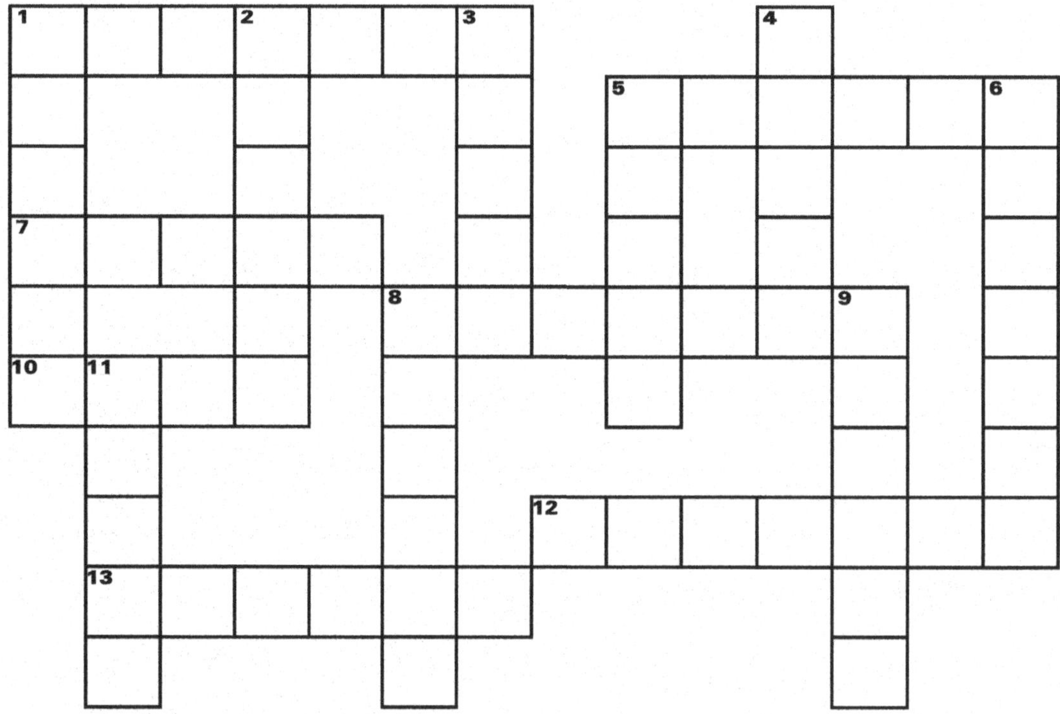

BEVERAGES

JUMBLE BrainBusters

Unscramble the Jumbles, one letter to each square, to spell things you can drink.

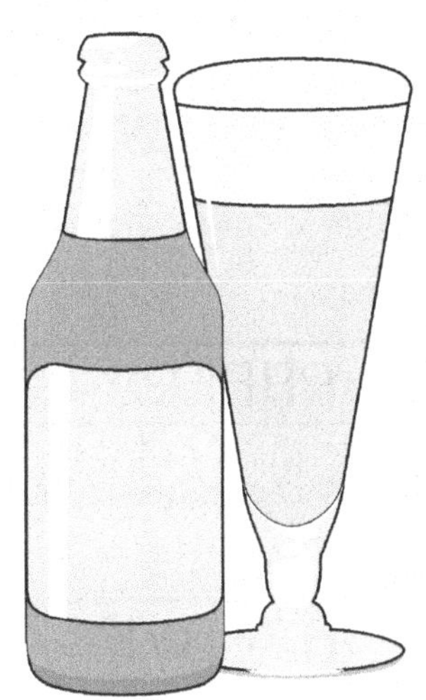

#1 CJEIU

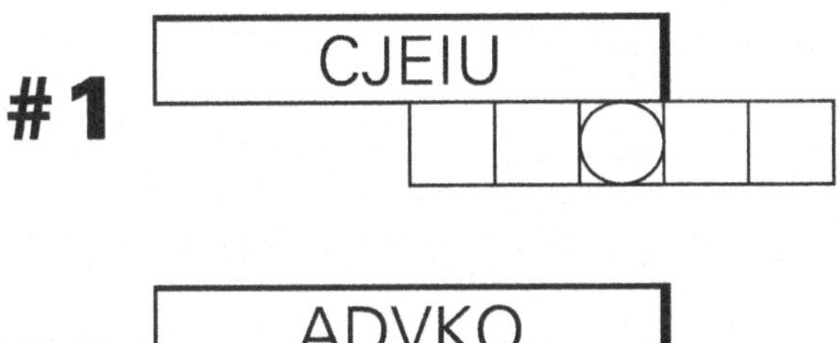

#2 ADVKO

#3 ETRWA

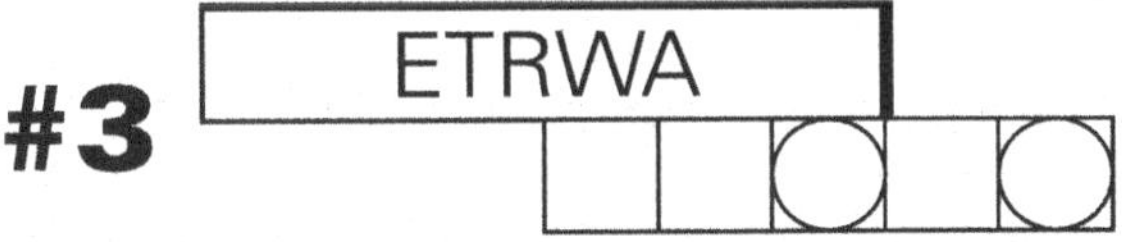

#4 FOECEF

#5 SESREOSP

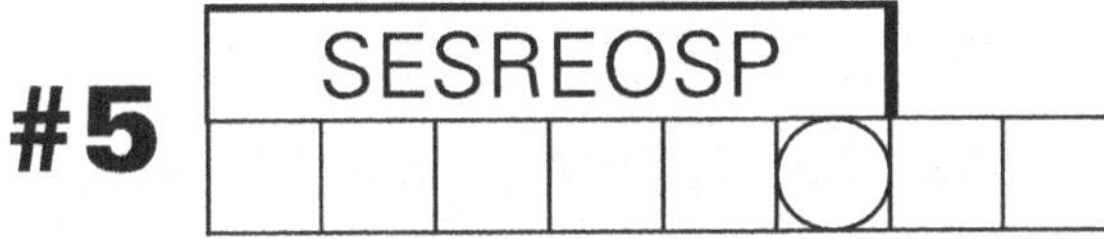

#6 DNLAEEOM

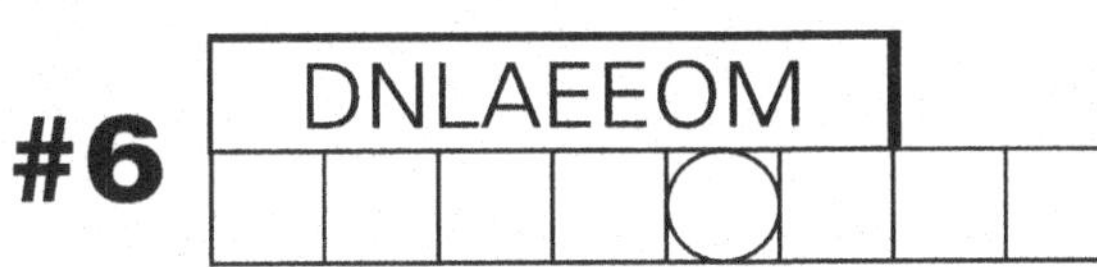

Interesting Beverage Facts

Some of the many people who have endorsed Coke include Roy Orbison, Diana Ross, and Ray Charles.

Milk is the official beverage of North Carolina.

Arrange the circled letters to solve the mystery answer.

MYSTERY ANSWER

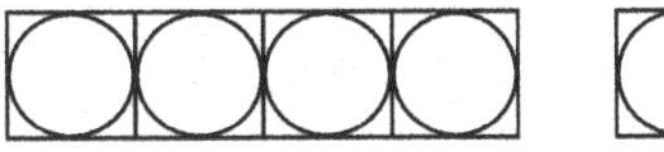 

ALL ABOUT FOOD

JUMBLE BrainBusters

Unscramble the Jumbles, one letter to each square, to spell words related to food.

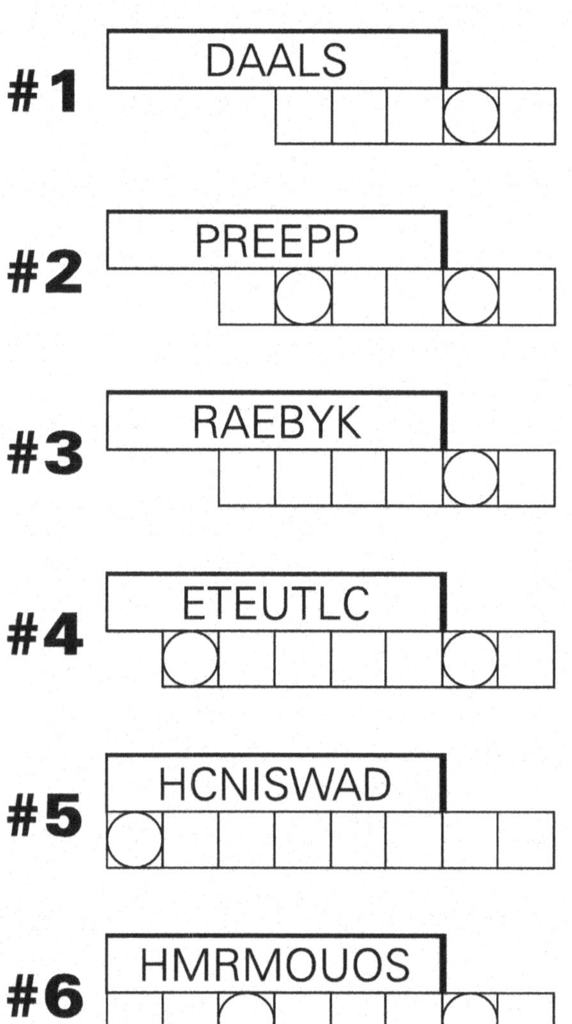

#1 DAALS

#2 PREEPP

#3 RAEBYK

#4 ETEUTLC

#5 HCNISWAD

#6 HMRMOUOS

Box of Clues

Stumped? Maybe you can find a clue below. (No clue for the mystery answer.)

-Starts with *P*; ends with *R*
-Starts with *M*; ends with *M*
-Starts with *B*; ends with *Y*
-Starts with *L*; ends with *E*
-Starts with *S*; ends with *D*
-Starts with *S*; ends with *H*

Arrange the circled letters to solve the mystery answer.

MYSTERY ANSWER

JUMBLE BrainBusters

LANGUAGES

Unscramble the Jumbles, one letter to each square, to spell the names of languages.

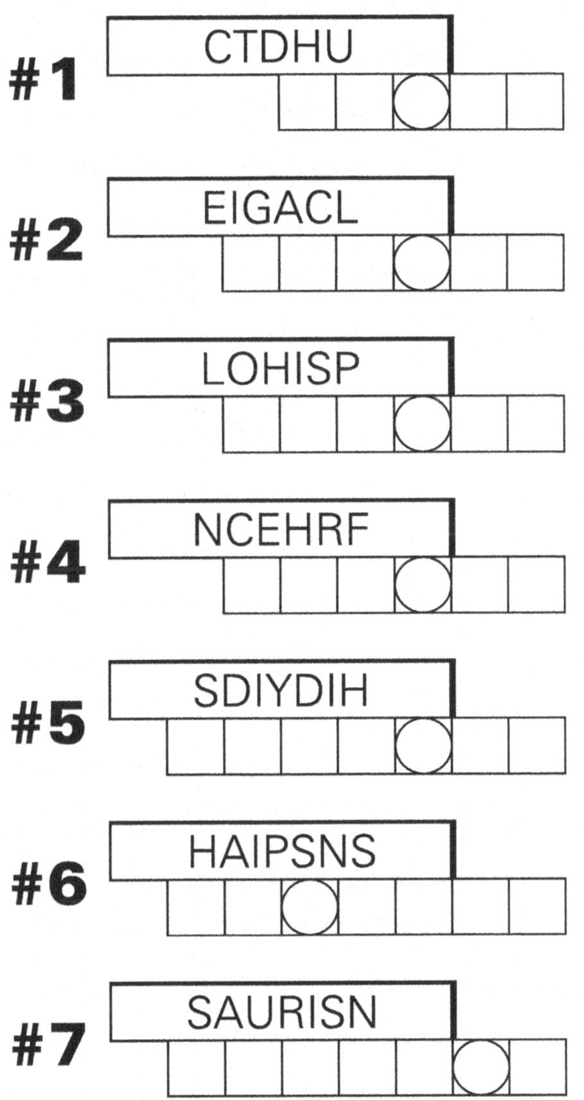

Arrange the circled letters to solve the mystery answer.

Interesting Language Facts

The Navajo Indian language was used as a code by the United States during World War II.

More than 700 languages are spoken in Papua New Guinea.

In a majority of the world's languages, the word for *mother* starts with *M*.

MYSTERY ANSWER

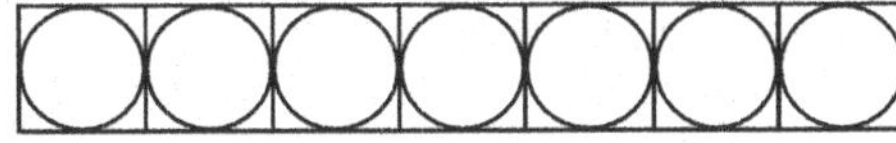

PUZZLE 102

ITALY

Unscramble the Jumbles, one letter to each square, to spell words related to Italy.

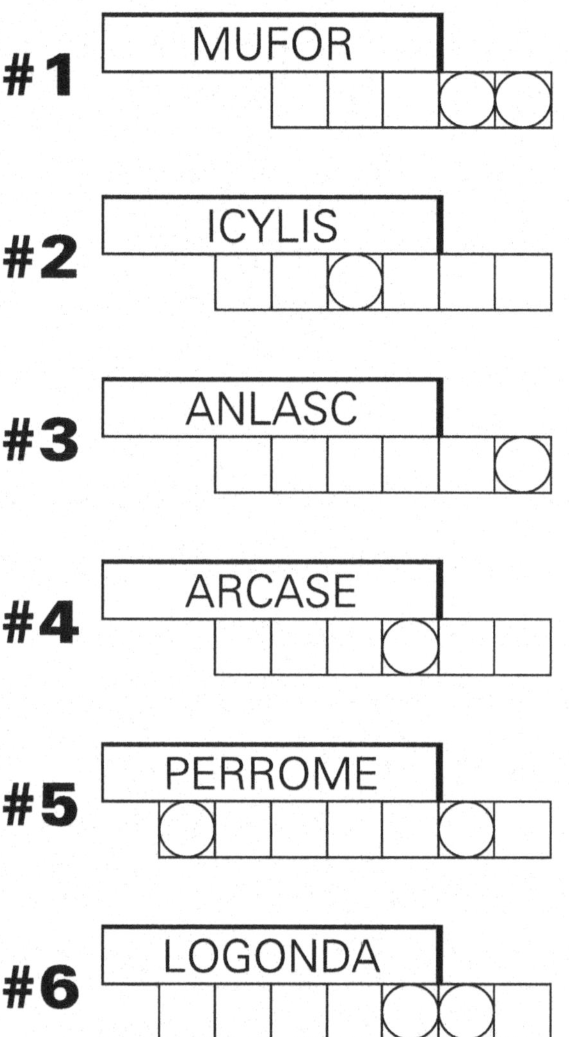

JUMBLE BrainBusters

Box of Clues

Stumped? Maybe you can find a clue below. (No clue for the mystery answer.)

- Italian island
- Waterways
- Italian leader born on Corsica
- Roman place of assembly
- Narrow boat
- Type of leader common in Italy in ancient times

Arrange the circled letters to solve the mystery answer.

MYSTERY ANSWER

PUZZLE 103

JUMBLE BrainBusters

HUMAN BODY

Unscramble the Jumbles, one letter to each square, to spell words related to the human body.

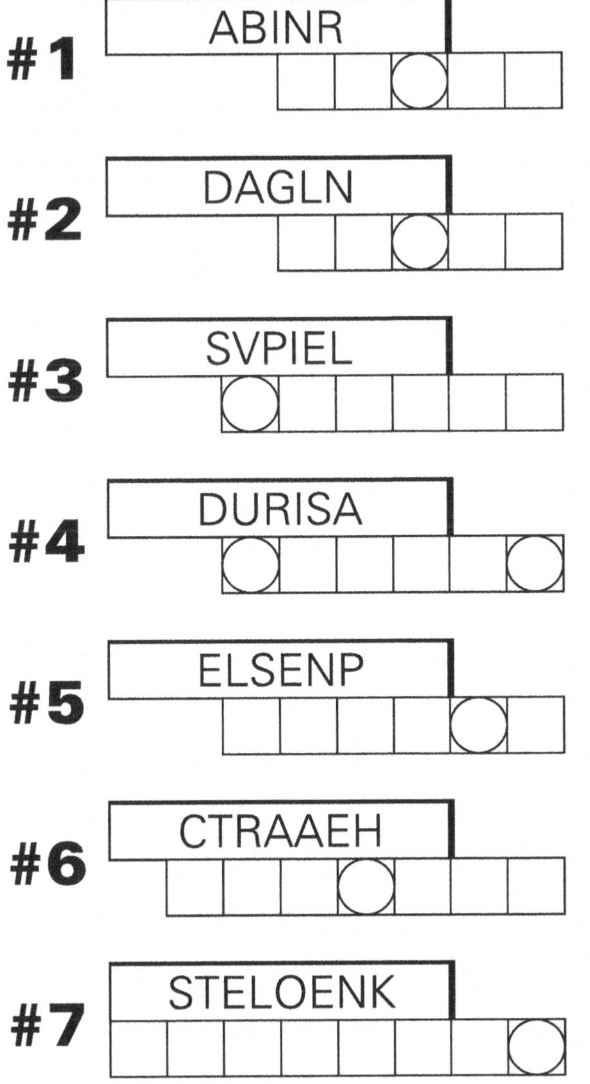

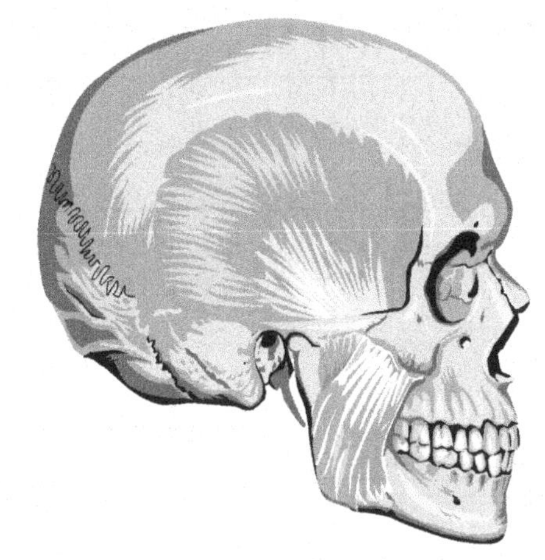

Box of Clues

Stumped? Maybe you can find a clue below.

-Starts with *S*; ends with *N*
-Starts with *B*; ends with *N*
-Starts with *G*; ends with *D*
-Starts with *P*; ends with *S*
-Starts with *T*; ends with *A*
-Starts with *S*; ends with *N*
-Starts with *P*; ends with *S*
-Starts with *R*; ends with *S*

Arrange the circled letters to solve the mystery answer.

MYSTERY ANSWER

UN-MIX AND MATCH
ACTRESSES

JUMBLE BrainBusters

Section 1: Unscramble the mixed-up letters, one letter to each square, to spell names of actresses.

#1 LIOENC DAINKM

#2 UAILJ RBRESOT

#3 NDSAAR KUCLOBL

#4 POIWOH RGBOELGD

Arrange the circled letters to solve the mystery answer. **MYSTERY ANSWER**

Section 2: Match the answers in the puzzle (including the mystery answer) to the following clues. (Write " MA." to represent the mystery answer.)

#____ This actress was born on June 20, 1967, in Honolulu, Hawaii. Her family moved to Australia when she was a child.

#____ This actress was born on July 26, 1964, in Arlington, Virginia. Her mother was an opera singer and her father was a voice coach.

#____ This actress was born on November 21, 1945, in Washington, D.C. She has a daughter who is an actress.

#____ This actress was born on November 13, 1955, in New York City. Her real name is Caryn Elaine Johnson.

#____ This actress was born on October 28, 1967, in Smyrna, Georgia. Her brother is an actor.

PUZZLE 105

MYSTERY PERSON

JUMBLE BrainBusters

Unscramble the Jumbles, one letter to each square, to spell words that relate to the mystery person.

#1
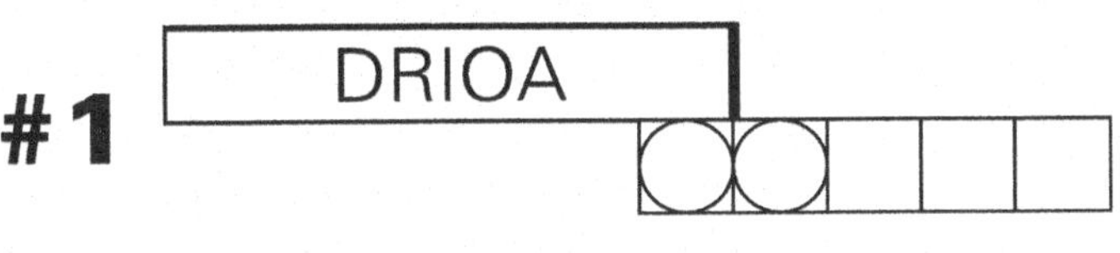

#2

#3
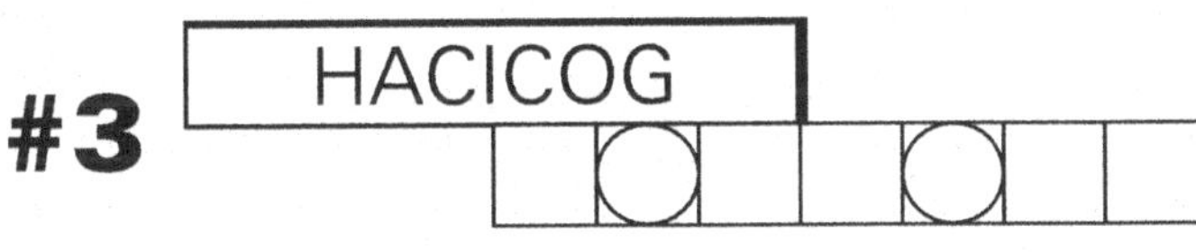

#4

#5

Box of Clues

Stumped? Maybe you can find a clue below.

- -He moved to this city in 1944
- -His ______ career began in 1933 at KVOO-AM
- -He attended college at the ______ of Tulsa
- -He was born and raised in Tulsa, ______
- -He moved to Hawaii in 1940 to cover the U.S. Navy's ______ fleet

Arrange the circled letters to solve the mystery person.

MYSTERY PERSON

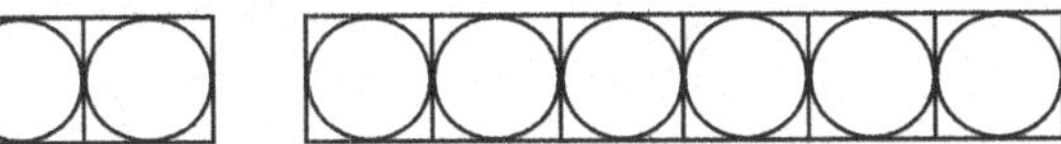

PUZZLE
106

MOVIES

JUMBLE BrainBusters

Unscramble the mixed-up letters, one letter to each square, to spell movie titles.

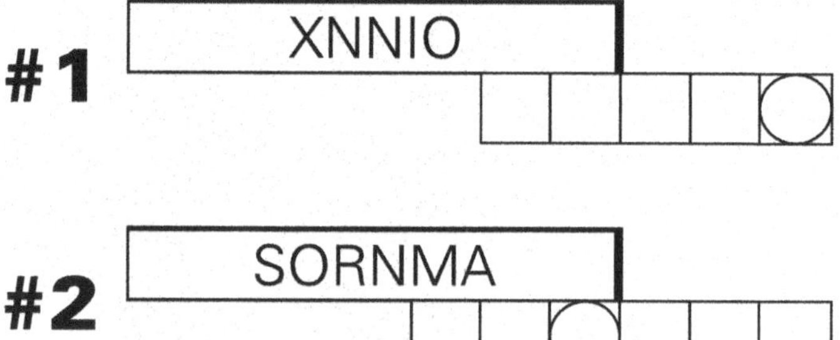

#1 XNNIO

#2 SORNMA

#3 TEH NTSIG

#4 HTE OSRUH

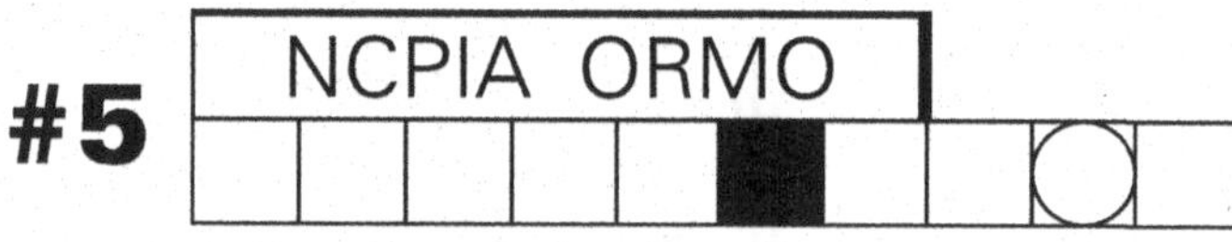

#5 NCPIA ORMO

#6 TPHAC DAASM

Box of Clues

Stumped? Maybe you can find a clue below.

- -1996 Mel Gibson movie
- -1995 movie about a U.S. president
- -2002 movie starring Nicole Kidman, Julianne Moore, and Meryl Streep
- -1996 John Travolta movie
- -2002 Jodie Foster movie
- -1973 Best Picture
- -1998 Robin Williams movie

Arrange the circled letters to solve the mystery answer.

MYSTERY ANSWER

PUZZLE 107

WARS AND THE MILITARY

JUMBLE® BrainBusters

Unscramble the Jumbles, one letter to each square, to spell words related to wars and the military.

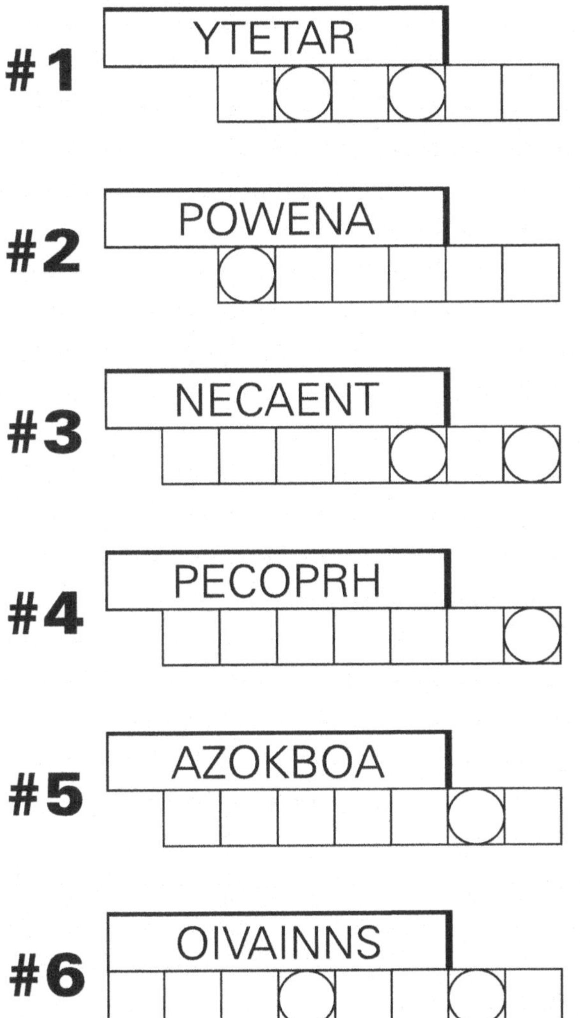

#1 YTETAR

#2 POWENA

#3 NECAENT

#4 PECOPRH

#5 AZOKBOA

#6 OIVAINNS

Box of Clues

Stumped? Maybe you can find a clue below.

-Type of container
-Peace ______
-Entrance of an armed force into a territory to conquer
-Aircraft nickname
-Conflict that lasted three years
-Shoulder-held weapon
-Instrument of attack or defense in combat

Arrange the circled letters to solve the mystery answer.

MYSTERY ANSWER

PUZZLE 108

MEANS THE OPPOSITE

JUMBLE BrainBusters

Unscramble the Jumbles, one letter to each square, to spell pairs of words that have opposite or nearly opposite meanings.

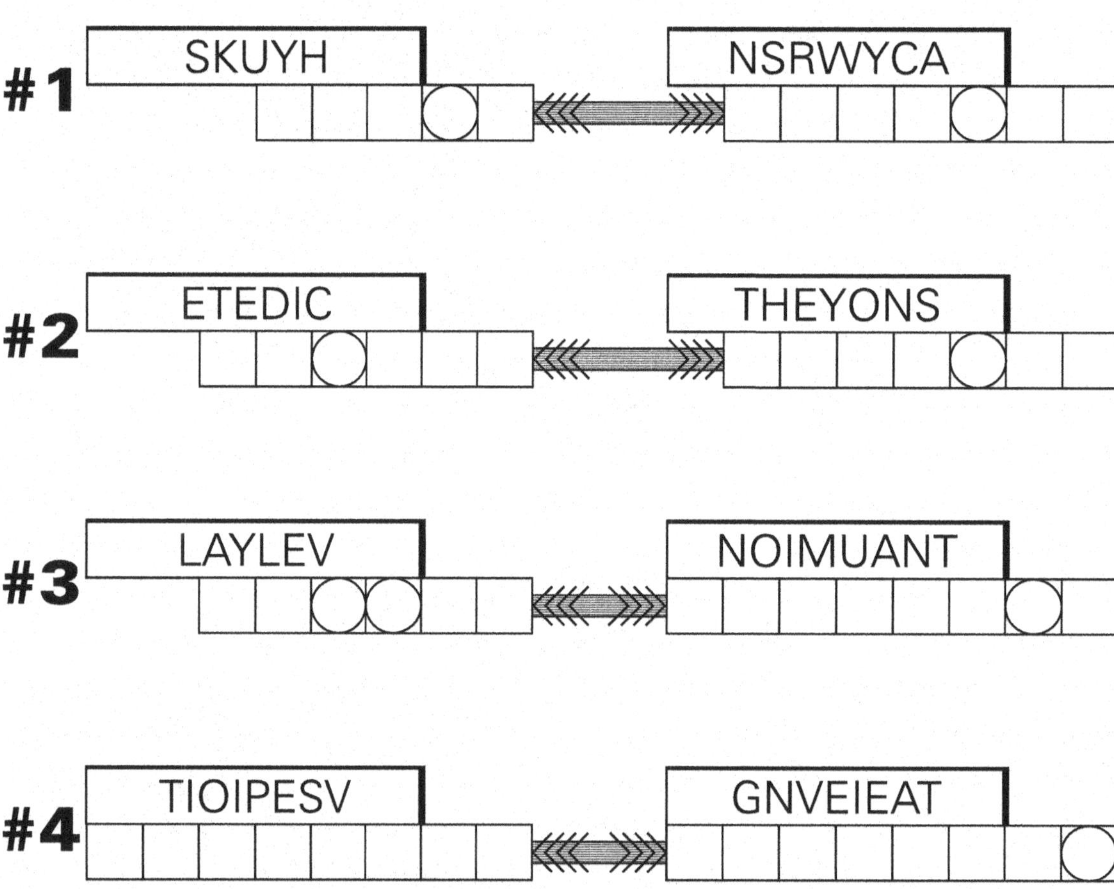

Arrange the circled letters to solve the mystery answer. (Form two words that have the opposite or nearly opposite meanings.)

MYSTERY ANSWER

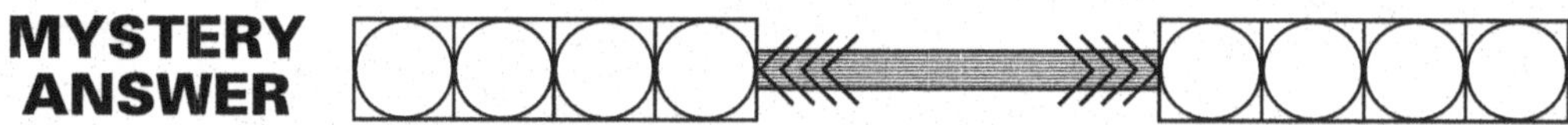

MATH

JUMBLE BrainBusters

Unscramble the Jumbles, one letter to each square, so that each equation is correct.

For example: NOTLSWOEOPNEU
ONE PLUS ONE = TWO

#1 XNFEOUSPSIVLIE

#2 NPOLENSSVUNEWIET

#3 ZNNINSNUIEREMOEIN

#4 FEVSEWUITIESMVONN

#5 EUHRETWSFOIGTMTIO

Then arrange the circled letters to solve the mystery equation.

MYSTERY EQUATION

PLANET EARTH

JUMBLE BrainBusters

Unscramble the Jumbles, one letter to each square, to spell words related to planet Earth.

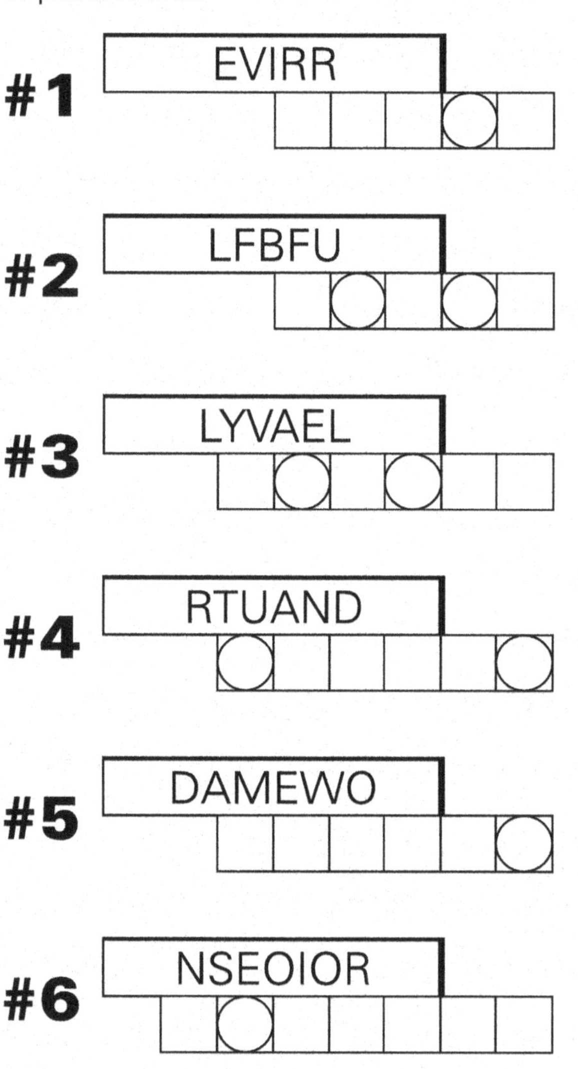

Interesting Planet Earth Facts

Most of the South Pole is a desert environment, averaging about the same amount of monthly rainfall as the Sahara Desert.

There is about one quarter-pound of salt in a gallon of seawater.

Arrange the circled letters to solve the mystery answer.

MYSTERY ANSWER

PUZZLE 111

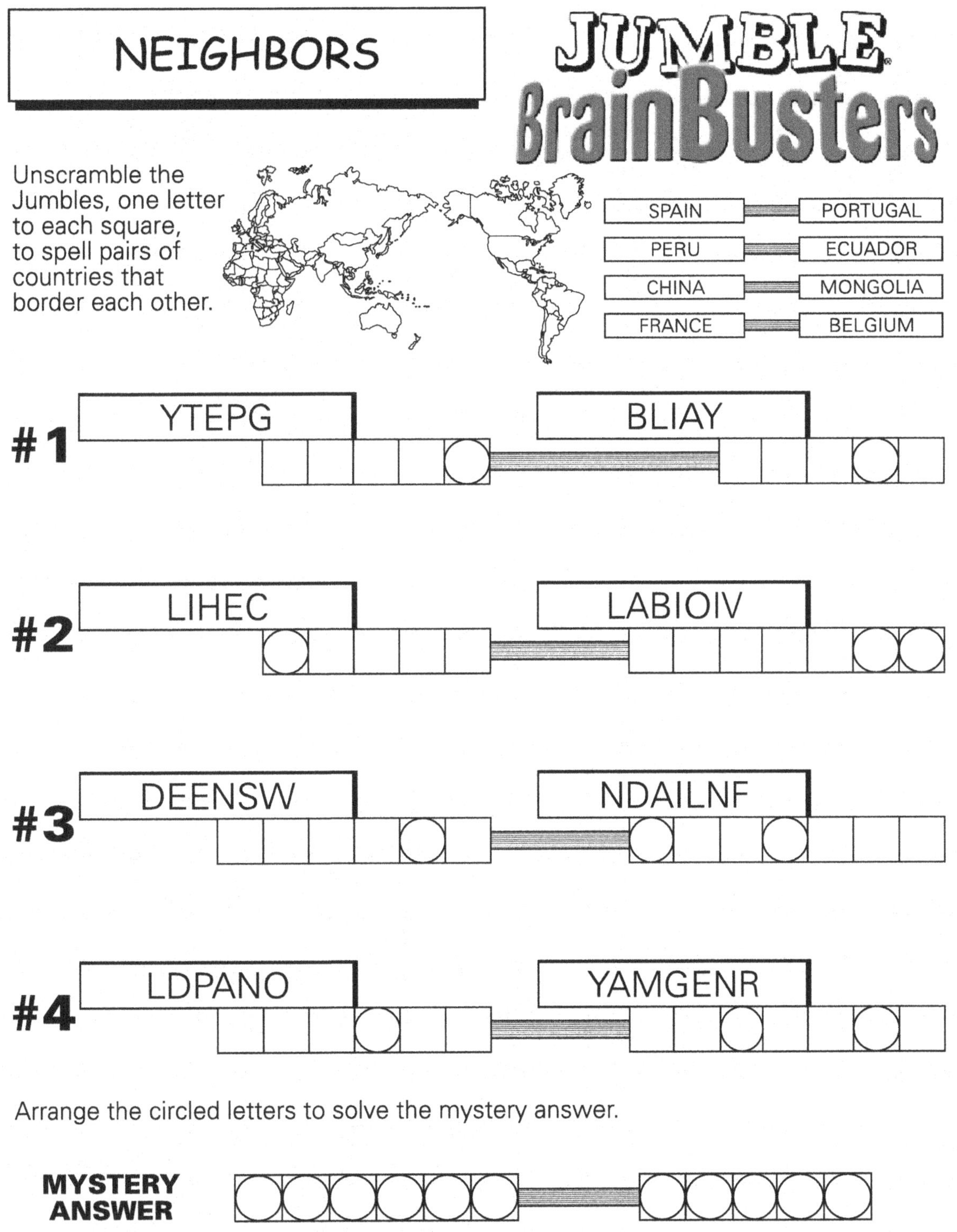
NEIGHBORS
JUMBLE BrainBusters
Unscramble the Jumbles, one letter to each square, to spell pairs of countries that border each other.
SPAIN
PORTUGAL
PERU
ECUADOR
CHINA
MONGOLIA
FRANCE
BELGIUM
#1
YTEPG
BLIAY
#2
LIHEC
LABIOIV
#3
DEENSW
NDAILNF
#4
LDPANO
YAMGENR
Arrange the circled letters to solve the mystery answer.
MYSTERY ANSWER

SOCCER

JUMBLE® BrainBusters

Unscramble the Jumbles, one letter to each square, to spell words related to soccer.

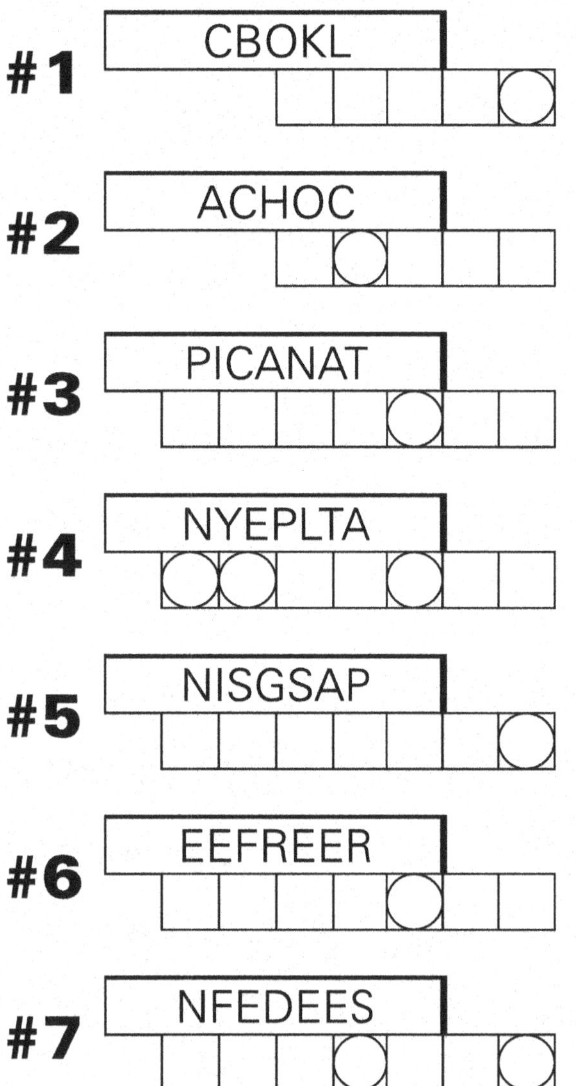

#1 CBOKL

#2 ACHOC

#3 PICANAT

#4 NYEPLTA

#5 NISGSAP

#6 EEFREER

#7 NFEDEES

Interesting Soccer Fact

Brazil has never (as of 2003) won a gold Olympic medal in soccer, despite being home to Péle, one of the world's most famous soccer players.

Arrange the circled letters to solve the mystery answer.

MYSTERY ANSWER

PUZZLE 113

MEANS THE SAME

JUMBLE BrainBusters

Unscramble the Jumbles, one letter to each square, to spell pairs of words that have the same or similar meanings.

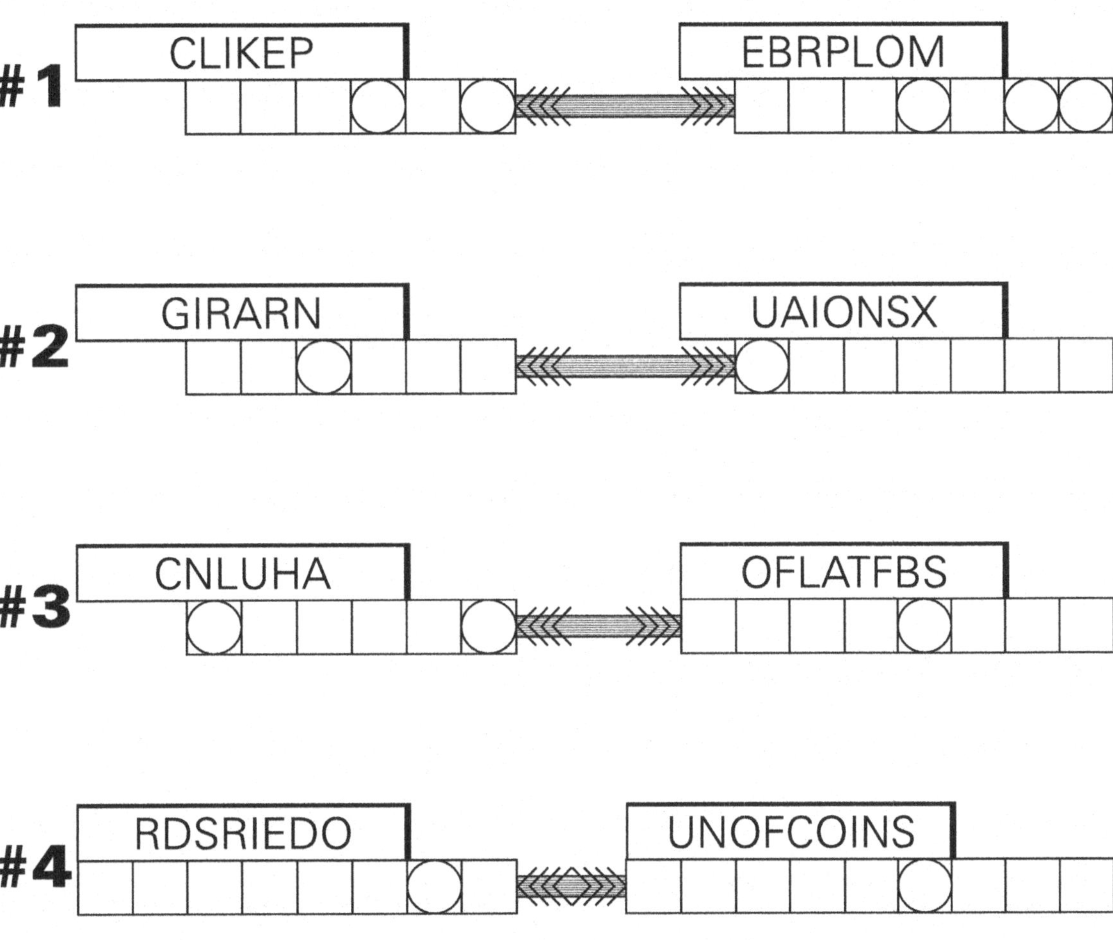

Arrange the circled letters to solve the mystery answer. (Form two words that have the same or similar meanings.)

MYSTERY ANSWER

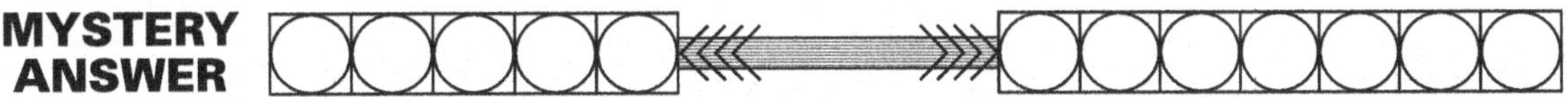

PUZZLE 114

MATH

JUMBLE BrainBusters

Unscramble the Jumbles, one letter to each square, so that each equation is correct.

For example: NONTEOEOW

ONE + ONE = TWO

#1 ENTENENINO

☐☐☐☐ + ◯☐☐ = ◯☐☐

#2 HWTGNTEOIET

☐◯☐☐◯ + ☐◯☐ = ◯☐☐

#3 OZZRZREROOEE

☐☐☐◯ − ☐◯☐☐ = ☐☐☐☐

#4 TOGFERHTIOWU

☐☐◯☐☐ ÷ ☐☐☐☐ = ◯◯☐

#5 XTYRTWTOHISTIY

☐☐☐◯☐ ÷ ☐◯◯ = ☐◯☐☐☐

Arrange the circled letters to solve the mystery equation.

MYSTERY EQUATION

(◯◯◯ + ◯◯◯) × ◯◯◯ = ◯◯◯◯◯

PUZZLE 115

SUPER JUMBLE® CHALLENGE

JUMBLE® BrainBusters

Unscramble the Jumbles, one letter to each square, to spell words.

#1 AGP

#2 LBBO

#3 RGMOO

#4 DMIELD

#5 BIEGERC

#6 EDOSLRHU

#7 THFIULRFG

#8 CNMEIEETXT

#9 NITPUCLIOBA

Box of Clues

Stumped? Maybe you can find a clue below.

- -A magazine or newspaper
- -______ blade
- -The Cumberland ______
- -Soft, amorphous mass
- -Terrifying
- -Type of sandwich
- -Frozen mass
- -An intense feeling
- -Bride's partner
- -Center

Arrange the circled letters to solve the mystery answer.

MYSTERY ANSWER

PUZZLE 116

RHYMING WORDS

JUMBLE BrainBusters

Unscramble the Jumbles, one letter to each square, to spell pairs of words that rhyme.

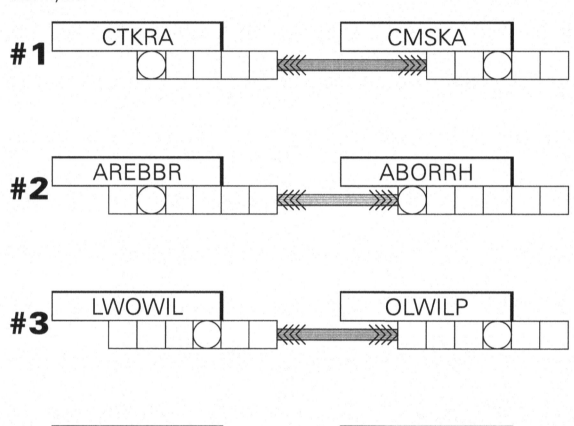

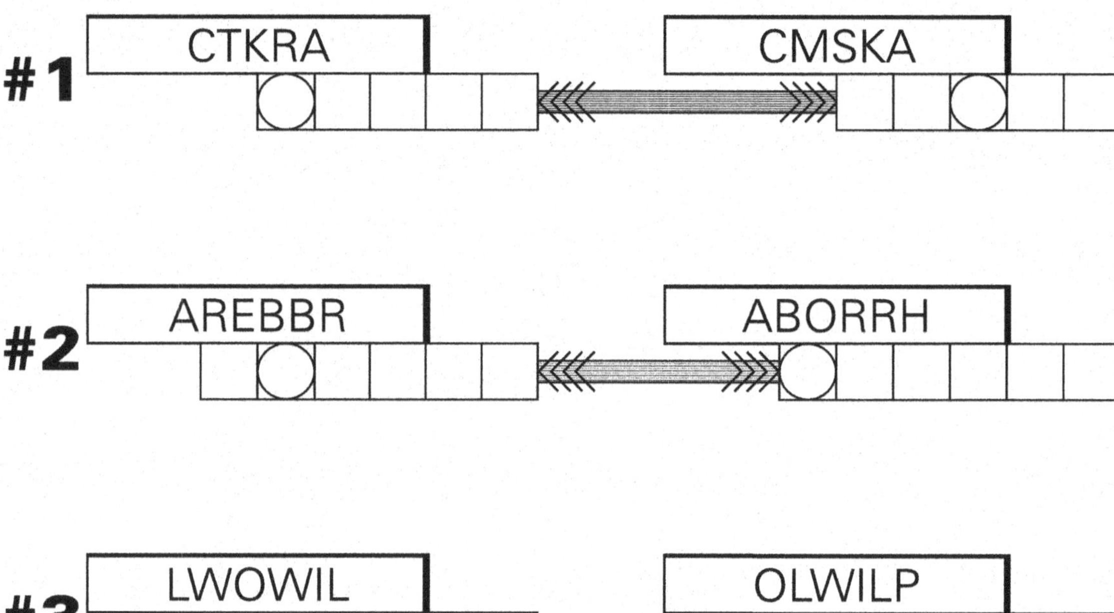

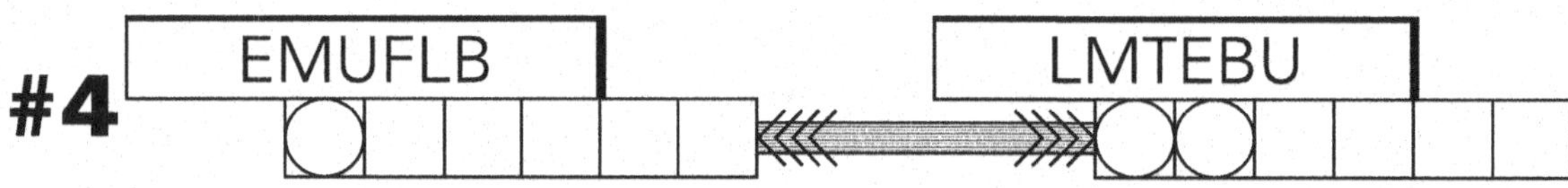

Arrange the circled letters to solve the mystery answer.
(Form two words that rhyme.)

MYSTERY ANSWER

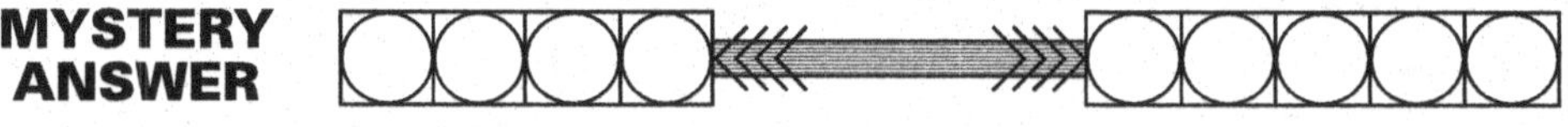

PUZZLE 117

JUMBLE® JOKES

JUMBLE® BrainBusters

Unscramble the mixed up letters to reveal the punch lines as suggested by the jokes.

#1 What is the hottest part of a man's face?

NHISBIEUSRSD

#2 What kind of house weighs the least?

SHGLAIOHUET

#3 What branch of the army do babies join?

FRETIANNTYH

#4 What doesn't get any wetter no matter how much it rains?

AOTEENHC

#5 What happened to the sardine when it didn't show up for work?

NWSITACNDEA

#6 What kind of phone makes music?

AHNSOAPOEX

PUZZLE 118

ANIMALS

JUMBLE BrainBusters

Unscramble the Jumbles, one letter to each square, to spell names of animals.

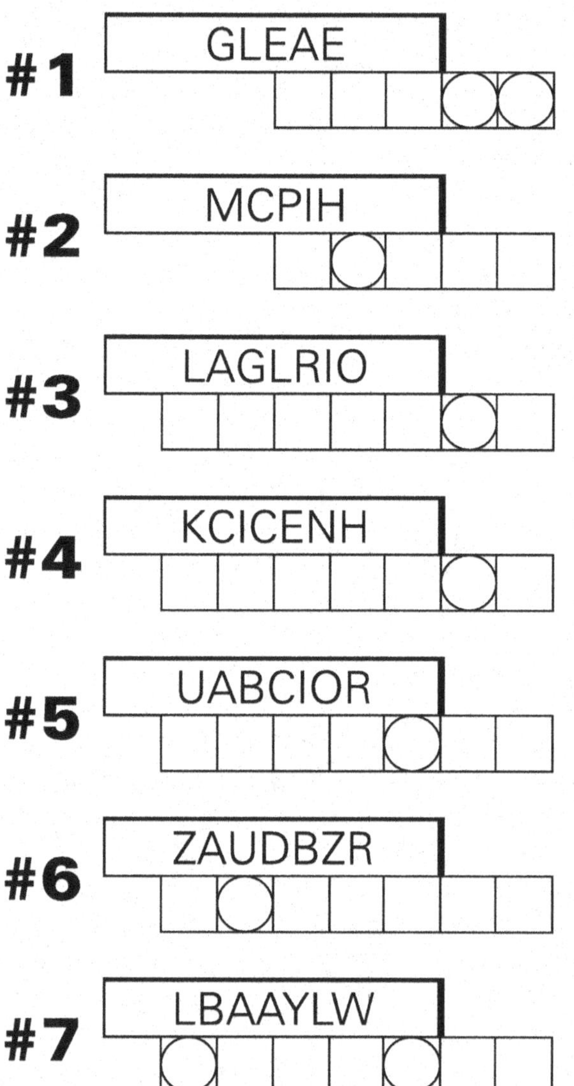

Box of Clues

Stumped? Maybe you can find a clue below.

-Type of African ape that can weigh up to 150 pounds
-The only deer in which both sexes have antlers
-Hopping marsupial
-Domesticated fowl
-Largest mammal that has ever lived
-Type of hawk
-Powerful bird of prey
-Largest ape

Arrange the circled letters to solve the mystery answer.

MYSTERY ANSWER

PUZZLE 119

JUMBLE® TRIVIA

JUMBLE® BrainBusters

Unscramble the Jumbles, one letter to each square, to spell words as suggested by the trivia clues.

#1 ______ is a mixture of volatile hydrocarbons having 4 to 12 carbon atoms per molecule.

#1 SONGAIEL

#2 This consists of about 75 percent potassium (or sodium) nitrate, 10 percent sulfur, and 15 percent charcoal.

#2 WUENPGORD

#3 This U.S. space station was launched on May 14, 1973.

#3 YSLBKA

#4 This fiber is produced by the polymerization of alcohol and organic acid.

#4 STPOELERY

#5 Walter Camp devised the main rules and tactics for American ______ in the late 1800s.

#5 LTBFOALO

Arrange the circled letters to solve the mystery answer.

This academy is located north of New York City on the bank of the Hudson River.

MYSTERY ANSWER

PUZZLE 120

TRIPLE JUMBLE® BRAINBUSTERS

Unscramble the Jumbles, one letter to each square, to spell words.

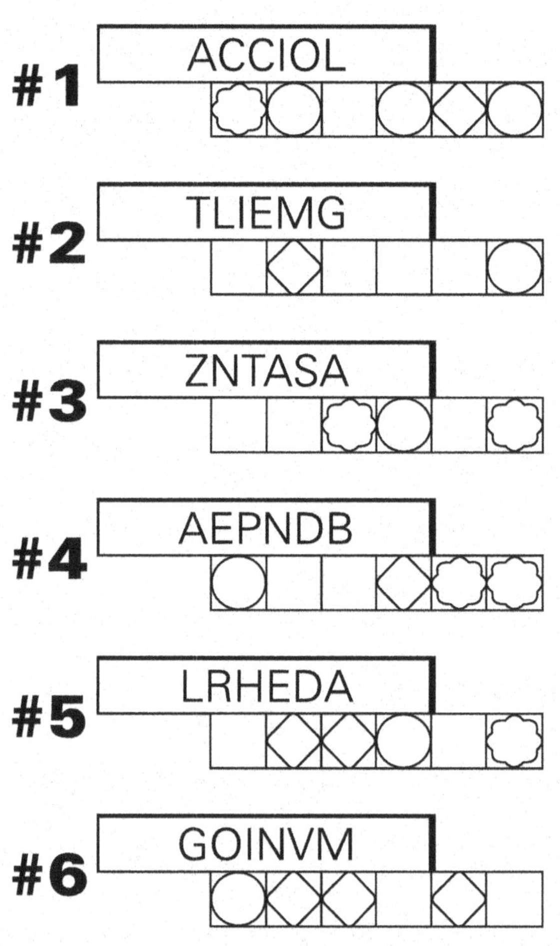

JUMBLE® BrainBusters

MYSTERY ANSWER #1 CHEF
MYSTERY ANSWER #2 BROIL
MYSTERY ANSWER #3 SEAFOOD

MYSTERY ANSWER #1 FISH
MYSTERY ANSWER #2 TROUT
MYSTERY ANSWER #3 UPSTREAM

Box of Clues

Stumped? Maybe you can find a clue below. (No clues for the mystery answers.)

-Division of a poem
-______ van
-Hospital room receptacle
-Type of cocktail
-Proclaim, announce
-______ cat

Arrange the clouded letters to solve mystery answer #1. Arrange the diamonded letters to solve mystery answer #2. Arrange the circled letters to solve mystery answer #3.
(The mystery answers will relate to each other.)

MYSTERY ANSWER #1

MYSTERY ANSWER #2

MYSTERY ANSWER #3

JUMBLE®
BrainBusters™
Advanced Puzzles

PUZZLE 121

STARTS AND ENDS WITH THE SAME LETTER

Unscramble the Jumbles, one letter to each square, to spell words that start and end with the same letter.

JUMBLE BrainBusters

RADAR ARENA POP GOING RIVER HIGH DICED CRYPTIC

#1 PMTET

#2 UIPPKC

#3 LFLAUW

#4 EBORRB

#5 RGEEEM

#6 DEIOSPE

Box of Clues

Stumped? Maybe you can find a clue below.

- -Separate part of a serialized work
- -Thief
- -______ truck
- -Something a spy might use
- -Come into view
- -Lure
- -Allowed

Arrange the circled letters to solve the mystery answer.

MYSTERY ANSWER

PUZZLE 122

THE STOCK MARKET

JUMBLE BrainBusters

Unscramble the Jumbles, one letter to each square, to spell words related to the stock market.

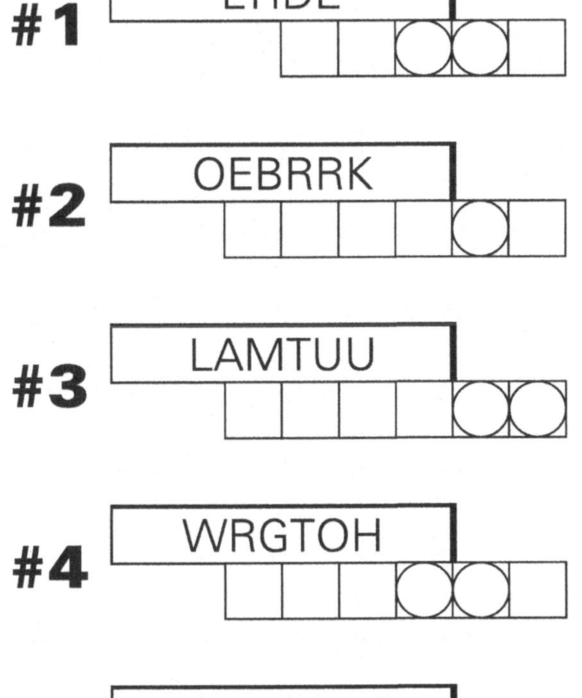

#1 LYIDE

#2 OEBRRK

#3 LAMTUU

#4 WRGTOH

#5 CNUAOTC

#6 NGENRISA

Box of Clues

Stumped? Maybe you can find a clue below. (No clue for the mystery answer.)

-An increase in value
-Type of agent
-Brokerage ______
-______ fund
-Business profits
-Return

Arrange the circled letters to solve the mystery answer.

MYSTERY ANSWER

PUZZLE 123

UN-MIX AND MATCH

COUNTRIES

Section 1: Unscramble the mixed-up letters, one letter to each square, to spell names of countries.

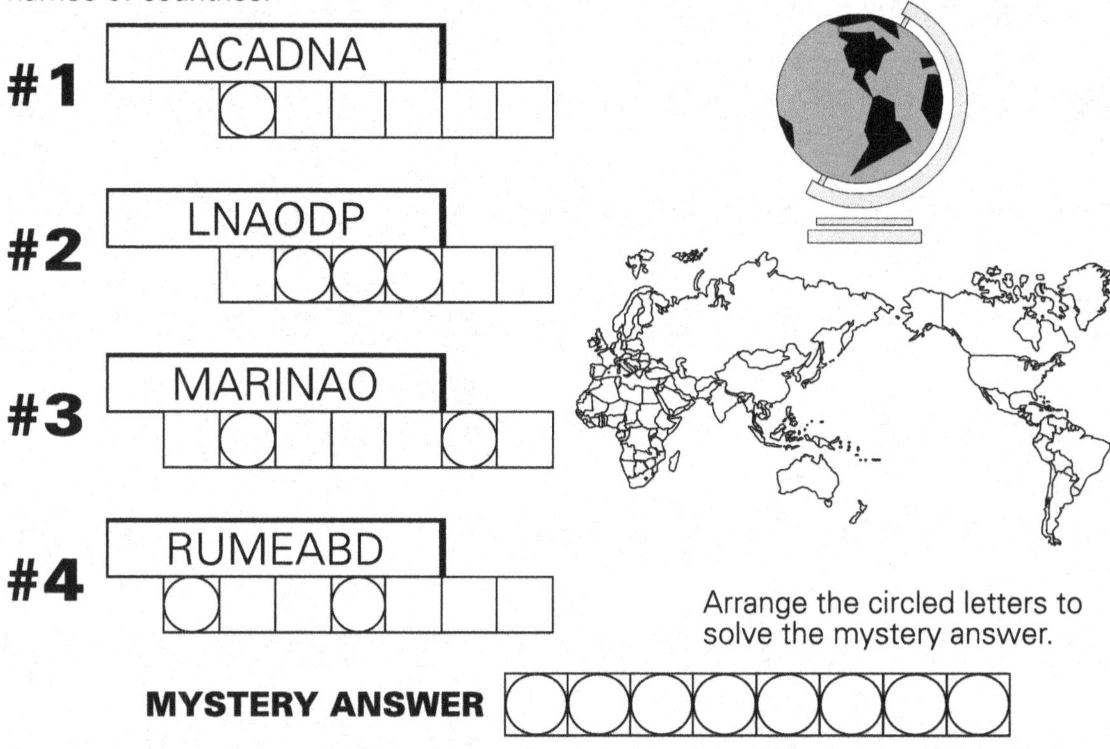

Arrange the circled letters to solve the mystery answer.

MYSTERY ANSWER

Section 2: Match the answers in the puzzle (including the mystery answer) to the following clues. (Write "M.A." to represent the mystery answer.)

#____ Country that borders Hungary, Serbia and Montenegro, Bulgaria, Moldova, and the Ukraine.

#____ Island country home to Hamilton (capital).

#____ Country that is home to more lakes than any other.

#____ Country with coastlines on the Pacific and Caribbean and home to both tropical jungles and snowcapped mountains.

#____ European country that is home to Gdańsk, Gdynia, and Szczecin.

PUZZLE 124

THE COSBY SHOW

JUMBLE BrainBusters

Unscramble the Jumbles, one letter to each square, to spell words related to the television show *The Cosby Show*.

#1 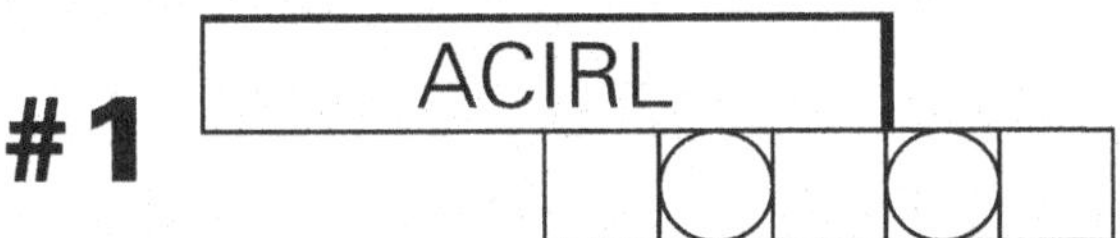

#2 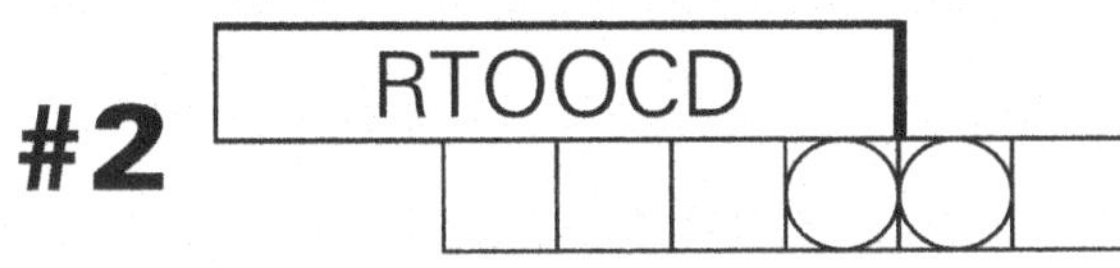

#3 

#4 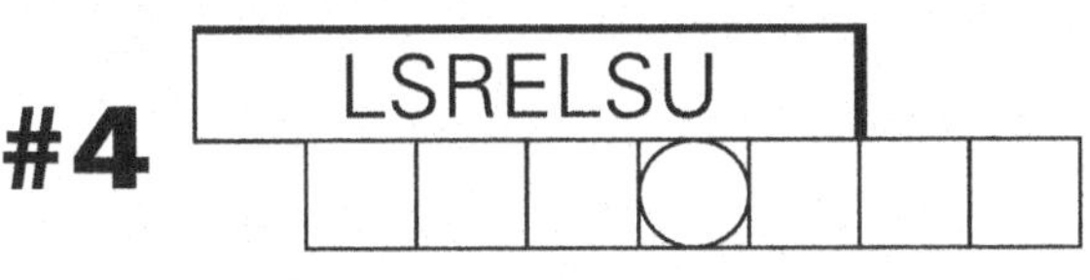

#5 

Box of Clues

Stumped? Maybe you can find a clue below. (No clue for the mystery answer.)

-Cliff's father's first name
-Huxtable child
-Phylicia Rashad role
-Cliff's profession
-Sisters

Arrange the circled letters to solve the mystery answer.

MYSTERY ANSWER

PUZZLE 125

JUMBLE BrainBusters

WEATHER

Unscramble the Jumbles, one letter to each square, to spell words related to weather.

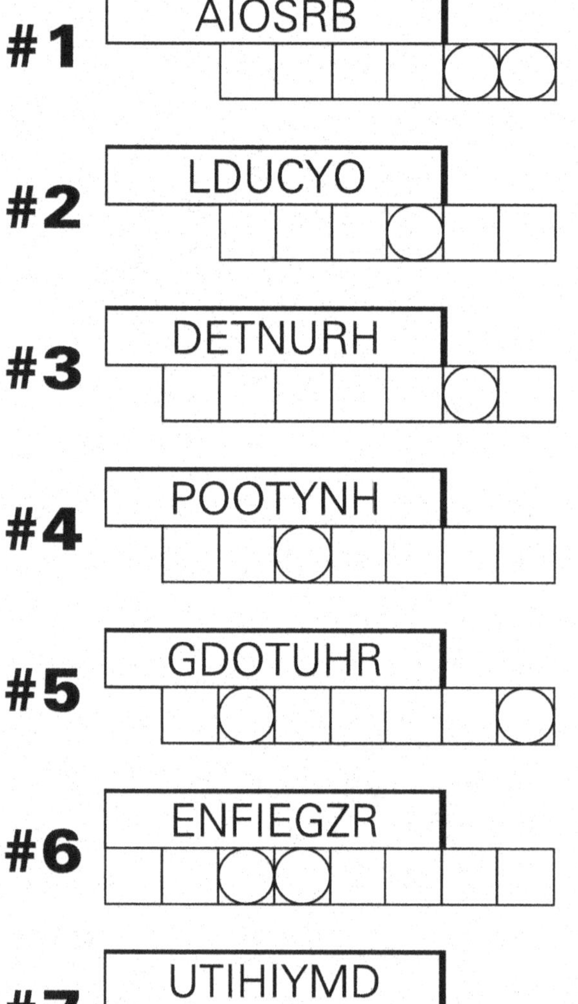

Interesting Weather Facts

The Weather Channel debuted on cable TV in 1982.

In a typical year, the United States can expect about 10,000 violent thunderstorms, 1,000 tornadoes, and several hurricanes.

Arrange the circled letters to solve the mystery answer.

MYSTERY ANSWER

PUZZLE 126

AUSTRALIA

JUMBLE BrainBusters

Unscramble the Jumbles, one letter to each square, to spell words related to Australia.

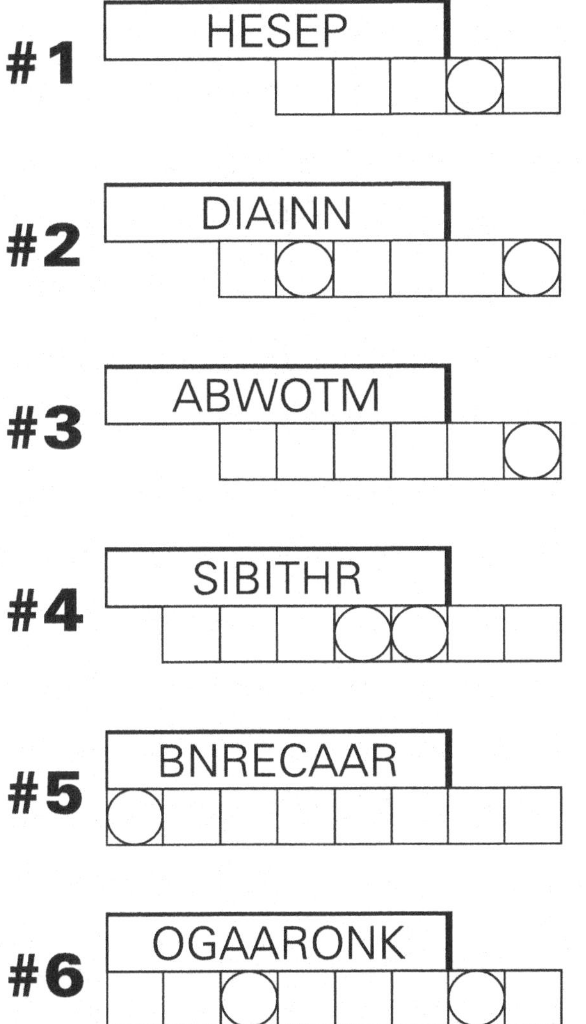

Box of Clues

Stumped? Maybe you can find a clue below. (No clue for the mystery answer.)

-Hopper
-First ______ settlement made in 1788
-Grazing animals
-______ Ocean
-Australia's capital
-Koala relative

MYSTERY ANSWER

Arrange the circled letters to solve the mystery answer.

PUZZLE 127

UN-MIX AND MATCH
U.S. STATES

JUMBLE BrainBusters

Section 1: Unscramble the mixed-up letters, one letter to each square, to spell names of U.S. states.

#1 GOWNYIM

#2 URISIMOS

#3 MOLHAAOK

#4 SWCIONNIS

Arrange the circled letters to solve the mystery answer.

MYSTERY ANSWER

Section 2: Match the answers in the puzzle (including the mystery answer) to the following clues. (Write "MA." to represent the mystery answer.)

#____ State that achieved statehood on November 16, 1907, and home to the Chickasaw National Recreation Area.

#____ The "Pelican State."

#____ State that achieved statehood on May 29, 1848, and home to Lake Winnebago.

#____ Rectangular U.S. state that is home to Grand Teton National Park.

#____ The "Show Me" state.

PUZZLE 128

ALL ABOUT BOOKS

JUMBLE® BrainBusters

Unscramble the Jumbles, one letter to each square, to spell words related to books.

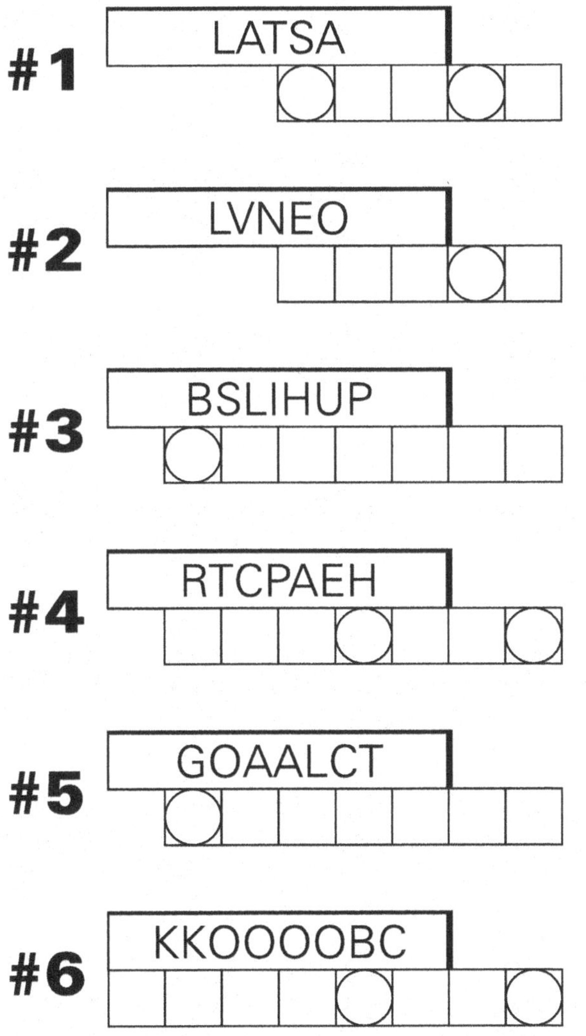

Interesting Book Facts

Millie's Book, Barbara Bush's book about her English springer spaniel, was on the best-seller list for more than 20 weeks.

Clint Eastwood is the subject of an unauthorized 1997 biography written by Sondra Locke entitled *The Good, the Bad, and the Very Ugly.*

Arrange the circled letters to solve the mystery answer.

MYSTERY ANSWER

PUZZLE 129

FISH

JUMBLE BrainBusters

Unscramble the Jumbles, one letter to each square, to spell types of fish.

#1 RKHAS

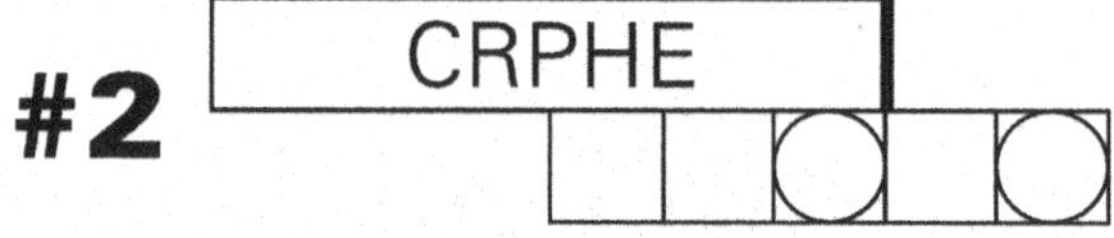

#2 CRPHE

#3 MOANSL

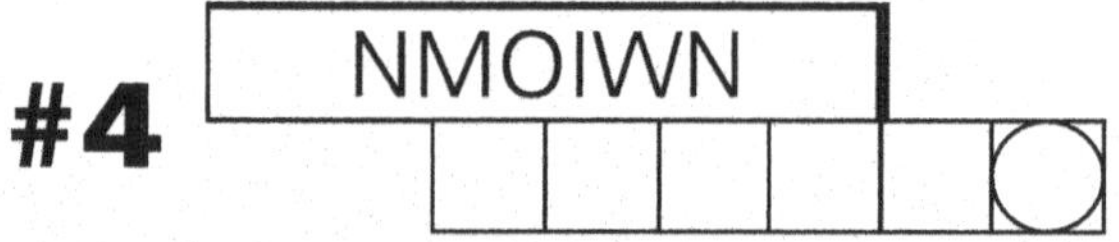

#4 NMOIWN

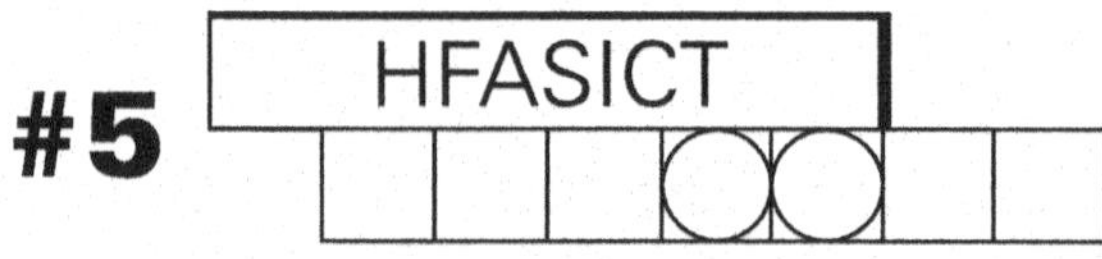

#5 HFASICT

#6 EDFUROLN

Interesting Fish Facts

There are more species of fish than mammals, reptiles, and birds combined.

There are 200 known species of catfish.

Arrange the circled letters to solve the mystery answer.

MYSTERY ANSWER

PUZZLE 130

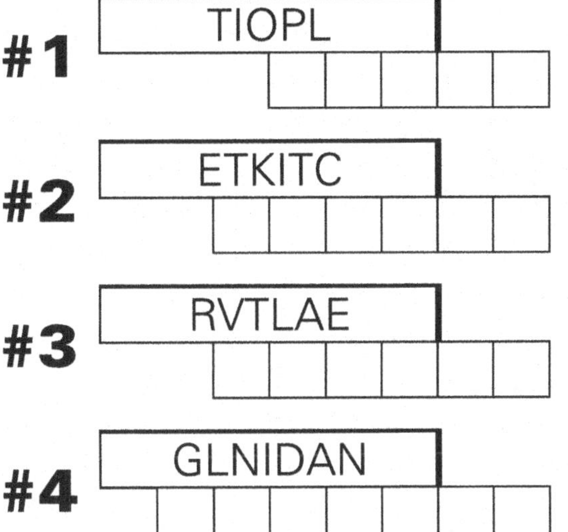

FIND THE JUMBLES®

JUMBLE® BrainBusters

Unscramble the Jumbles, one letter to each square, to spell words.

#1 TIOPL

#2 ETKITC

#3 RVTLAE

#4 GLNIDAN

#5 RRAITOP

#6 TURTIOS

#7 NATICAOV

#8 TRSAPPSO

Find and circle the answers (from above) in the grid of letters below.

A	D	S	P	P	V	S	E	A	R	H	U	G	M	A	E
M	I	G	S	I	K	A	C	M	V	D	B	R	T	K	T
C	K	N	H	W	L	M	C	L	G	Y	Z	E	O	H	R
F	L	I	P	B	V	O	E	A	U	N	K	R	U	E	O
B	R	D	A	C	F	V	T	U	T	C	T	S	R	T	P
I	S	N	X	E	A	S	R	X	I	I	G	P	I	I	S
O	L	A	I	R	P	O	R	T	L	Y	O	N	S	U	S
H	O	L	T	R	G	I	O	F	H	M	P	N	T	B	A
A	L	I	D	F	L	H	G	N	A	C	I	O	A	G	P

PUZZLE 131

JUMBLE® JOKES

JUMBLE® BrainBusters

Unscramble the mixed up letters to reveal the punch lines as suggested by the jokes.

#1 How can you tune into the sun?

EAAUSNDIULS

#2 What horses keep late hours?

SEGMNIARHT

#3 If you want to learn how to fight, what book should you read?

ORACAOBKSP

#4 What is the best way to raise strawberries?

TAWOIHONPS

#5 How can you fix a short circuit?

TGHLNTEEIN

#6 What is the biggest fly swatter?

ASLLAAEABTBB

PUZZLE 132

UN-MIX AND MATCH ACTORS

Section 1: Unscramble the mixed-up letters, one letter to each square, to spell names of actors.

#1 ENGE NAMCAHK

#2 DIEED HUYRMP

#3 TESEV NARIMT

#4 ANYDN ELROGV

Arrange the circled letters to solve the mystery answer.

MYSTERY ANSWER

Section 2: Match the answers in the puzzle (including the mystery answer) to the following clues. (Write "M.A." to represent the mystery answer.)

#____ This actor was born on April 3, 1961, in Brooklyn, New York. He was a regular on *Saturday Night Live.*

#____ This actor was born on August 14, 1945, in Waco, Texas. He was a stand-up comedian before becoming an actor.

#____ This actor was born on September 9, 1960, in London, England. He graduated from Oxford University with a degree in English.

#____ This actor was born on July 22, 1947, in San Francisco, California. He made his film debut in *Escape from Alcatraz* in 1979.

#____ This actor was born on January 30, 1930, in San Bernardino, California. He turned down the part of President Franklin Roosevelt in *Pearl Harbor.*

MOVIES

Unscramble the mixed-up letters, one letter to each square, to spell movie titles.

#1
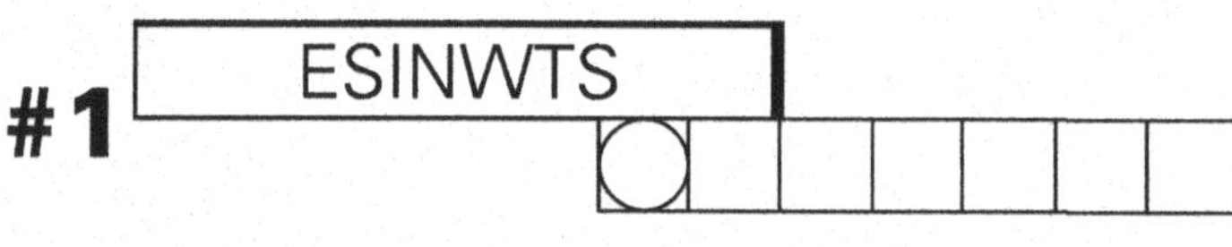

#2
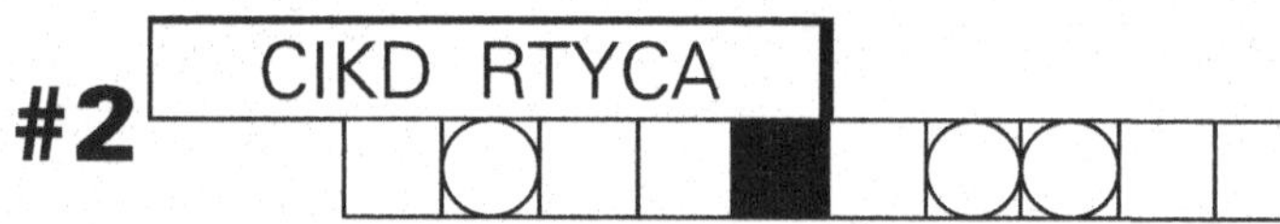

#3

#4
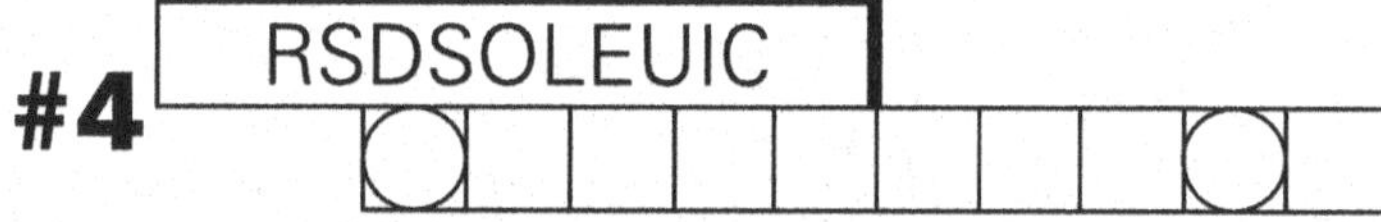

#5

#6
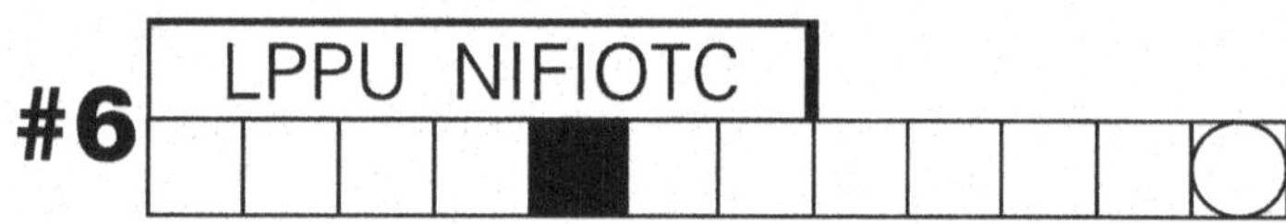

Box of Clues

Stumped? Maybe you can find a clue below.

- 1987 Michael Douglas movie
- 1985 Harrison Ford movie
- 1994 movie based on a Michael Crichton novel
- 1954 movie starring Jimmy Stewart and Grace Kelly
- 1990 Warren Beatty movie
- 1994 movie directed by Quentin Tarantino
- 1990 Macaulay Culkin movie

MYSTERY ANSWER

Arrange the circled letters to solve the mystery answer.

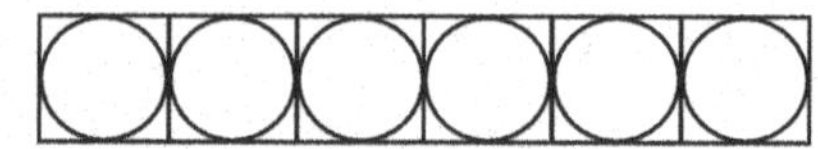

PUZZLE 134

MATH

JUMBLE® BrainBusters

Unscramble the Jumbles, one letter to each square, so that each equation is correct.

For example: NONTEOEOW

ONE + ONE = TWO

#1 FWNEOTVTIE

◯☐☐ ÷ ☐☐☐☐ = ☐◯☐

#2 EEIORXOZSZR

☐☐◯ × ☐☐☐◯ = ☐☐☐☐

#3 VNRVNELOESUEFEE

◯☐☐☐☐ + ☐◯☐☐ = ☐☐☐☐☐☐

#4 NIERWLEVHETNEET

☐◯☐☐ + ☐☐☐☐☐ = ◯◯☐☐☐☐

#5 ELVETEEVWOENLNE

◯☐☐ + ☐☐☐☐☐☐ = ◯◯☐☐☐☐

Arrange the circled letters to solve the mystery equation.

MYSTERY EQUATION

◯◯◯ + ◯◯◯ + ◯◯◯ = ◯◯◯

PUZZLE 135

OUTER SPACE

JUMBLE® BrainBusters

Unscramble the Jumbles, one letter to each square, to spell words related to outer space.

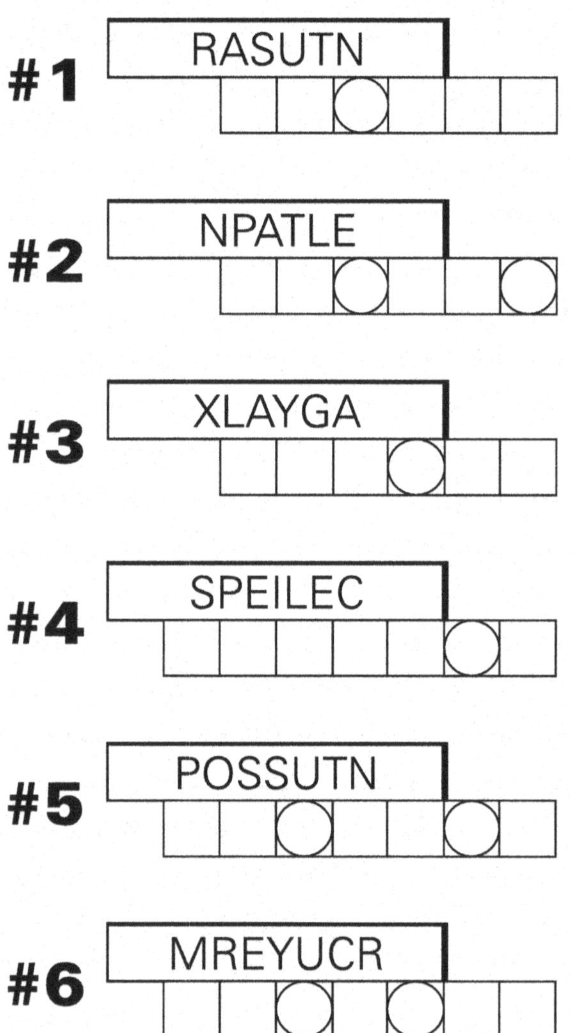

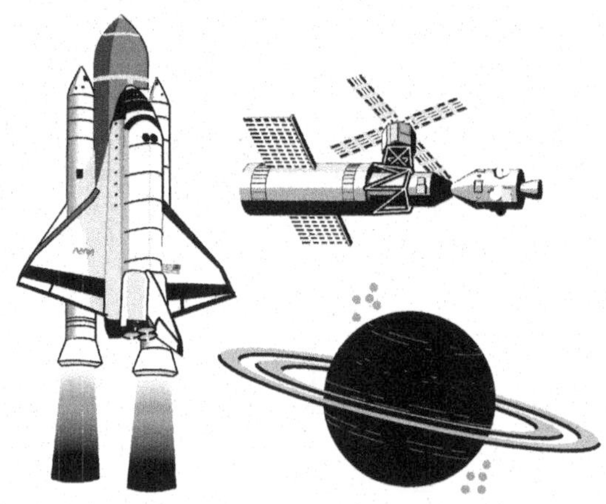

Interesting Outer Space Facts

Astronomers believe Jupiter's moon, Europa, may have an ocean of liquid beneath the ice that covers the whole moon.

Titan, Saturn's largest moon, has an atmosphere.

Arrange the circled letters to solve the mystery answer.

MYSTERY ANSWER

SPORTS

JUMBLE BrainBusters

Unscramble the Jumbles, one letter to each square, to spell words related to sports.

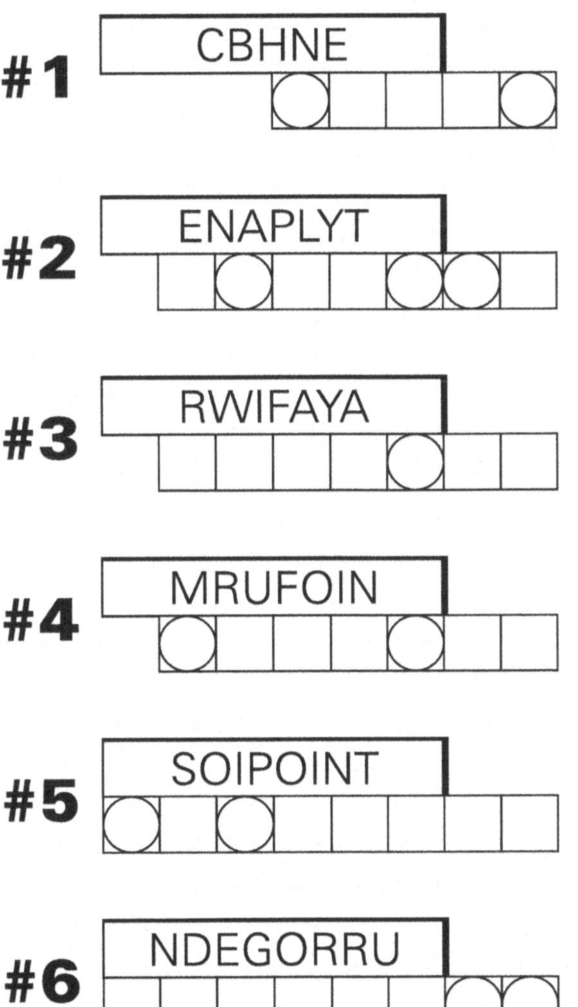

Box of Clues

Stumped? Maybe you can find a clue below.

-Low baseball hit
-_______ box
-A yearly competition
-Outfit
-Golfing goal off the tee
-Watching area
-Pitcher, for example

Arrange the circled letters to solve the mystery answer.

MYSTERY ANSWER

PUZZLE 137

JUMBLE® TRIVIA

JUMBLE® BrainBusters

Unscramble the Jumbles, one letter to each square, to spell words as suggested by the trivia clues.

#1 This independent principality takes up about 480 acres.

#1 COMAON

#2 Alfred Butts invented this popular game in the early thirties.

#2 LCBSREAB

#3 Deserts comprise about 95 percent of this country.

#3 PGTYE

#4 When he was in his early twenties, this U.S. president worked as a village postmaster.

#4 NOLINLC

#5 ______, which is home to about 700,000 people, is Scotland's largest city.

#5 LWGSAOG

Arrange the circled letters to solve the mystery answer.

This reptile is so rare that it is protected by law in many areas.

MYSTERY ANSWER

PUZZLE 138

JUMBLE BrainBusters

RADAR
ARENA
POP
GOING
RIVER
HIGH
DICED
CRYPTIC

STARTS AND ENDS WITH THE SAME LETTER

Unscramble the Jumbles, one letter to each square, to spell words that start and end with the same letter.

#1 MPIPR

#2 TEECIX

#3 LEVOEV

#4 TLHAHE

#5 NTAISTR

#6 EOSIRSU

Box of Clues

Stumped? Maybe you can find a clue below.

- -Develop
- -_______ spa
- -Groom
- -Spacious
- -_______ system
- -Stir to activity
- -Earnest

Arrange the circled letters to solve the mystery answer.

MYSTERY ANSWER

DOGS

JUMBLE BrainBusters

Unscramble the Jumbles, one letter to each square, to spell types of dogs.

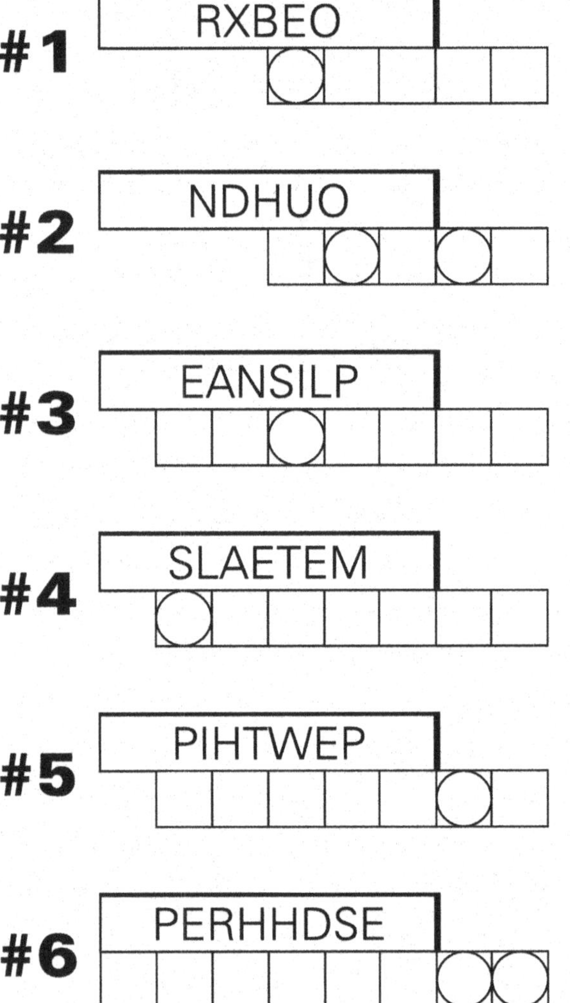

#1 RXBEO

#2 NDHUO

#3 EANSILP

#4 SLAETEM

#5 PIHTWEP

#6 PERHHDSE

Box of Clues

Stumped? Maybe you can find a clue below.

-Starts with *B*; ends with *R*
-Starts with *W*; ends with *T*
-Starts with *S*; ends with *L*
-Starts with *M*; ends with *E*
-Starts with *S*; ends with *D*
-Starts with *D*; ends with *N*
-Starts with *H*; ends with *D*

Arrange the circled letters to solve the mystery answer.

MYSTERY ANSWER

PUZZLE 140

JUMBLE® CONNECTIONS

JUMBLE® BrainBusters

Unscramble the Jumbles, one letter to each square, to spell words that fit into the puzzle below.

ACROSS		DOWN	
#1	RANEULM	#1	DSINTU
#5	HCSONE	#2	NREOEC
#7	MIOID	#3	ARALV
#8	LCABAEN	#4	NITOC
#10	RUET	#5	LCOAK
#12	MLADIAR	#6	TLUNRAA
#13	TONCAE	#8	NEBODY
		#9	YREEGN
		#11	NARYO

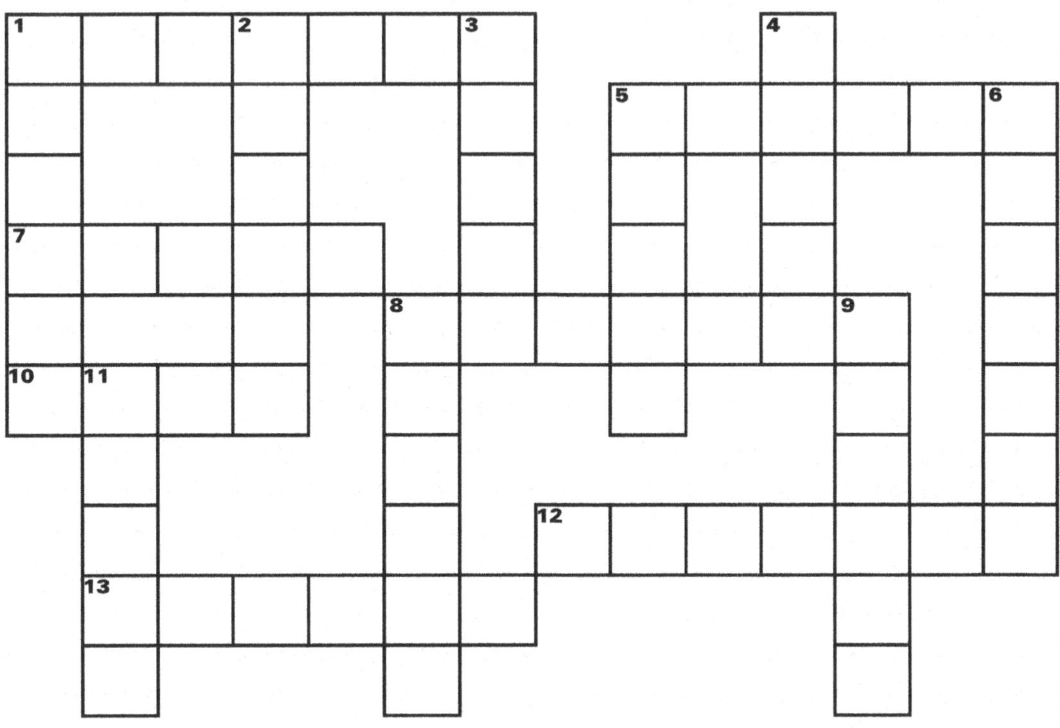

MYSTERY PERSON

JUMBLE BrainBusters

Unscramble the Jumbles, one letter to each square, to spell words that relate to the mystery person.

#1

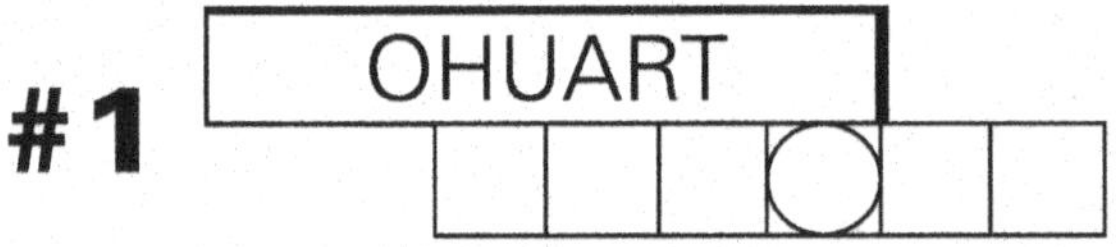

#2

#3

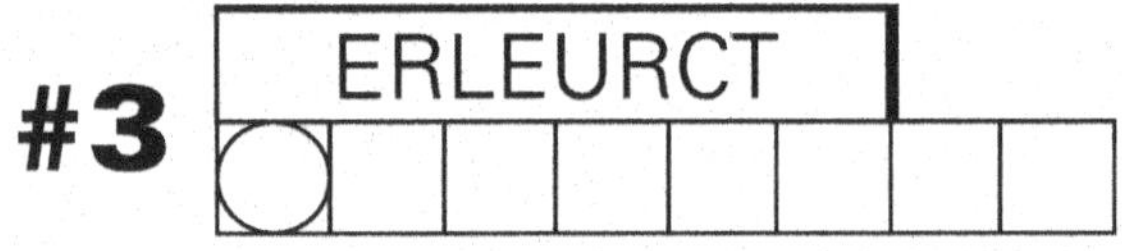

#4

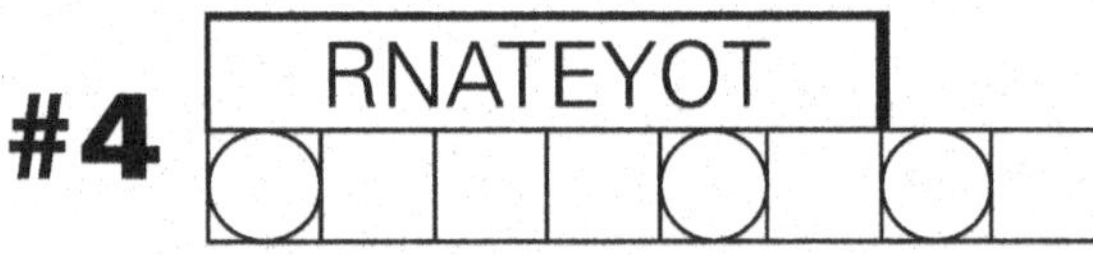

#5

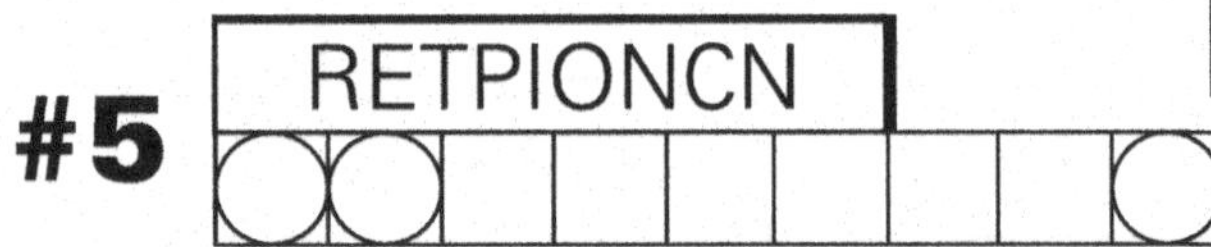

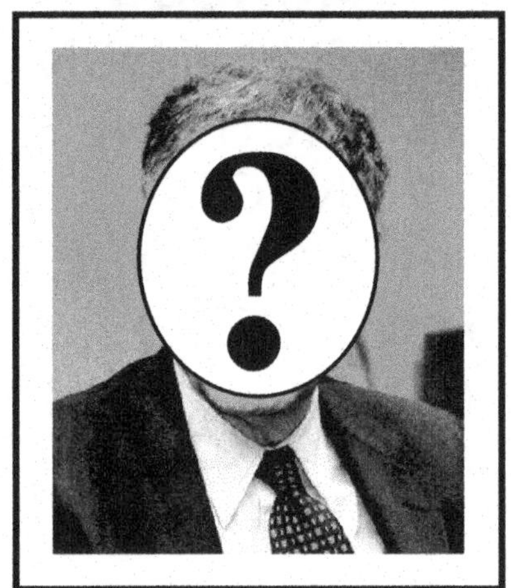

Box of Clues

Stumped? Maybe you can find a clue below.

-He was one at the University of Hartford in the sixties
-Writer
-He was the editor of the ______ *Law Review*
-What he became in 1958
-He graduated magna cum laude from this university in 1955

Arrange the circled letters to solve the mystery person.

MYSTERY PERSON

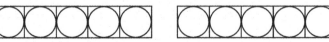

PUZZLE 142

TREES

JUMBLE BrainBusters

Unscramble the Jumbles, one letter to each square, to spell varieties of trees.

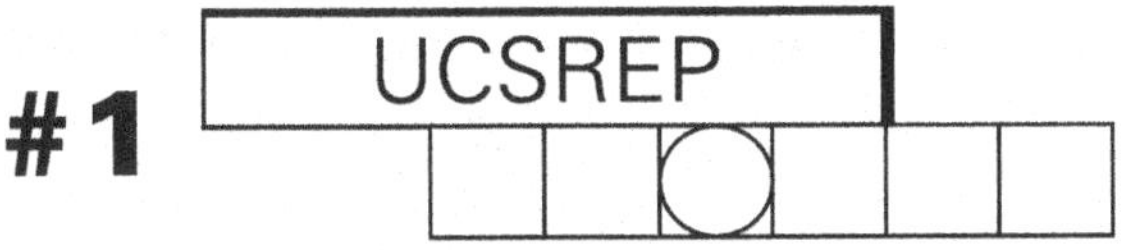

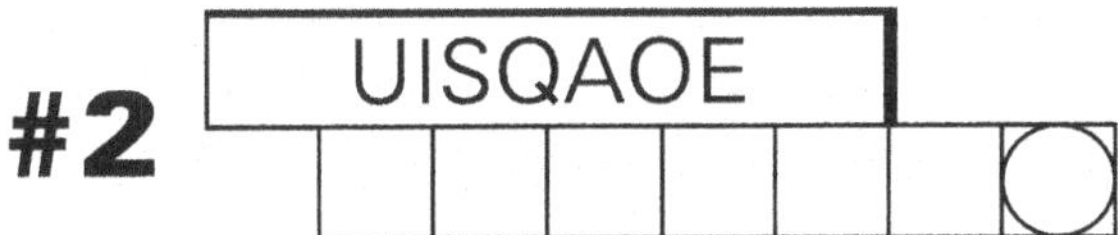

Box of Clues

Stumped? Maybe you can find a clue below.

- -Starts with *S*; ends with *A*
- -Starts with *S*; ends with *E*
- -Starts with *C*; ends with *S*
- -Starts with *S*; ends with *E*
- -Starts with *C*; ends with *T*
- -Starts with *R*; ends with *D*
- -Starts with *H*; ends with *K*

Arrange the circled letters to solve the mystery answer.

MYSTERY ANSWER

PUZZLE 143

SUPER JUMBLE® CHALLENGE

JUMBLE® BrainBusters

Unscramble the Jumbles, one letter to each square, to spell words.

#1 MMO

#2 RIGL

#3 COFKL

#4 XFREEL

#5 DRHOACR

#6 THCSUTEN

#7 KNMHAUIDN

#8 OPSUESINNS

#9 AMTSEIETLNN

Box of Clues

Stumped? Maybe you can find a clue below.

- -______ tree
- -Flower ______
- -The human race
- -Mushy, romantic
- -Group of birds
- -Dad's partner
- -______ bridge
- -Automatic response
- -Example
- -Apple ______

Arrange the circled letters to solve the mystery answer.

MYSTERY ANSWER

PUZZLE 144

FAMILY TIES

JUMBLE BrainBusters

Unscramble the Jumbles, one letter to each square, to spell words related to the television show *Family Ties.*

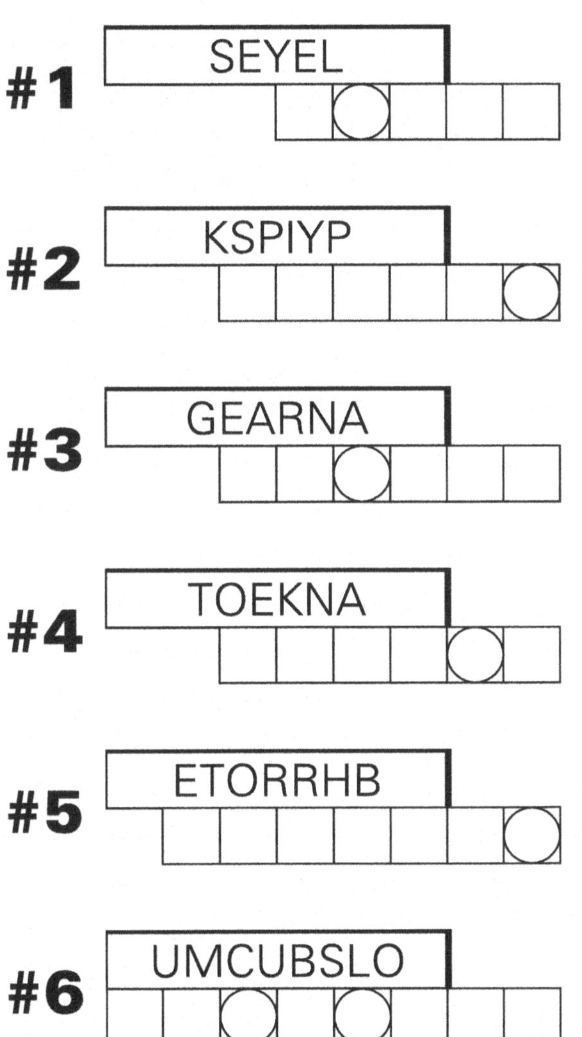

Box of Clues

Stumped? Maybe you can find a clue below. (No clue for the mystery answer.)

- -Family last name
- -Meredith Baxter-Birney role
- -This president said *Family Ties* was his favorite show
- -Alex's friend
- -*Family Ties* setting
- -Andrew to Alex

Arrange the circled letters to solve the mystery answer.

MYSTERY ANSWER

PUZZLE 145

UN-MIX AND MATCH

U.S. PRESIDENTS

JUMBLE® BrainBusters

Section 1: Unscramble the mixed-up letters, one letter to each square, to spell last names of U.S. presidents.

#1 DEGRILAF

#2 GODCOLIE

#3 CANUAHNB

#4 RSEOFENJF

Arrange the circled letters to solve the mystery answer.

MYSTERY ANSWER

Section 2: Match the answers in the puzzle (including the mystery answer) to the following clues. (Write "M.A." to represent the mystery answer.)

#____ This U.S. president was responsible for the purchase of the Louisiana Territory from France in 1803.

#____ This U.S. president took office after the death of Warren Harding.

#____ This U.S. president served from 1857 to 1861.

#____ This U.S. president died after just one month in office in 1841.

#____ This U.S. president was assassinated in office in 1881.

PUZZLE 146

JUMBLE® TRIVIA

JUMBLE® BrainBusters

Unscramble the Jumbles, one letter to each square, to spell words as suggested by the trivia clues.

#1 The LEGO company was founded by Ole Kirk Christiansen in Billund, ______, in 1932.

#1 KERNDMA

#2 The ______ seal is the heaviest seal in the world.

#2 TPNHEELA

#3 During the 1958-59 TV season, the top four shows were all ______.

#3 TSERSEWN

#4 John ______ turned down the lead roles in *American Gigolo* and *An Officer and a Gentleman*.

#4 LTAOARTV

#5 The ______, botanically speaking, is a fruit.

#5 BURUCCEM

Arrange the circled letters to solve the mystery answer.

______ ______ move 1,100 feet per second in the air. They move even faster through solids and liquids.

MYSTERY ANSWER

PUZZLE 147

JUMBLE® CONNECTIONS

JUMBLE® BrainBusters

Unscramble the Jumbles, one letter to each square, to spell words that fit into the puzzle below.

ACROSS		DOWN	
#1	NEBALTK	#1	TABRRE
#5	LNUNAA	#2	NTNOIO
#7	RTIHE	#3	MPTUH
#8	PLAOTES	#4	EKNLE
#10	NRIU	#5	BSAYS
#12	HAIEECV	#6	ALLVOEB
#13	XSEIEC	#8	ESACSC
		#9	DETXNE
		#11	PUREP

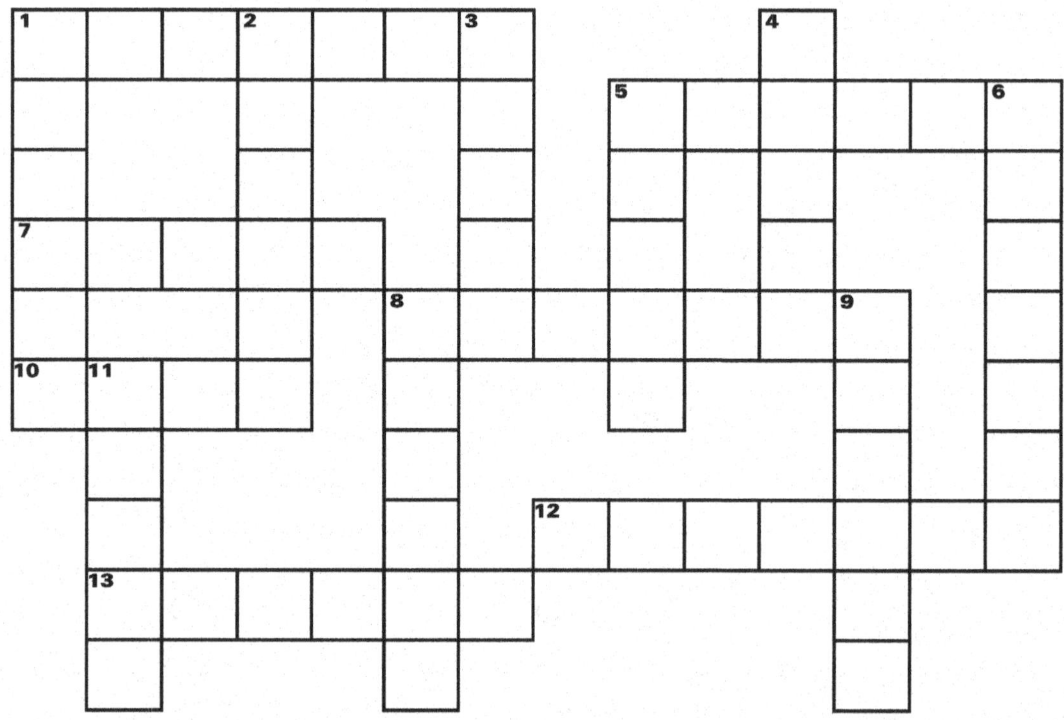

PUZZLE 148

AROUND THE HOME

JUMBLE BrainBusters

Unscramble the Jumbles, one letter to each square, to spell words related to the home.

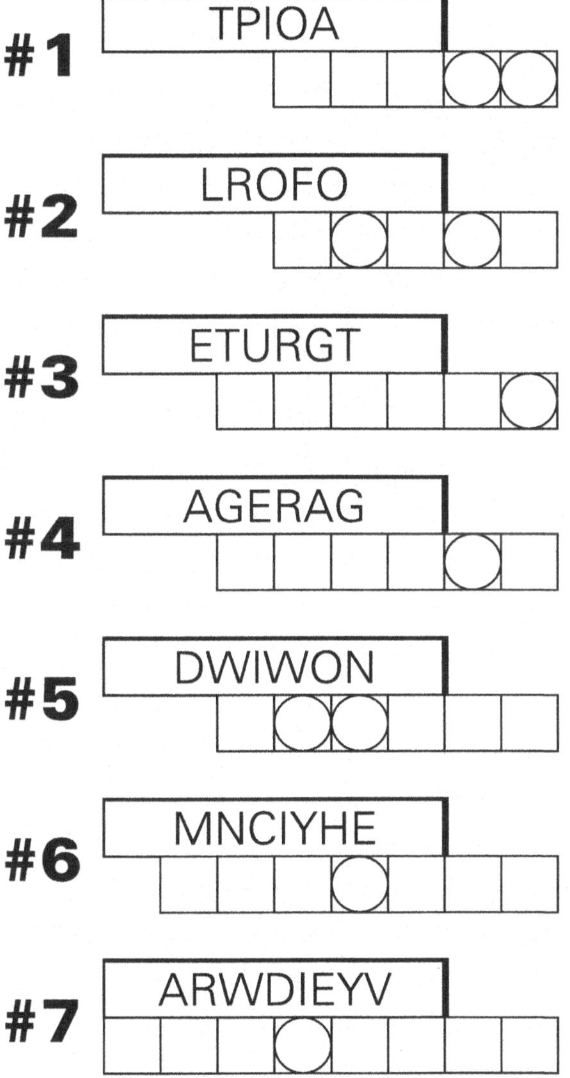

Interesting Home Facts

Actor/comedian/writer Dan Aykroyd bought a home in Hollywood that was once owned by Cass Elliot of the Mamas and the Papas.

It is believed that about 50 percent of homes in the U.S. have significant numbers of dust mites residing in them.

Arrange the circled letters to solve the mystery answer.

MYSTERY ANSWER

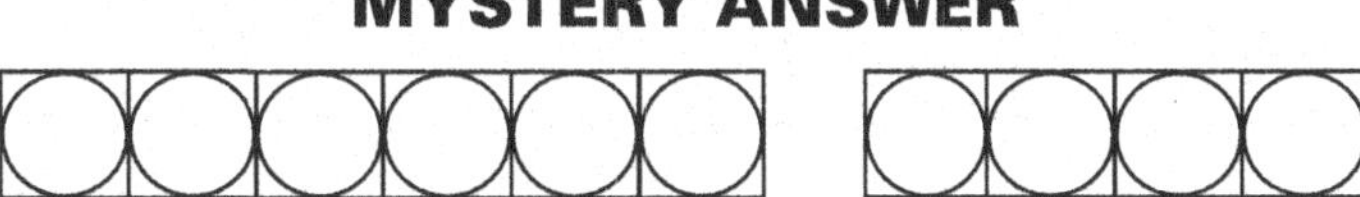

FAMOUS ARTISTS

JUMBLE BrainBusters

Unscramble the Jumbles, one letter to each square, to spell names of famous artists.

#1 AHWROL

#2 SCAPISO

#3 LCPKOLO

#4 NESAGTR

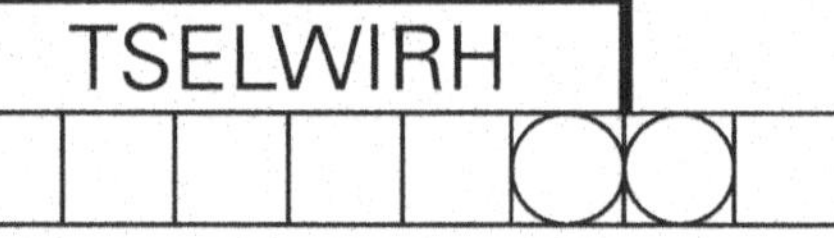

Box of Clues

Stumped? Maybe you can find a clue below. (No clue for the mystery answer.)

- -James Abbott McNeill ______
- -Jackson ______
- -John Singer ______
- -Andy ______
- -Pablo ______

Arrange the circled letters to solve the mystery answer.

MYSTERY ANSWER

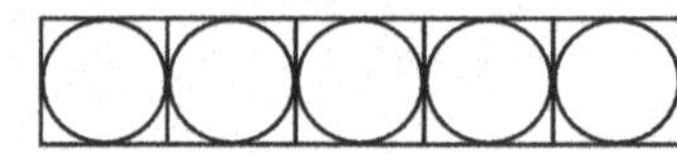

PUZZLE 150

UN-MIX AND MATCH

U.S. STATE CAPITALS

JUMBLE BrainBusters

Section 1: Unscramble the mixed-up letters, one letter to each square, to spell U.S. state capitals.

#1 ANBAYL

#2 RNETONT

#3 CRMBIAKS

#4 ALNLSIEHV

Arrange the circled letters to solve the mystery answer.

MYSTERY ANSWER

Section 2: Match the answers in the puzzle (including the mystery answer) to the following clues. (Write "MA."to represent the mystery answer.)

#____ U.S. state capital on the Delaware River.

#____ U.S. state capital that shares its name with the river that flows through it.

#____ U.S. state capital situated on hills overlooking the Missouri River.

#____ U.S. state capital that lies on the west bank of the Hudson River.

#____ U.S. state capital on the Cumberland River.

ANIMALS

JUMBLE BrainBusters

Unscramble the Jumbles, one letter to each square, to spell names of animals.

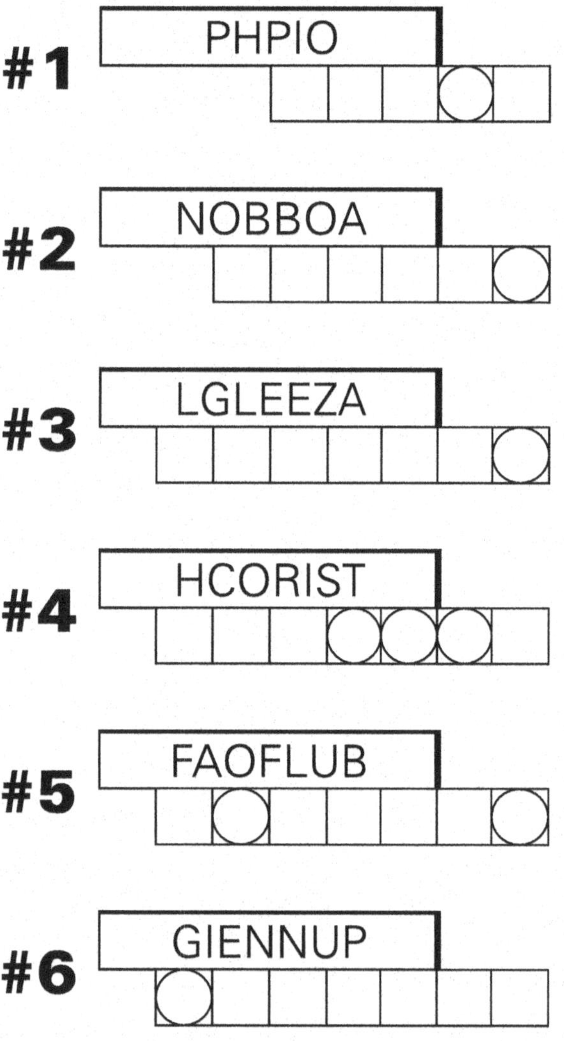

Interesting Animal Facts

The European eagle owl is the largest owl in the world. It can measure more than two feet tall with a wingspan of about five feet.

The scream of a hippopotamus has been recorded at 115 decibels. This is louder than a jet plane at takeoff.

MYSTERY ANSWER

Arrange the circled letters to solve the mystery answer.

PUZZLE 152

DOUBLE JUMBLE® BRAINBUSTERS

JUMBLE® BrainBusters

Unscramble the Jumbles, one letter to each square, to spell words.

#1 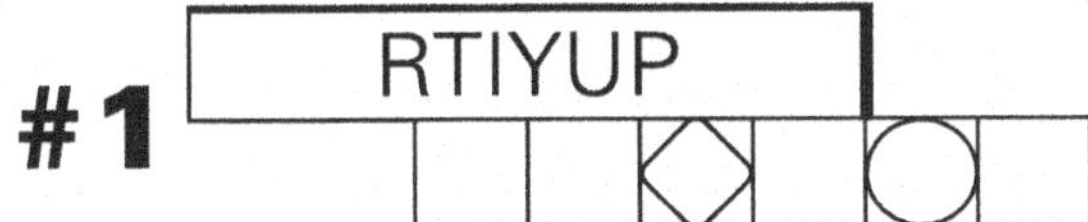

#2 

#3 

#4 

#5 

#6 

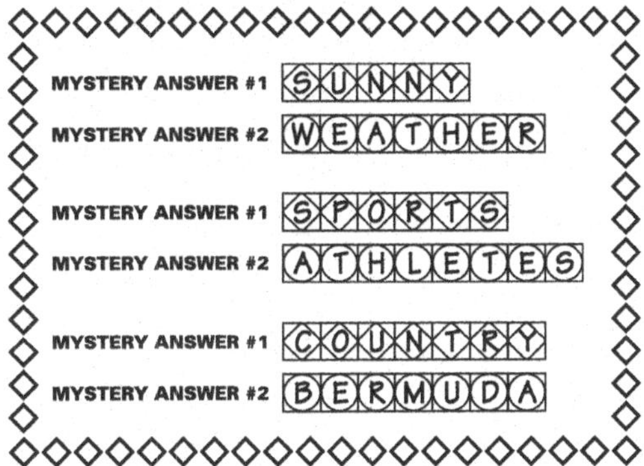

Box of Clues

Stumped? Maybe you can find a clue below. (No clues for the mystery answers.)

-______ tree
-Condition of being clean and free of contaminants
-Arrive at through reasoning
-______ staircase
-Myth
-Type of flower

Arrange the diamonded letters to solve mystery answer #1. Arrange the circled letters to solve mystery answer #2. (The mystery answers will relate to each other.)

MYSTERY ANSWER #1 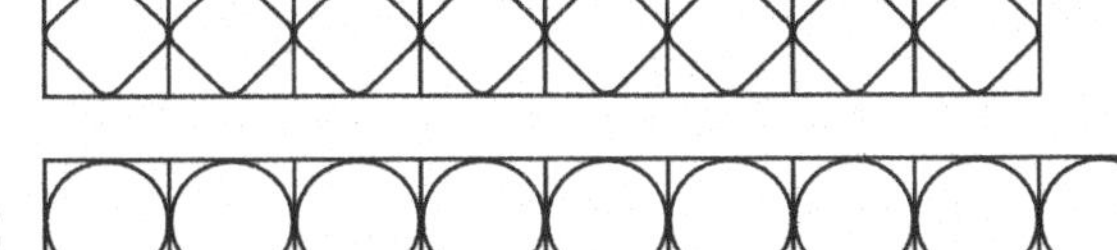

MYSTERY ANSWER #2

PUZZLE 153

JUMBLE® CONNECTIONS

JUMBLE® BrainBusters

Unscramble the Jumbles, one letter to each square, to spell words that fit into the puzzle below.

ACROSS

#1 NBGADIL
#5 EWFORO
#7 KOYOK
#8 PPAELAR
#10 ATPL
#12 RMGUTEO
#13 NVATAC

DOWN

#1 UABCPK
#2 KDTCOE
#3 RUGOP
#4 EGDOD
#5 TEWAH
#6 DIARATN
#8 DNADIG
#9 NWLMAA
#11 ALVEE

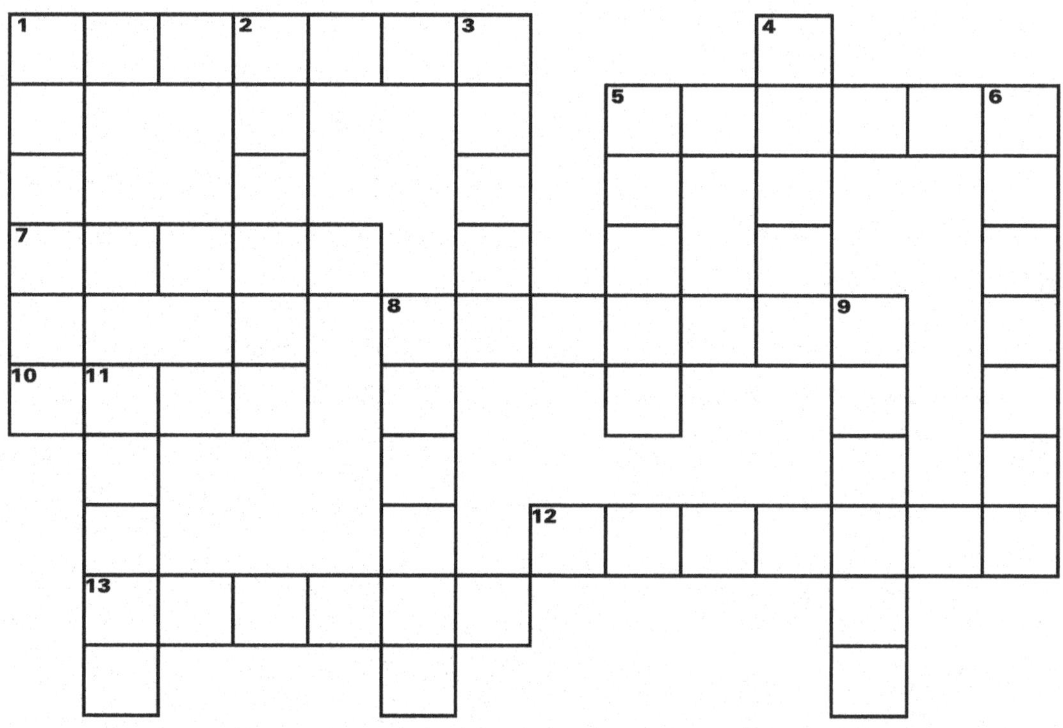

PUZZLE 154

COMPUTERS

JUMBLE® BrainBusters

Unscramble the Jumbles, one letter to each square, to spell words related to computers.

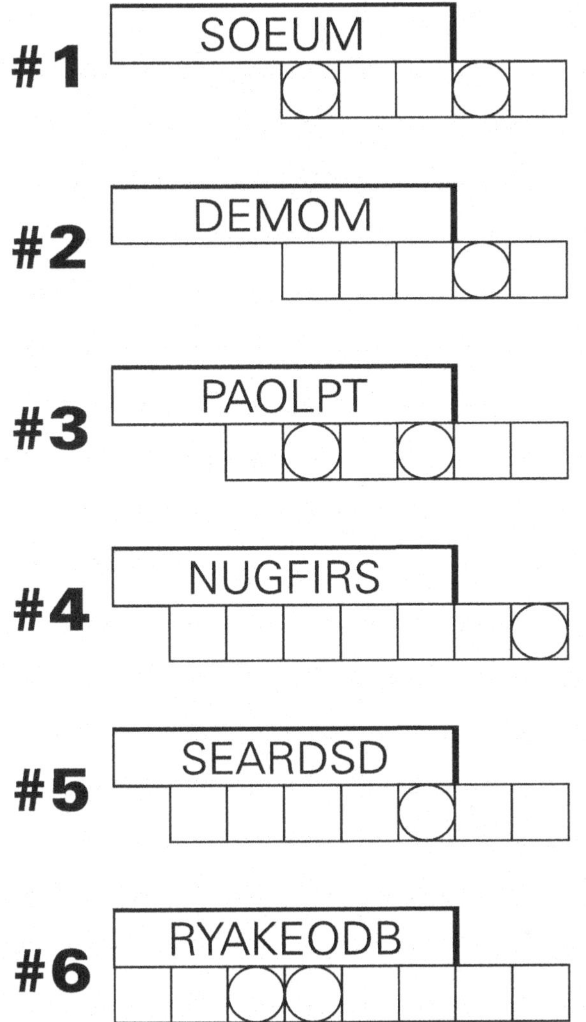

Interesting Computer Facts

The average computer chip factory produces about 4 million gallons of wastewater a day.

The highest-selling Internet domain name to date, www.business.com, sold for $7.5 million in 1999.

Arrange the circled letters to solve the mystery answer.

MYSTERY ANSWER

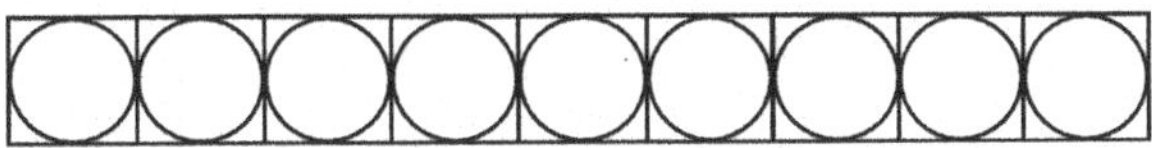

PUZZLE 155

ADJECTIVES

JUMBLE BrainBusters

Unscramble the Jumbles, one letter to each square, to spell adjectives.

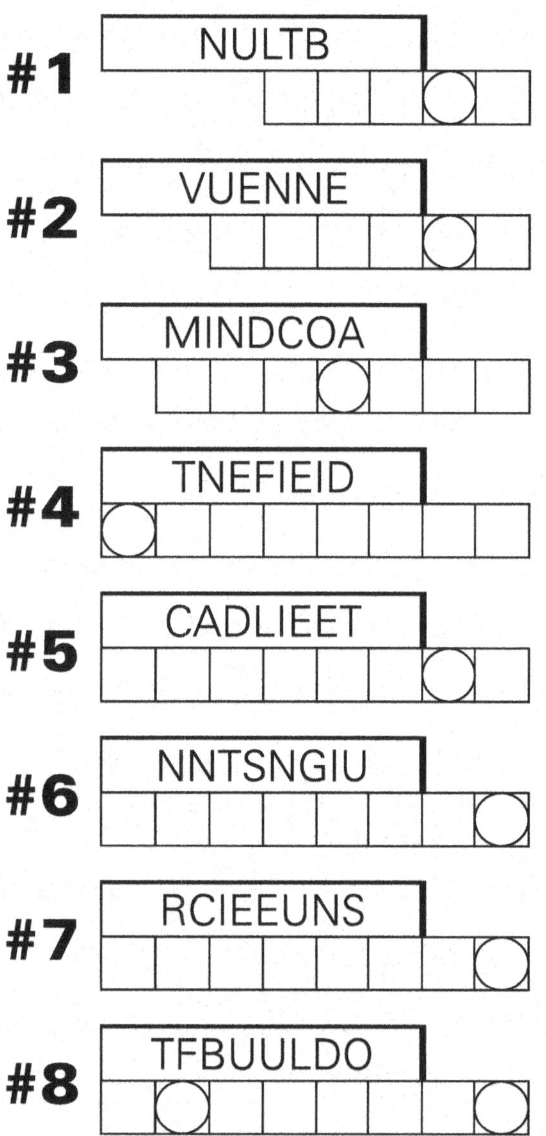

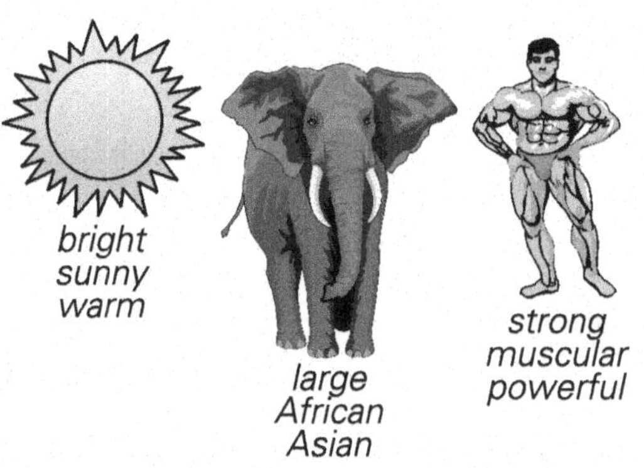

Box of Clues

Stumped? Maybe you can find a clue below.

- -Sure
- -Unlikely
- -Tending to travel and change settlements frequently
- -Frank
- -Extended
- -Fragile
- -Gorgeous
- -Patchy, spotty
- -Unprotected

Arrange the circled letters to solve the mystery answer.

MYSTERY ANSWER

ALL ABOUT FOOD

JUMBLE BrainBusters

Unscramble the Jumbles, one letter to each square, to spell words related to food.

#1
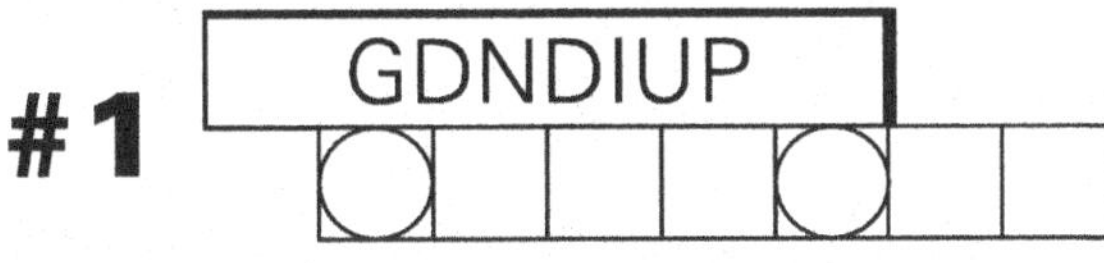

#2

#3

#4
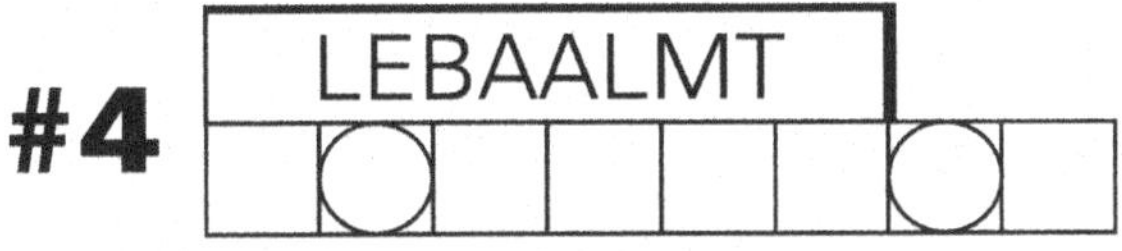

#5

Interesting Food Facts

In the sixties, cast members from *The Andy Griffith Show* and *Green Acres* served as spokespersons for Jell-O Instant Pudding in TV commercials.

Baked bat is a popular Samoan dish.

Arrange the circled letters to solve the mystery answer.

MYSTERY ANSWER

PUZZLE 157

JUMBLE® JOKES

JUMBLE® BrainBusters

Unscramble the mixed up letters to reveal the punch lines as suggested by the jokes.

#1 What did Batman go buy at the pet shop?

OBRINA

#2 What is another name for a telephone booth?

EBCXHROTAAT

#3 What food is good for the brain?

UDSNOELOPO

#4 What can you hold without touching it?

NONCAVESOAITR

#5 What kind of ant can count?

TANNAANOCTCU

#6 What does a wicked chicken lay?

SGEDEIDGLVE

PUZZLE 158

MOVIES

JUMBLE BrainBusters

Unscramble the mixed-up letters, one letter to each square, to spell movie titles.

#1 LGLOZAID

#2 CSTA WAYA

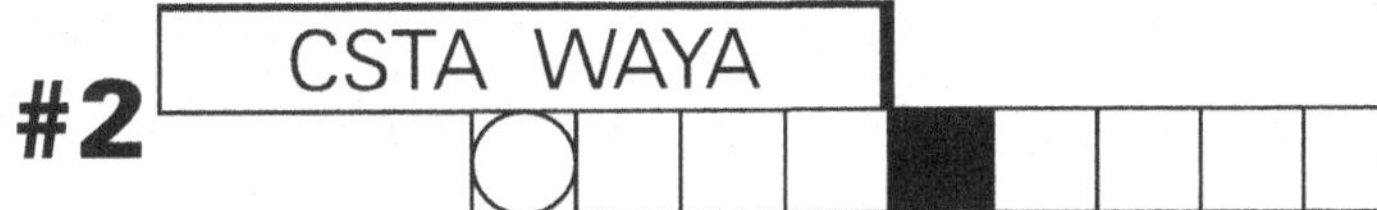

#3 PEDE MCIATP

#4 TEH VGUIEFIT

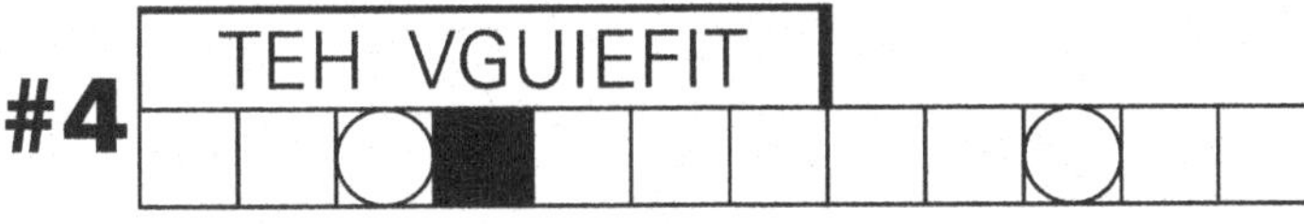

#5 GNTNTIO LIHL

#6 AKFYER RADIYF

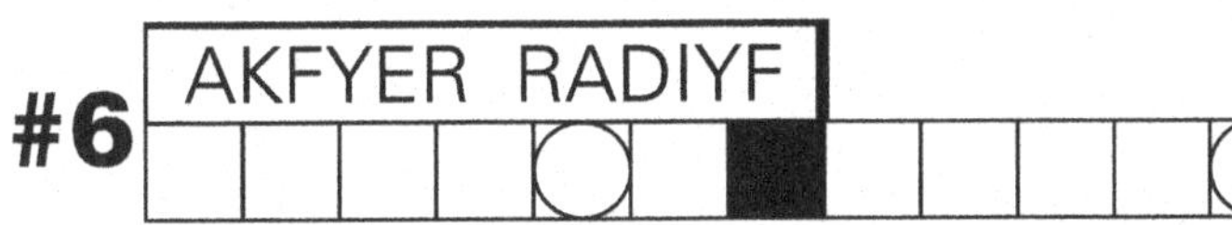

Box of Clues

Stumped? Maybe you can find a clue below.

- -1999 movie starring Julia Roberts and Hugh Grant
- -1998 movie about a comet striking Earth
- -1941 movie about the owner of a newspaper
- -1998 monster movie
- -2000 Tom Hanks movie
- -1993 Harrison Ford movie
- -2003 remake starring Jamie Lee Curtis

Arrange the circled letters to solve the mystery answer.

MYSTERY ANSWER

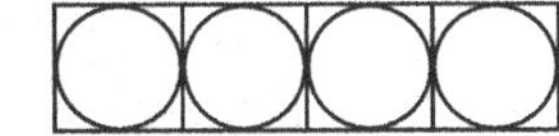

PUZZLE 159

RHYMING WORDS

JUMBLE BrainBusters

Unscramble the Jumbles, one letter to each square, to spell pairs of words that rhyme.

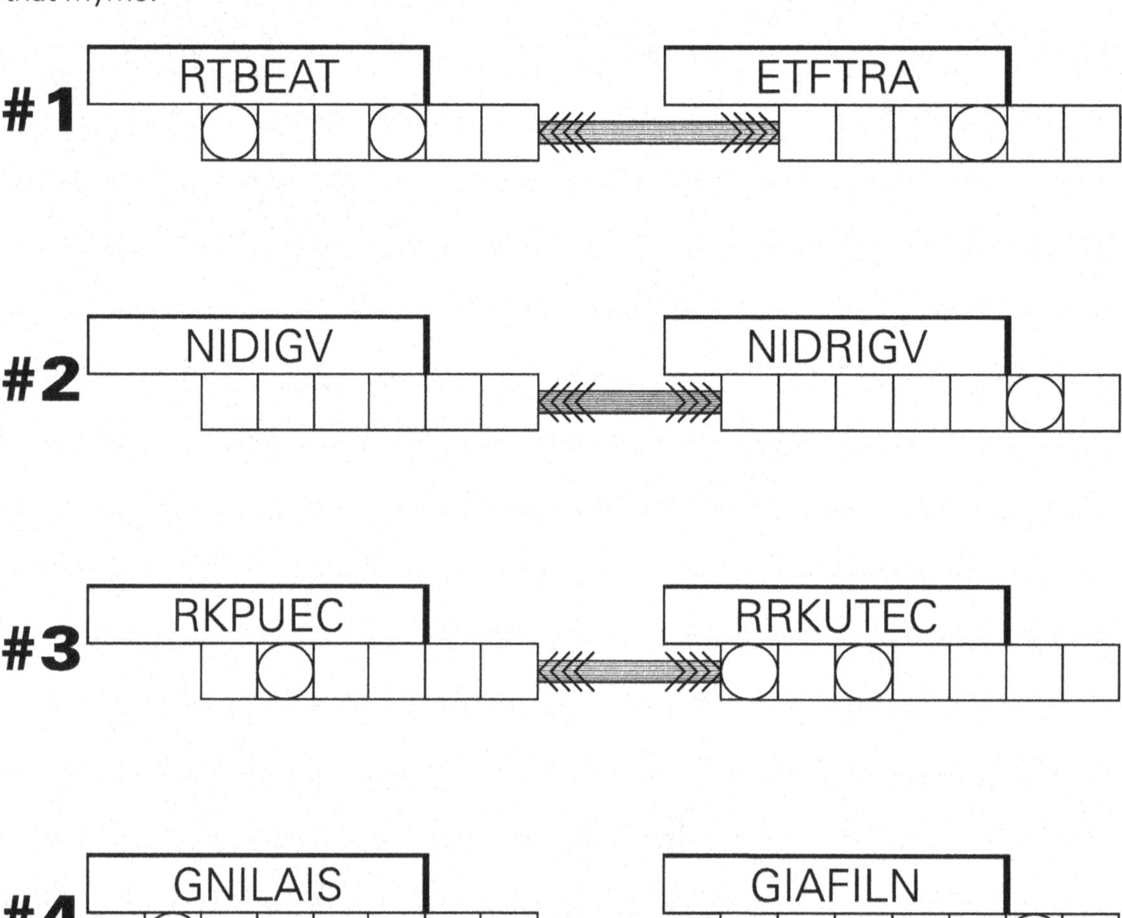

Arrange the circled letters to solve the mystery answer. (Form two words that rhyme.)

MYSTERY ANSWER

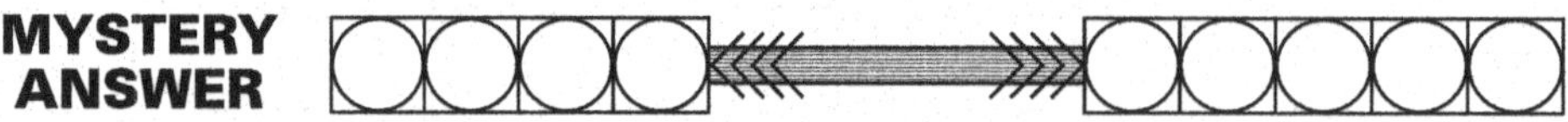

JUMBLE® TRIVIA

JUMBLE BrainBusters

Unscramble the Jumbles, one letter to each square, to spell words as suggested by the trivia clues.

#1 Lake ______ is the deepest lake in North America (1,645 feet).

#1 HTOEA

#2 In a standard deck of playing cards, the king of hearts is the only king without a ______.

#2 CTSAOHEUM

#3 There are only about 50 ______ fields known to exist on Earth.

#3 RSEEYG

#4 Mead, a wine made from honey, is the national drink of ______.

#4 LPDNOA

#5 Mt. ______ was first ascended in 1913.

#5 SYPOULM

Arrange the circled letters to solve the mystery answer.

Scientists have determined that ______ ______ is moving east at about one-fifth of an inch per year.

MYSTERY ANSWER

MATH

JUMBLE BrainBusters

Unscramble the Jumbles, one letter to each square, so that each equation is correct.

For example: NONTEOEOW

ONE + ONE = TWO

#1 LSTWXXEVIESI

☐☐☐ + ☐☐☐ = ☐◯☐☐◯

#2 ZERRIYEXZOTOS

◯☐☐☐ × ☐☐◯☐ = ☐☐☐◯

#3 EEIFNHETREIEVTFF

◯☐☐☐☐☐☐ ÷ ◯☐☐☐☐ = ☐☐☐◯

#4 HENOENEDUDRTNETN

☐◯☐ × ☐☐◯ = ☐◯☐ ☐◯☐☐☐◯☐

#5 TNAEIETWGOEVNOENO

☐☐☐ − ◯☐☐ = ☐☐☐☐☐☐◯☐ ◯☐☐

Arrange the circled letters to solve the mystery equation.

MYSTERY EQUATION

◯◯◯◯◯ × ◯◯◯ = ◯◯◯◯◯◯◯◯

PUZZLE 162

BIRDS

JUMBLE BrainBusters

Unscramble the Jumbles, one letter to each square, to spell varieties of birds.

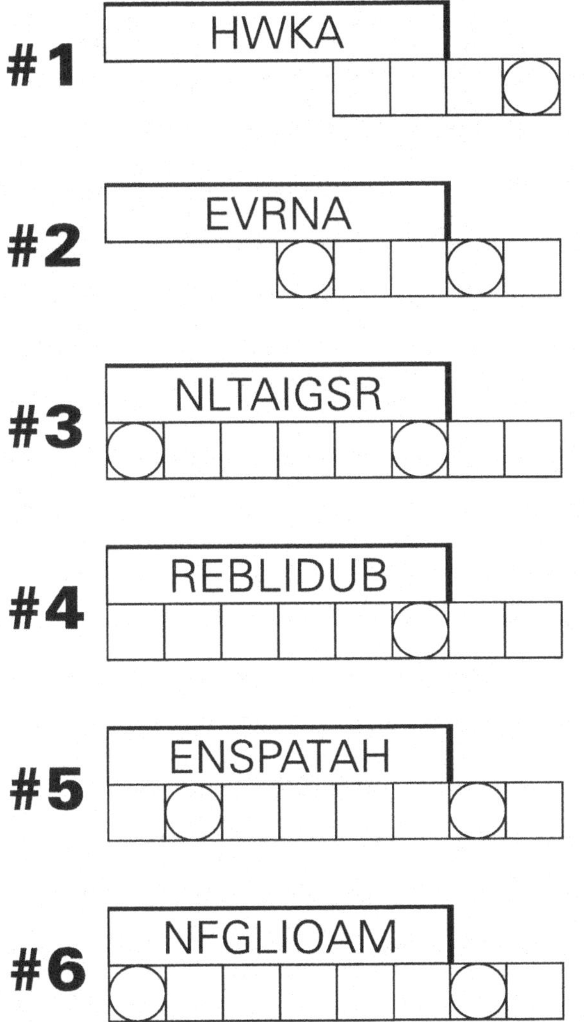

Interesting Bird Facts

The central shaft of a bird's feather is called the rachis.

There are about 300 species of doves and pigeons in the world.

Arrange the circled letters to solve the mystery answer.

MYSTERY ANSWER

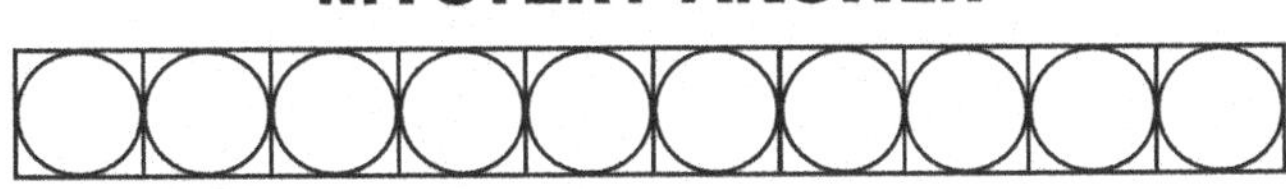

PUZZLE 163

WARS AND THE MILITARY

JUMBLE BrainBusters

Unscramble the Jumbles, one letter to each square, to spell words related to wars and the military.

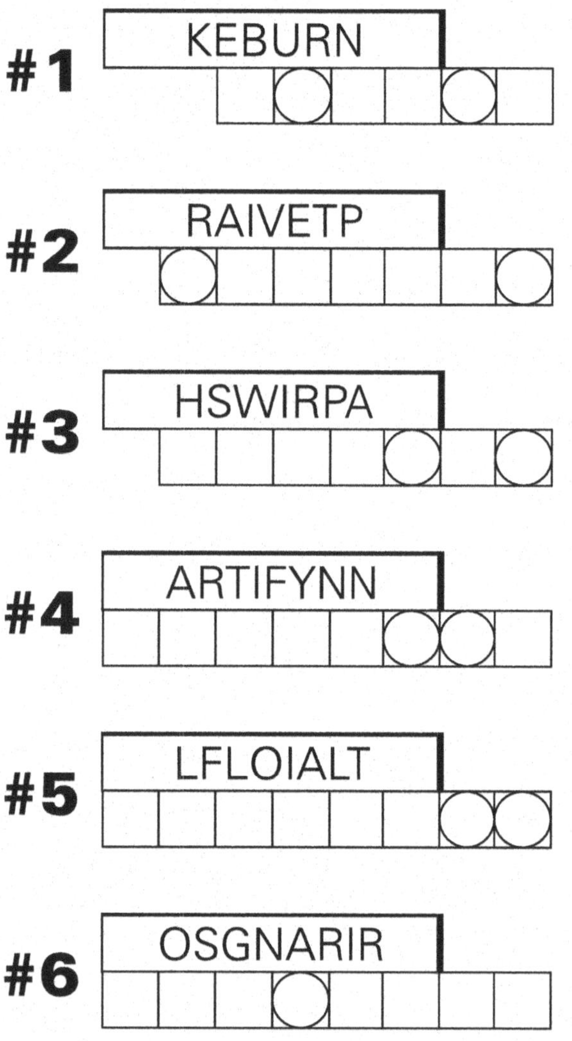

Box of Clues

Stumped? Maybe you can find a clue below.

-Military vessel
-Defensive position with a fortified projection above ground level
-The branch of an army made up of units trained to fight on foot
-A U.S. military decoration
-Noncommissioned rank in the U.S. Army or Marine Corps
-Fleet of ships
-Military post or the troops assigned to the post

Arrange the circled letters to solve the mystery answer.

MYSTERY ANSWER

PUZZLE 164

MATH

JUMBLE BrainBusters

Unscramble the Jumbles, one letter to each square, so that each equation is correct.

For example: NOTLSWOEOPNEU

ONE PLUS ONE = TWO

#1 TMITEISTOEEVNFW

#2 WMFRTOTIETUOOWS

#3 RWSOTUWIUOTNOFM

#4 TNNRIUSHLEEIESPX

#5 NNEIEEMTWIUNSVONEL

Then arrange the circled letters to solve the mystery equation.

MYSTERY EQUATION

PUZZLE
165

STARTS AND ENDS WITH THE SAME LETTER

Unscramble the Jumbles, one letter to each square, to spell words that start and end with the same letter.

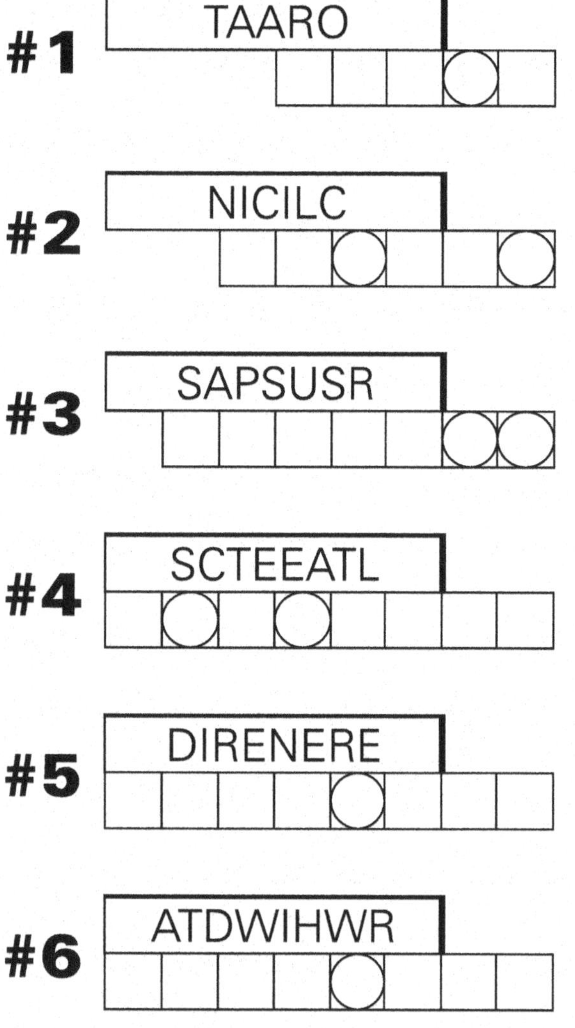

JUMBLE BrainBusters

RADAR
ARENA
POP
GOING
RIVER
HIGH
DICED
CRYPTIC

Box of Clues

Stumped? Maybe you can find a clue below.

- -Northern, cold-weather mammal
- -Main trunk of the systemic arteries in the heart
- -Medical facility
- -Analyzed
- -Go beyond, as in degree or quality
- -Remove
- -Broadcast

Arrange the circled letters to solve the mystery answer.

MYSTERY ANSWER

PUZZLE 166

SUPER JUMBLE® CHALLENGE

JUMBLE® BrainBusters

#1 GRI

#2 BEOO

#3 LOHEL

#4 MUUTNA

#5 GCAAKPE

#6 COHEALES

#7 STEEXIENV

#8 UBSEOLDPNL

#9 RSTOREOEPHU

Unscramble the Jumbles, one letter to each square, to spell words.

Box of Clues

Stumped? Maybe you can find a clue below.

- -Fall
- -Enchanted, fascinated
- -Program for young students
- -Type of string, cord
- -A musical instrument
- -______ steak
- -Hi
- -Large-scale, broad
- -Oil ______
- -Container

Arrange the circled letters to solve the mystery answer.

MYSTERY ANSWER

PUZZLE 167

UN-MIX AND MATCH
ELEMENTS

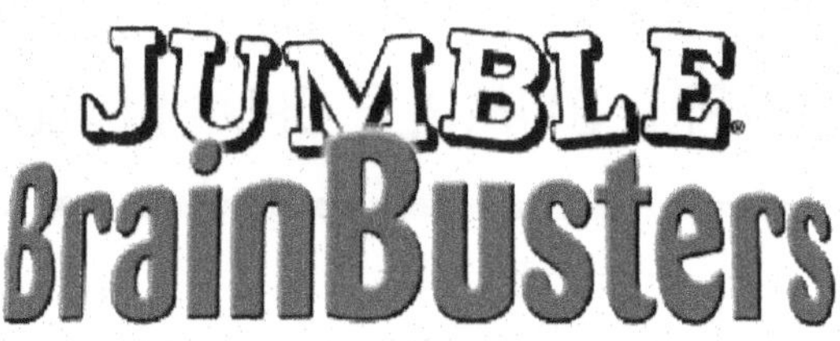

Section 1: Unscramble the mixed-up letters, one letter to each square, to spell names of elements.

#1 DSIMUO

#2 LCSIOIN

#3 MUPAINTL

#4 GDNREOHY

THE PERIODIC TABLE

Atomic #
Atomic Symbol

H																	He
Li	Be											B	C	N	O	F	Ne
Na	Mg											Al	Si	P	S	Cl	Ar
K	Ca	Sc	Ti	V	Cr	Mn	Fe	Co	Ni	Cu	Zn	Ga	Ge	As	Se	Br	Kr
Rb	Sr	Y	Zr	Nb	Mo	Tc	Ru	Rh	Pd	Ag	Cd	In	Sn	Sb	Te	I	Xe
Cs	Ba		Hf	Ta	W	Re	Os	Ir	Pt	Au	Hg	Tl	Pb	Bi	Po	At	Rn
Fr	Ra		Unq	Unp	Unh	Uns		Une									

Arrange the circled letters to solve the mystery answer.

MYSTERY ANSWER

Section 2: Match the answers in the puzzle (including the mystery answer) to the following clues. (Write "MA." to represent the mystery answer.)

#____ The most common element in the universe.

#____ Element used commonly in glass, semiconducting devices, concrete, brick, refractories, and pottery.

#____ This silver-white metallic element reacts explosively with water and is soft, light, and extremely malleable.

#____ This soft, silver-white metallic element occurs in nature only in compounds and is explosively reactive.

#____ Used as a catalyst and in electrical components, this silver-white metallic element occurs worldwide and is usually mixed with other metals.

PUZZLE 168

JUMBLE® TRIVIA

JUMBLE® BrainBusters

Unscramble the Jumbles, one letter to each square, to spell words as suggested by the trivia clues.

#1 This was the first U.S. airline to serve alcoholic beverages in flight (1949).

#1 STNOEWTRH

#2 This country is home to about 50 million people.

#2 NLEAGDN

#3 This area was under Chinese control from 1691 to 1911 and from 1919 to 1921.

#3 LGMOOAIN

#4 This musician's final performance was November 2, 1986, at Radio City Music Hall.

#4 CRLIEEBA

#5 This region is home to more than 20 percent of the world's forests.

#5 RSIEIAB

Arrange the circled letters to solve the mystery answer.

About 400 people survive being hit by this each year.

MYSTERY ANSWER

PUZZLE 169

UN-MIX AND MATCH
COUNTRIES

Section 1: Unscramble the mixed-up letters, one letter to each square, to spell names of countries.

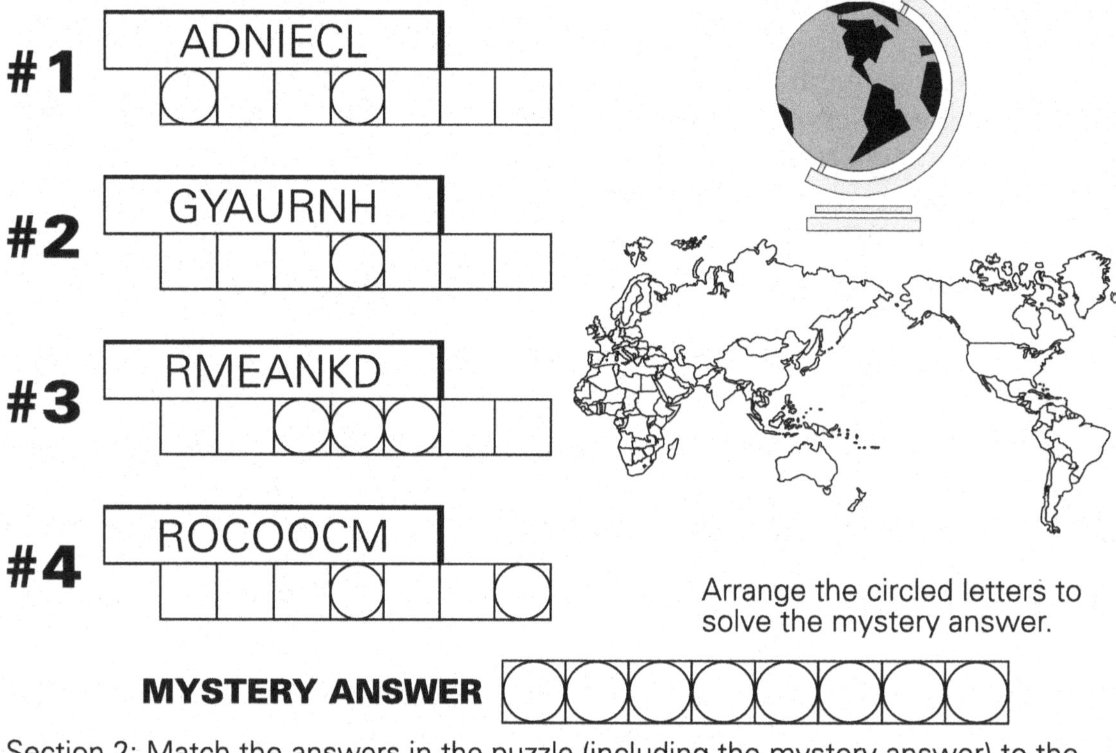

Arrange the circled letters to solve the mystery answer.

MYSTERY ANSWER

Section 2: Match the answers in the puzzle (including the mystery answer) to the following clues. (Write "MA." to represent the mystery answer.)

#____ The southernmost Scandinavian country.

#____ Island country that lies just south of the Arctic Circle.

#____ High Asian country with an average elevation of more than 4,000 feet.

#____ Country situated on a plain near the geographic center of Europe.

#____ Country with coastlines on the Mediterranean and Atlantic.

PUZZLE 170

JUMBLE® CONNECTIONS

JUMBLE® BrainBusters

Unscramble the Jumbles, one letter to each square, to spell words that fit into the puzzle below.

ACROSS		DOWN	
#1	NVEIOLV	#1	PICCEA
#5	RGAEUD	#2	TFOSEF
#7	LACSS	#3	EELGA
#8	NGHEIAR	#4	NAAIG
#10	EPTL	#5	RMALA
#12	MLVESUO	#6	SDIESIA
#13	NGGEGO	#8	THOOGD
		#9	MAUNNG
		#11	TEEAN

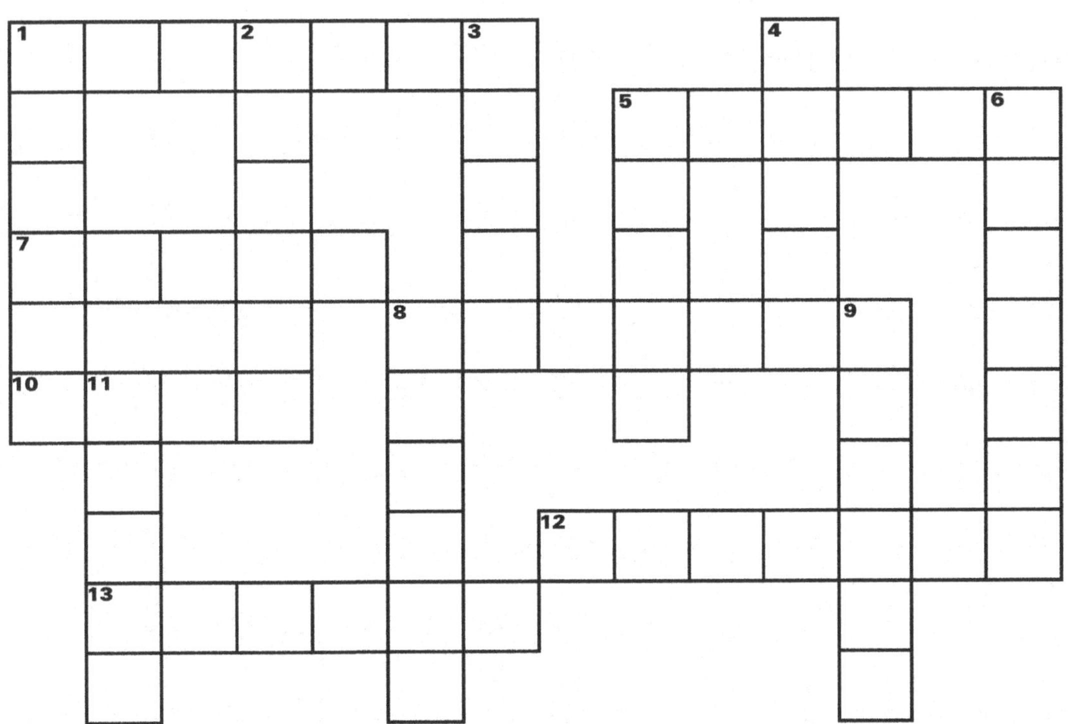

PUZZLE 171

FIND THE JUMBLES®

JUMBLE® BrainBusters

Unscramble the Jumbles, one letter to each square, to spell words.

#1 REAAN ☐☐☐☐☐

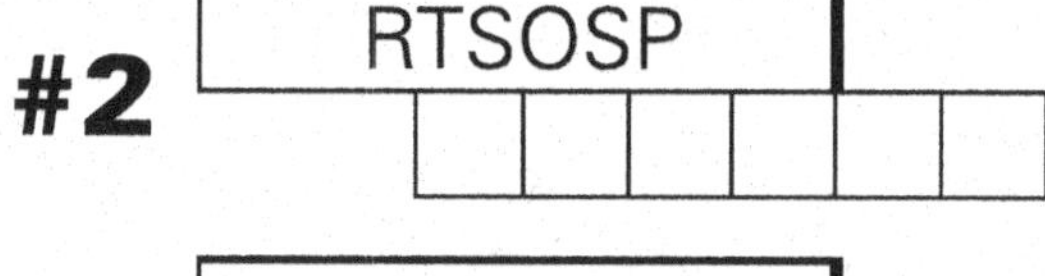

#2 RTSOSP ☐☐☐☐☐☐

#3 LTEEHTA ☐☐☐☐☐☐☐

#4 NEEEDFS ☐☐☐☐☐☐☐

#5 SFOEEFN ☐☐☐☐☐☐☐

#6 NTETOSC ☐☐☐☐☐☐☐

#7 UDSAIMT ☐☐☐☐☐☐☐

#8 PCEEMOT ☐☐☐☐☐☐☐

Find and circle the answers (from above) in the grid of letters below.

D G H P A V B O H E E I G L S A
H A S D J K D I L G I L A N T F
C O T O G F J T N C T N M E A H
O M R H P B S O F F E N S E D C
A G O C L E K G R R S N U A I U
D J P D T E H I A V E V B E U G
L H S N A B T M N F W A M I M Z
B C O M P E T E E R D N G J K C
G C P F I A K D X I A C N D B I

PUZZLE 172

MOVIES

JUMBLE BrainBusters

Unscramble the mixed-up letters, one letter to each square, to spell movie titles.

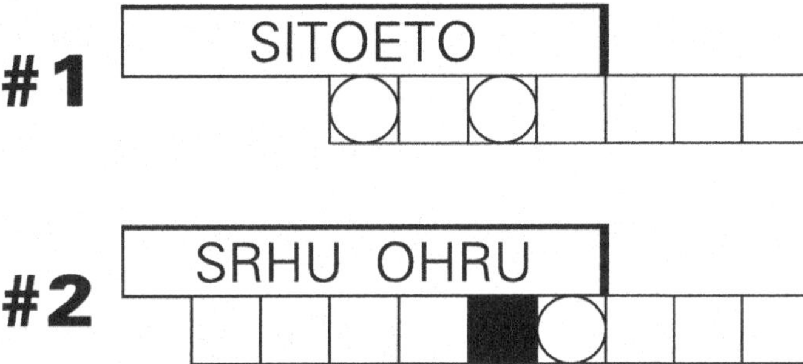

#2 SRHU OHRU

#3 RIDGAATOL

#4 NIAEN LALH

#5 OVNRIUNFEG

#6 NIRGAG ULBL

Box of Clues

Stumped? Maybe you can find a clue below.

- 1992 Best Picture
- 1982 Dustin Hoffman movie
- 2000 Best Picture
- 1998 movie starring Chris Tucker and Jackie Chan
- 1972 Best Picture
- 1980 Robert Di Nero movie
- 1977 Best Picture

Arrange the circled letters to solve the mystery answer.

MYSTERY ANSWER

PUZZLE 173

SUPER JUMBLE® CHALLENGE

JUMBLE® BrainBusters

Unscramble the Jumbles, one letter to each square, to spell words.

#1 JGU

#2 HPCO

#3 NIJOT

#4 CRUSKU

#5 TSTINOA

#6 NCOIRELH

#7 ANSEUORVP

#8 RSREATANUT

#9 UBMHINIRDMG

Box of Clues

Stumped? Maybe you can find a clue below.

- -"Cl"
- -Ankle, for example
- -Cut
- -Fast food ______
- -Loud
- -Type of container
- -Small bird
- -Train ______
- -Exploding star
- -Commotion

Arrange the circled letters to solve the mystery answer.

MYSTERY ANSWER

MYSTERY PERSON

JUMBLE® BrainBusters

Unscramble the Jumbles, one letter to each square, to spell words that relate to the mystery person.

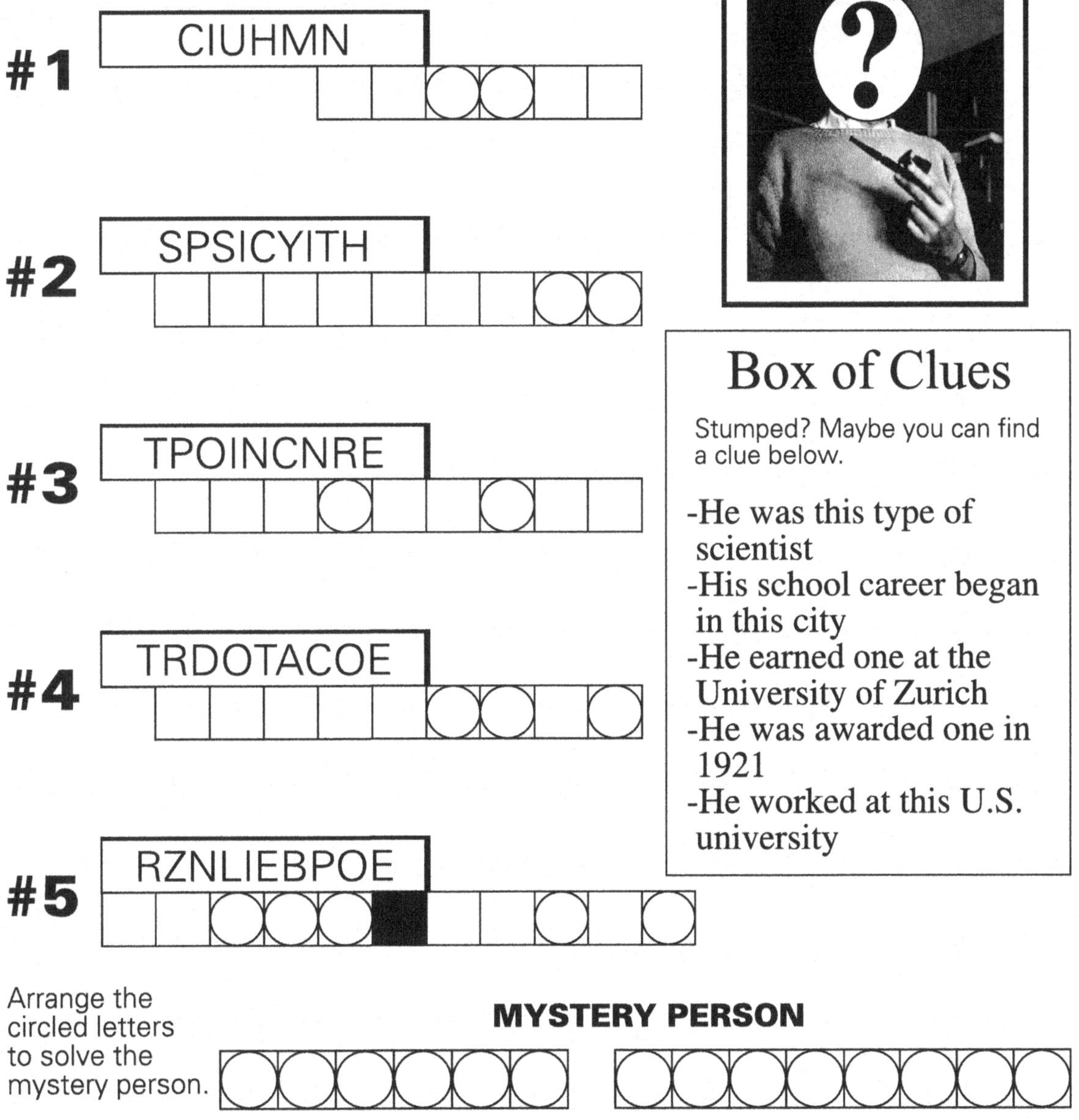

#1
CIUHMN
#2
SPSICYITH
#3
TPOINCNRE
#4
TRDOTACOE
#5
RZNLIEBPOE
?
Box of Clues
Stumped? Maybe you can find a clue below.
-He was this type of scientist
-His school career began in this city
-He earned one at the University of Zurich
-He was awarded one in 1921
-He worked at this U.S. university

Arrange the circled letters to solve the mystery person.

MYSTERY PERSON

PUZZLE 175

JUMBLE® CONNECTIONS

JUMBLE® BrainBusters

Unscramble the Jumbles, one letter to each square, to spell words that fit into the puzzle below.

ACROSS

#1 ESMIVAS
#5 PEAIEC
#7 LHLOE
#8 HKOBECA
#10 AMIN
#12 MNARGAA
#13 EOJTBC

DOWN

#1 HAMMEY
#2 ESOTNL
#3 MENAE
#4 PHOIP
#5 KAWEA
#6 RMEAURD
#8 ACBRHN
#9 REMEEG
#11 BAROH

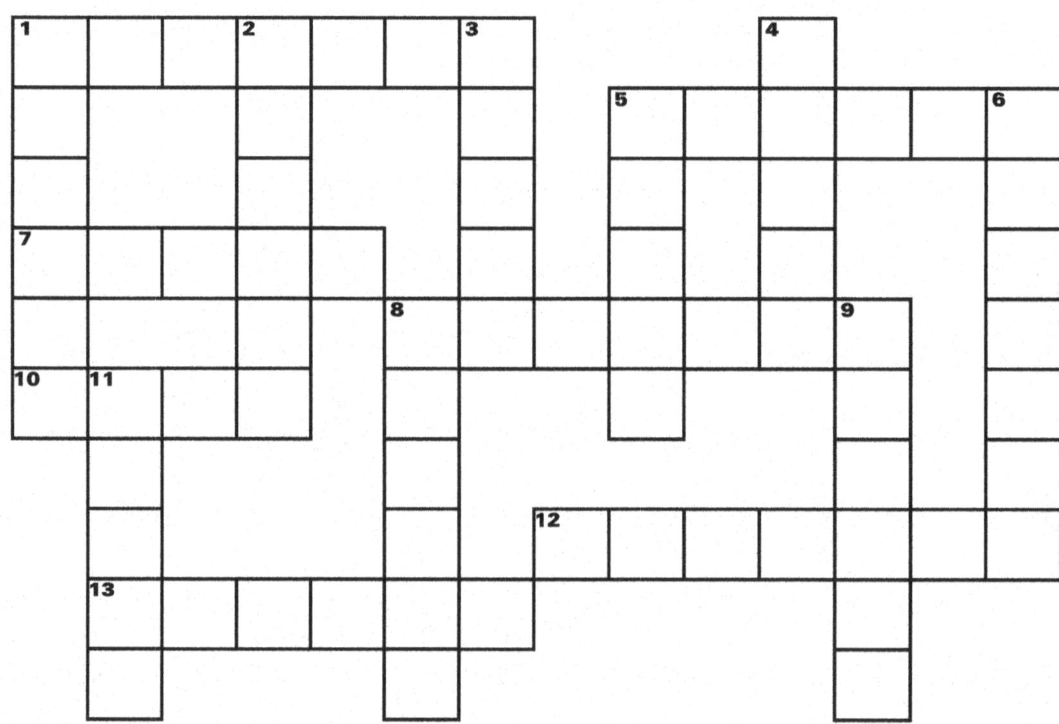

RHYMES WITH . . .

JUMBLE BrainBusters

Unscramble the Jumbles, one letter to each square, to spell words that will each have a corresponding rhyming clue.

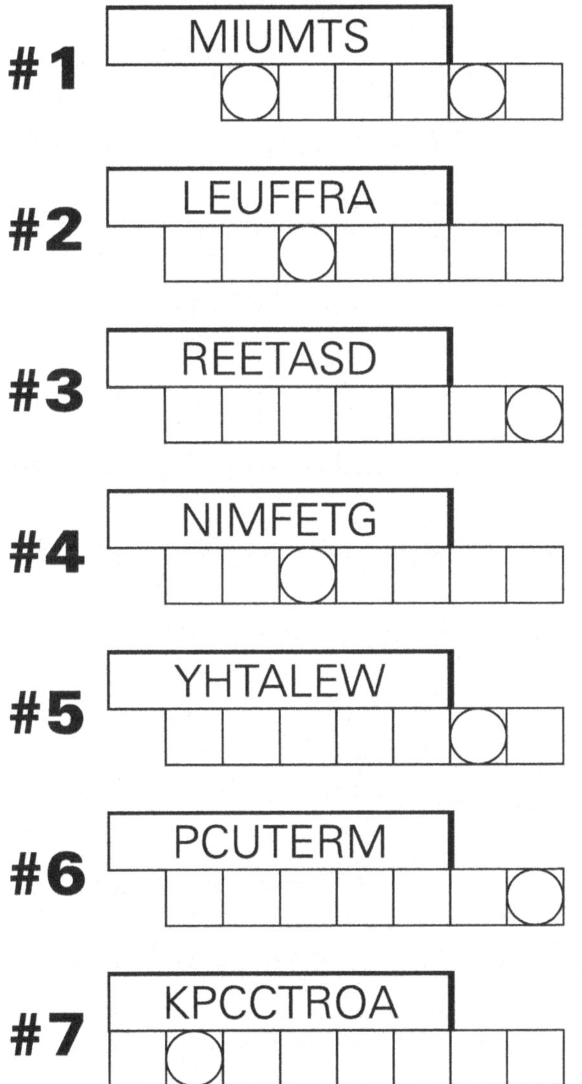

GO . . . NO
TON . . . FUN
BACK . . . STACK
STUCK . . . TRUCK
MISTER . . . SISTER
SCANDAL . . . SANDAL

Box of Clues

Stumped? Maybe you can find a clue below.

-Rhymes with *jackpot*
-Rhymes with *healthy*
-Rhymes with *tearful*
-Rhymes with *freight*
-Rhymes with *nearest*
-Rhymes with *pigment*
-Rhymes with *plummet*
-Rhymes with *trumpet*

Arrange the circled letters to solve the mystery answer.

MYSTERY ANSWER

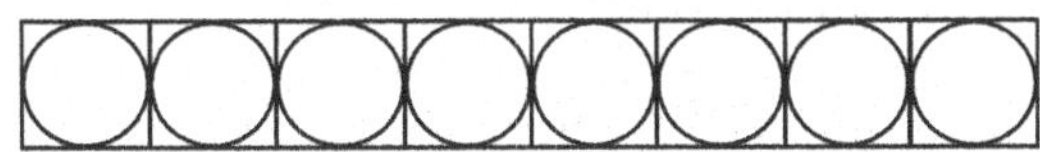

ANSWERS

1. **Jumbles:** #1. KELLOGG #2. CONCORDE #3. NEPTUNE #4. ZAMBIA #5. CATFISH **Mystery Answer:** CONNECTICUT
2. **Jumbles:** #1. *ALIEN* #2. *ROCKY* #3. *GHOST* #4. *ICE AGE* #5. *CHAPLIN* #6. *TWISTER* **Mystery Answer:** *CHICAGO*
3. **Jumbles:** #1. SIX – SIX = ZERO
#2. ONE + EIGHT = NINE
#3. FIVE + TWO = SEVEN
#4. THREE × THREE = NINE
#5. SEVEN – ZERO = SEVEN
Mystery Equation: TWO × FIVE = TEN
4. **Jumbles:** #1. CRAB #2. OTTER #3. RHINO #4. PIGEON #5. PANTHER #6. MALLARD #7. RACCOON **Mystery Answer:** CROCODILE
5. **Jumbles:** #1. TICKET #2. AUGUST #3. POUNDS #4. NUMBER #5. CAPTAIN #6. FEBRUARY **Mystery Answer:** DIAMETER
6. **Jumbles:** #1. RAZOR #2. PLUMP #3. TYRANT #4. AGENDA #5. TONIGHT #6. RATTLER **Mystery Answer:** TREATMENT
7. **Jumbles:** #1. CLUCK—TRUCK
#2. POWDER—CHOWDER
#3. BEDDING—HEADING
#4. FACTION—TRACTION
Mystery Answer: OUNCE—BOUNCE
8. **Jumbles:** #1. RUGBY #2. TENNIS #3. TACKLE #4. JERSEY #5. HUDDLE #6. VICTORY **Mystery Answer:** CATCHER
9. **Jumbles:** #1. INLET #2. ISLAND #3. SPRING #4. JUNGLE #5. SEASON #6. GLACIER **Mystery Answer:** PLATEAU
10. **Jumbles:** #1. HELMET #2. MISSION #3. BARRAGE #4. ADMIRAL #5. SAMURAI #6. COMMAND **Mystery Answer:** SURRENDER
11. **Jumbles:** #1. BREATH #2. A STAIRCASE #3. A CHAIR #4. SUNDAY #5. A FLEA #6. A CUPCAKE
12. **Jumbles:** #1. RUSSELL #2. WOUNDED #3. MAJORITY #4. FOOTBALL #5. REPUBLICAN **Mystery Person:** BOB DOLE
13. **Jumbles:** #1. FRUIT #2. FUDGE #3. SNACK #4. BUTTER #5. BUFFET #6. MUFFIN **Mystery Answer:** DRUMSTICK
14. **Jumbles:** #1. NAVY #2. ROBIN #3. POLICE #4. FERRARI #5. SECURITY #6. THURSDAY **Mystery Answer:** DETECTIVE
15. **Jumbles:** #1. SALLY FIELD #2. SALMA HAYEK #3. DIANE KEATON #4. ASHLEY JUDD **Mystery Answer:** HELEN HUNT **Section 2 Answers:** 4 3 1 M.A. 2
16. **Jumbles:** #1. WILLIAM #2. MAINE #3. HOPKINS #4. DAMASCUS #5. WEBSTER **Mystery Answer:** WINDSOR CASTLE
17. **Jumbles:** #1. WISE—PRUDENT
#2. HUMAN—PERSON #3. FREELY—EASILY
#4. GIGGLE—CHUCKLE
Mystery Answer: NICE—PLEASANT
18. **Jumbles:** #1. TRUNK #2. AZALEA #3. BRANCH #4. JUNIPER #5. FOLIAGE #6. NURSERY **Mystery Answer:** FERTILIZER
19. **Jumbles:** #1. FINAL—INITIAL
#2. PEACE—WARTIME #3. STURDY—FLIMSY
#4. DIVIDE—MULTIPLY
Mystery Answer: FAR—NEAR
20. **Jumbles:** #1. GOOD #2. GOURD #3. GOBLIN #4. GOLFER #5. GOTTEN #6. GOPHER **Mystery Answer:** GOLDENROD
21. **Jumbles:** #1. PUPPY #2. BREED #3. CANINE #4. KENNEL #5. COLLAR #6. BISCUIT #7. TRAINING **Mystery Answer:** PEDIGREE
22. **Jumbles:** #1. FUSION #2. ACTING #3. SPLINT #4. TARGET #5. LEGACY #6. CHORUS **Mystery Answers:** #1. AFRICA #2. ETHIOPIA
23. **Jumbles:** #1. DATA #2. MEMORY #3. MONITOR #4. NETWORK #5. COMMAND #6. SHORTCUT **Mystery Answer:** INTERNET
24. **Jumbles:** #1. DOVE #2. TURKEY #3. OSPREY #4. MAGPIE #5. SPARROW #6. CARDINAL **Mystery Answer:** WOODPECKER
25. **Jumbles:** #1. CRISIS #2. ATTAIN #3. CANDID #4. CACKLE #5. FLOPPY #6. CANOPY **Mystery Answers:** #1. PILOT #2. COCKPIT #3. AIRPLANE
26. **Jumbles:** #1. LANSING #2. OLYMPIA #3. RICHMOND #4. COLUMBUS **Mystery Answer:** INDIANAPOLIS **Section 2 Answers:** 4 1 M.A. 2 3
27. **Jumbles:** #1. BINGO #2. CARGO #3. AGONY #4. GOBLET #5. DRAGON #6. VERTIGO **Mystery Answer:** DECAGON
28. **Jumbles:** #1. DESK #2. PUPIL #3. CLASS #4. SCHOOL #5. EDUCATE #6. SUBJECT #7. COLLEGE #8. LEARNING
29. **Jumbles:** #1. ROMANS #2. A BALD MAN #3. YOUR NAME #4. A HORSE #5. A RULER #6. A MIRROR
30. **Jumbles:** #1. HOOVER #2. GERBIL #3. DALLAS #4. MOOSE #5. MISSOURI **Mystery Answer:** BERMUDA
31. **Jumbles:** #1. *TWINS* #2. *ALADDIN* #3. *TRAFFIC* #4. *PLATOON* #5. *MEMENTO* #6. *SUPERMAN* **Mystery Answer:** *STAR WARS*
32. **Jumbles:** #1. FOUR / TWO = TWO
#2. ONE + THREE = FOUR
#3. ZERO × ZERO = ZERO
#4. FIVE – TWO = THREE
#5. FOUR + ZERO = FOUR
Mystery Equation: FOUR – THREE = ONE
33. **Jumbles:** #1. UTAH—COLORADO
#2. INDIANA—MICHIGAN
#3. VIRGINIA—MARYLAND
#4. OKLAHOMA—ARKANSAS
Mystery Answer: IDAHO—MONTANA
34. **Jumbles:** #1. MURKY #2. BRIGHT #3. BENIGN #4. HUMBLE #5. INTENSE #6. CONCISE #7. FATEFUL #8. CHRONIC **Mystery Answer:** CHEERFUL
35. **Jumbles:** #1. A HORSEFLY #2. A CANNIBAL #3. MUSTARD #4. A TYRANT #5. A GOLDFISH #6. LIE STILL
36. **Jumbles:** #1. BILL MURRAY #2. ALEC BALDWIN #3. KEVIN BACON #4. CLINT EASTWOOD **Mystery Answer:** BRUCE WILLIS **Section 2 Answers:** 3 2 4 M.A. 1
37. **Jumbles:** #1. LARRY #2. DARRIN #3. ARTHUR #4. ENDORA #5. SITCOM #6. KRAVITZ **Mystery Answer:** SAMANTHA

38. **Jumbles:** #1. SLOTH #2. MOUSE #3. MOOSE #4. GIBBON #5. JAGUAR #6. REINDEER #7. ELEPHANT
Mystery Answer: HEDGEHOG

39. **Jumbles:** #1. RADAR #2. FLOOD #3. CHILLY #4. TWISTER #5. CYCLONE #6. MONSOON #7. RAINFALL
Mystery Answer: COLD FRONT

40. **Jumbles:** #1. PULSE #2. MOUTH #3. FIBULA #4. ARTERY #5. TONGUE #6. MUSCLE #7. EARDRUM
Mystery Answer: ESOPHAGUS

41. **Jumbles:** #1. A SIDEWALK #2. RUN DOWN #3. A TOMBSTONE #4. TO THE DOCK #5. FRANKLY #6. JITTERBUGS

42. **Jumbles:** #1. PILOT #2. JOINED #3. DEGREE #4. COLONEL #5. HONORARY
Mystery Person: JOHN GLENN

43. **Jumbles:** #1. EDDIE #2. RADIO #3. *CHEERS* #4. DAPHNE #5. SEATTLE #6. MAHONEY
Mystery Answer: PSYCHIATRIST

44. **Jumbles:** #1. *BAMBI* #2. *AIRPORT* #3. *CONTACT* #4. *POLLOCK* #5. *GET SHORTY* #6. *THE PATRIOT*
Mystery Answer: *POCAHONTAS*

45. **Jumbles:** #1. ADVICE #2. NICKNAME #3. DAUGHTER #4. LAST NAME #5. COLUMNIST
Mystery Person: ANN LANDERS

46. **Jumbles:** #1. SASSY #2. AWARE #3. SULLEN #4. SEVERE #5. SPEEDY #6. PROPER #7. VISIBLE #8. ENDLESS
Mystery Answer: PREPARED

47. **Jumbles:** #1. A CARPET #2. WELL WATER #3. BALDNESS #4. HE BUCKED #5. IMPORTANT #6. POLLUTION

48. **Jumbles:** #1. DRAFT #2. BULLET #3. TARGET #4. DEFECT #5. GUNFIRE #6. VETERAN
Mystery Answer: BATTLEFIELD

49. **Jumbles:** #1. TARDY—PROMPT
#2. FINISH—COMMENCE
#3. RELEASE—CAPTURE
#4. NERVOUS—RELAXED
Mystery Answer: ODD—EVEN

50. **Jumbles:** #1. ONE TIMES SIX = SIX
#2. FOUR PLUS TWO = SIX
#3. FIVE PLUS FIVE = TEN
#4. TWENTY MINUS TEN = TEN
#5. TEN PLUS FIVE = FIFTEEN
Mystery Equation: TWO TIMES TWO = FOUR

51. **Jumbles:** #1. TIGER #2. SHEEP #3. PANDA #4. GOOSE #5. TURTLE #6. CHEETAH #7. CHIPMUNK
Mystery Answer: SALAMANDER

52. **Jumbles:** #1. PUNCH #2. BASKET #3. BUNKER #4. HOCKEY #5. HELMET #6. STADIUM
Mystery Answer: BADMINTON

53. **Jumbles:** #1. CREEK #2. BEACH #3. SWAMP #4. GEYSER #5. LAGOON #6. MOUNTAIN
Mystery Answer: ECOSYSTEM

54. **Jumbles:** #1. OUNCE #2. AVENUE #3. SUNDAY #4. BUILDING #5. DISTANCE #6. DECEMBER
Mystery Answer: BOULEVARD

55. **Jumbles:** #1. CARRY—TRANSPORT
#2. BLAZING—BURNING #3. EXPLAIN—JUSTIFY
#4. VICTORY—TRIUMPH
Mystery Answer: FUNNY—COMICAL

56. **Jumbles:** #1. PORCH #2. SIDING #3. PANTRY #4. CARPET #5. CLOSET #6. CABINET #7. BALCONY
Mystery Answer: BASEBOARD

57. **Jumbles:** #1. FILLY—SILLY #2. SAVOR—FAVOR #3. TOKEN—BROKEN #4. CREEPY—SLEEPY
Mystery Answer: RALLY—VALLEY

58. **Jumbles:** #1. LIBYA #2. RIVER #3. CAIRO #4. AFRICA #5. SPHINX #6. KINGDOM
Mystery Answer: PYRAMIDS

59. **Jumbles:** #1. GECKO #2. TURTLE #3. RATTLER #4. DINOSAUR #5. TORTOISE
Mystery Answer: ALLIGATOR

60. **Jumbles:** #1. TWO − ZERO = TWO
#2. SIX / TWO = THREE #3. TEN × FIVE = FIFTY
#4. NINE / THREE = THREE
#5. ONE + ELEVEN = TWELVE
Mystery Equation: TWELVE − THREE = NINE

61. **Jumbles:** #1. INDIGO #2. IMPALE #3. UNLESS #4. OPPOSE #5. CROUCH #6. GROWTH
Mystery Answers: #1. COMPASS #2. DIRECTION

62. **Jumbles:** #1. SLOWLY #2. NOTICE #3. FOREVER #4. REALIZE #5. CLEVER #6. BECOMES
Mystery Answer: TIME FLIES

63. **Jumbles:** #1. HYDROGEN #2. FOOTPRINT #3. FLAMINGO #4. AUSTRALIA #5. COSTNER
Mystery Answer: TOM CRUISE

64. **Jumbles:** #1. JOVIAL #2. DISCUS #3. TYRANT #4. GLOBAL #5. MANIAC #6. SHRIMP
Mystery Answers: #1. ISLAND #2. JAMAICA #3. TROPICS

65. **Jumbles:** #1. TITLE #2. AUTHOR #3. FICTION #4. ALMANAC #5. PULITZER #6. TEXTBOOK
Mystery Answer: LITERATURE

66. **Jumbles:** #1. EXHUME #2. COGNAC #3. WILLOW #4. TOURIST #5. DEVOTED #6. ANTENNA
Mystery Answer: EXTENSIVE

67. **Jumbles:** #1. BIRCH #2. PECAN #3. MYRTLE #4. WALNUT #5. COCONUT #6. DOGWOOD
Mystery Answer: MAGNOLIA

68. **Jumbles:** #1. GRAVY #2. PICKLE #3. DANISH #4. CHEESE #5. LASAGNA #6. CRACKER
Mystery Answer: PANCAKES

69. **Jumbles:** #1. WIN #2. CAVE #3. GROUP #4. POCKET #5. HIDEOUT #6. HARDWARE #7. SUNFLOWER #8. BATTLESHIP #9. CONTRAPTION
Mystery Answer: CONVERSATION

70. **Jumbles:** #1. COUSIN #2. TAYLOR #3. KNOTTS #4. HOWARD #5. SHERIFF #6. MAYBERRY
Mystery Answer: NORTH CAROLINA

71. **Jumbles:** #1. VERMONT #2. MICHIGAN #3. ARKANSAS #4. DELAWARE
Mystery Answer: WASHINGTON
Section 2 Answers: 2 1 M.A. 3 4

72. **Jumbles:** #1. HOOVER #2. HARDING #3. JACKSON #4. FILLMORE
Mystery Answer: CLEVELAND
Section 2 Answers: 3 4 M.A. 1 2

73. **Jumbles:** #1. UPPITY #2. UPBEAT #3. UPDATE #4. UPSHOT #5. UPROAR #6. UPGRADE #7. UPSWING
Mystery Answer: UPROOTED

74. **Jumbles:** #1. TUNA #2. BASS #3. TROUT #4. TARPON #5. MARLIN #6. HERRING
Mystery Answer: STURGEON

75. **Jumbles:** #1. NIECE #2. UNCLE #3. COUSIN #4. FATHER #5. NEPHEW #6. MOTHER #7. BROTHER #8. RELATIVE

76. **Jumbles:** #1. RIGOR #2. GOOFY #3. JARGON #4. FOREGO #5. OREGON #6. CHICAGO
Mystery Answer: ONGOING

77. **Jumbles:** #1. *THE MASK* #2. *MAVERICK* #3. *STIR CRAZY* #4. *STRIPTEASE* #5. *SCARY MOVIE* #6. *FORREST GUMP*
Mystery Answer: *THE MUMMY*

78. **Jumbles:** #1. SIX – FOUR = TWO #2. FOUR / ONE = FOUR #3. FIFTY × ONE = FIFTY #4. EIGHT x ZERO = ZERO #5. TWENTY + TEN = THIRTY
Mystery Equation: EIGHT / TWO = FOUR

79. **Jumbles:** #1. CHINESE #2. BUSINESS #3. FRANKLIN #4. OREGON #5. TURTLE
Mystery Answer: GOLF CLUBS

80. **Jumbles:** #1. AROMA #2. LETHAL #3. WINDOW #4. ELUSIVE #5. NEUTRON #6. TRUMPET
Mystery Answer: RETRIEVER

81. **Jumbles:** #1. HYENA #2. PANDA #3. GOPHER #4. COYOTE #5. BABOON #6. WALRUS #7. MONKEY
Mystery Answer: BLACK BEAR

82. **Jumbles:** #1. A CABBAGE #2. A PENNY #3. LIKE A KID #4. A BALLROOM #5. MULTIPLIERS #6. SCHOLARSHIPS

83. **Jumbles:** #1. BUG #2. COMB #3. FRUIT #4. REMOVE #5. CHECKUP #6. LANDFILL #7. YOUNGSTER #8. PICKPOCKET #9. SIGNIFICANT
Mystery Answer: CONTEMPTIBLE

84. **Jumbles:** #1. OXYGEN #2. CALCIUM #3. URANIUM #4. TUNGSTEN
Mystery Answer: MAGNESIUM
Section 2 Answers: 2 1 M.A. 4 3

85. **Jumbles:** #1. PLUTO #2. COMET #3. URANUS #4. JUPITER #5. NEPTUNE #6. UNIVERSE
Mystery Answer: METEORITE

86. **Jumbles:** #1. A RIVER #2. YOUR TEETH #3. DELIGHTED #4. A HAMMER #5. IT GETS WET #6. BUGS BUNNY

87. **Jumbles:** #1. LEWIS #2. CHICAGO #3. CLOONEY #4. EDWARDS #5. HOSPITAL
Mystery Answer: DOCTORS

88. **Jumbles:** #1. JAGUAR #2. BARBIE #3. FLORIDA #4. PETROLEUM #5. OSPREY
Mystery Answer: PILLSBURY

89. **Jumbles:** #1A. SUPPORT #5A. BUZZER #7A. IMAGE #8A. ATTRACT #10A. EYED #12A. AVIATOR #13A. HEARSE #1D. SPLICE #2D. PURGED #3D. THEFT #4D. AZTEC #5D. BOARD #6D. RANCHER #8D. ADVISE #9D. TWITCH #11D. YACHT

90. **Jumbles:** #1. VOWS #2. AISLE #3. MUSIC #4. FITTING #5. DIAMOND #6. REGISTRY
Mystery Answer: INVITATION

91. **Jumbles:** #1. PUTTER #2. DOUBLE #3. TROPHY #4. SOCCER #5. REFEREE #6. FOOTBALL
Mystery Answer: BABE RUTH

92. **Jumbles:** #1. BARK #2. TWIG #3. PRUNE #4. BLOOM #5. POLLEN #6. WILLOW
Mystery Answer: BEGONIA

93. **Jumbles:** #1. ABUNDANCE #2. A CAR POOL #3. A GLOVE #4. TOMORROW #5. A YARDSTICK #6. A SHADOW

94. **Jumbles:** #1. DOCTOR #2. WEAVER #3. MARSHAL #4. REYNOLDS #5. DODGE CITY
Mystery Answer: WESTERN

95. **Jumbles:** #1. CUPID #2. ABRUPT #3. COUPLE #4. COUPON #5. JUPITER #6. SUPPORT
Mystery Answer: OCCUPANT

96. **Jumbles:** #1. SUNNY #2. FUNNY #3. USEFUL #4. BROKEN #5. EXPLICIT #6. GRATEFUL #7. INFAMOUS #8. HANDSOME
Mystery Answer: SELFLESS

97. **Jumbles:** #1. EROTIC #2. CRANKY #3. CRADLE #4. SUNSET #5. CLUTCH #6. BRONZE
Mystery Answers: #1. CRITTER #2. CREATURE

98. **Jumbles:** #1A. FREEDOM #5A. BABOON #7A. NAVAL #8A. BECAUSE #10A. HOOK #12A. ACCOUNT #13A. NEARLY #1D. FLINCH #2D. EMBARK #3D. MOVIE #4D. OBOES #5D. BEGAN #6D. NEGLECT #8D. BRIDLE #9D. ENOUGH #11D. OZONE

99. **Jumbles:** #1. JUICE #2. VODKA #3. WATER #4. COFFEE #5. ESPRESSO #6. LEMONADE
Mystery Answer: SOFT DRINK

100. **Jumbles:** #1. SALAD #2. PEPPER #3. BAKERY #4. LETTUCE #5. SANDWICH #6. MUSHROOM
Mystery Answer: CASSEROLE

101. **Jumbles:** #1. DUTCH #2. GAELIC #3. POLISH #4. FRENCH #5. YIDDISH #6. SPANISH #7. RUSSIAN
Mystery Answer: ITALIAN

102. **Jumbles:** #1. FORUM #2. SICILY #3. CANALS #4. CAESAR #5. EMPEROR #6. GONDOLA
Mystery Answer: COLOSSEUM

103. **Jumbles:** #1. BRAIN #2. GLAND #3. PELVIS #4. RADIUS #5. SPLEEN #6. TRACHEA #7. SKELETON
Mystery Answer: PANCREAS

104. **Jumbles:** #1. NICOLE KIDMAN #2. JULIA ROBERTS #3. SANDRA BULLOCK #4. WHOOPI GOLDBERG
Mystery Answer: GOLDIE HAWN
Section 2 Answers: 1 3 M.A. 4 2

105. **Jumbles:** #1. RADIO #2. PACIFIC #3. CHICAGO #4. OKLAHOMA #5. UNIVERSITY
Mystery Person: PAUL HARVEY

106. **Jumbles:** #1. *NIXON* #2. *RANSOM* #3. *THE STING* #4. *THE HOURS* #5. *PANIC ROOM* #6. *PATCH ADAMS*
Mystery Answer: *PHENOMENON*

107. **Jumbles:** #1. TREATY #2. WEAPON #3. CANTEEN #4. CHOPPER #5. BAZOOKA #6. INVASION
Mystery Answer: KOREAN WAR

108. **Jumbles:** #1. HUSKY—SCRAWNY #2. DECEIT—HONESTY #3. VALLEY—MOUNTAIN #4. POSITIVE—NEGATIVE
Mystery Answer: WELL—SICK

109. **Jumbles:** #1. FIVE PLUS ONE = SIX #2. TWO PLUS SEVEN = NINE #3. NINE MINUS NINE = ZERO #4. SEVEN MINUS TWO = FIVE #5. TWO TIMES FOUR = EIGHT
Mystery Equation: ELEVEN MINUS TEN = ONE

110. **Jumbles:** #1. RIVER #2. BLUFF #3. VALLEY #4. TUNDRA #5. MEADOW #6. EROSION
Mystery Answer: WATERFALL

111. **Jumbles:** #1. EGYPT—LIBYA #2. CHILE—BOLIVIA #3. SWEDEN—FINLAND #4. POLAND—GERMANY
Mystery Answer: FRANCE—ITALY

112. **Jumbles:** #1. BLOCK #2. COACH #3. CAPTAIN #4. PENALTY #5. PASSING #6. REFEREE #7. DEFENSE
Mystery Answer: GOALKEEPER

113. **Jumbles:** #1. PICKLE—PROBLEM #2. RARING—ANXIOUS #3. LAUNCH—BLASTOFF #4. DISORDER—CONFUSION
Mystery Answer: SHAKE—TREMBLE

114. **Jumbles:** #1. NINE + ONE = TEN
#2. EIGHT + TWO = TEN
#3. ZERO − ZERO = ZERO
#4. EIGHT / FOUR = TWO
#5. SIXTY / TWO = THIRTY
Mystery Equation: (TWO + TWO) × TWO = EIGHT

115. **Jumbles:** #1. GAP #2. BLOB #3. GROOM #4. MIDDLE #5. ICEBERG #6. SHOULDER #7. FRIGHTFUL #8. EXCITEMENT #9. PUBLICATION
Mystery Answer: CHEESEBURGER

116. **Jumbles:** #1. TRACK—SMACK #2. BARBER—HARBOR #3. WILLOW—PILLOW #4. FUMBLE—TUMBLE
Mystery Answer: HALT—FAULT

117. **Jumbles:** #1. HIS SIDEBURNS #2. A LIGHTHOUSE #3. THE INFANTRY #4. THE OCEAN #5. IT WAS CANNED #6. A SAXOPHONE

118. **Jumbles:** #1. EAGLE #2. CHIMP #3. GORILLA #4. CHICKEN #5. CARIBOU #6. BUZZARD #7. WALLABY
Mystery Answer: BLUE WHALE

119. **Jumbles:** #1. GASOLINE #2. GUNPOWDER #3. SKYLAB #4. POLYESTER #5. FOOTBALL
Mystery Answer: WEST POINT

120. **Jumbles:** #1. CALICO #2. GIMLET #3. STANZA #4. BEDPAN #5. HERALD #6. MOVING
Mystery Answers: #1. CANADA #2. PROVINCE #3. MANITOBA

121. **Jumbles:** #1. TEMPT #2. PICKUP #3. LAWFUL #4. ROBBER #5. EMERGE #6. EPISODE
Mystery Answer: MICROFILM

122. **Jumbles:** #1. YIELD #2. BROKER #3. MUTUAL #4. GROWTH #5. ACCOUNT #6. EARNINGS
Mystery Answer: WALL STREET

123. **Jumbles:** #1. CANADA #2. POLAND #3. ROMANIA #4. BERMUDA
Mystery Answer: COLOMBIA
Section 2 Answers: 3 4 1 M.A. 2

124. **Jumbles:** #1. CLAIR #2. DOCTOR #3. VANESSA #4. RUSSELL #5. SIBLINGS
Mystery Answer: LISA BONET

125. **Jumbles:** #1. ISOBAR #2. CLOUDY #3. THUNDER #4. TYPHOON #5. DROUGHT #6. FREEZING #7. HUMIDITY
Mystery Answer: TEMPERATURE

126. **Jumbles:** #1. SHEEP #2. INDIAN #3. WOMBAT #4. BRITISH #5. CANBERRA #6. KANGAROO
Mystery Answer: CONTINENT

127. **Jumbles:** #1. WYOMING #2. MISSOURI #3. OKLAHOMA #4. WISCONSIN
Mystery Answer: LOUISIANA
Section 2 Answers: 3 M.A. 4 1 2

128. **Jumbles:** #1. ATLAS #2. NOVEL #3. PUBLISH #4. CHAPTER #5. CATALOG #6. COOKBOOK
Mystery Answer: PAPERBACK

129. **Jumbles:** #1. SHARK #2. PERCH #3. SALMON #4. MINNOW #5. CATFISH #6. FLOUNDER
Mystery Answer: SWORDFISH

130. **Jumbles:** #1. PILOT #2. TICKET #3. TRAVEL #4. LANDING #5. AIRPORT #6. TOURIST #7. VACATION #8. PASSPORT

131. **Jumbles:** #1. USE A SUNDIAL #2. NIGHTMARES #3. A SCRAPBOOK #4. WITH A SPOON #5. LENGTHEN IT #6. A BASEBALL BAT

132. **Jumbles:** #1. GENE HACKMAN #2. EDDIE MURPHY #3. STEVE MARTIN #4. DANNY GLOVER
Mystery Answer: HUGH GRANT
Section 2 Answers: 2 3 M.A. 4 1

133. **Jumbles:** #1. *WITNESS* #2. *DICK TRACY* #3. *HOME ALONE* #4. *DISCLOSURE* #5. *WALL STREET* #6. *PULP FICTION*
Mystery Answer: *REAR WINDOW*

134. **Jumbles:** #1. TEN / FIVE = TWO
#2. SIX × ZERO = ZERO
#3. SEVEN + FOUR = ELEVEN
#4. NINE + THREE = TWELVE
#5. ONE + ELEVEN = TWELVE
Mystery Equation: TWO + TWO + TWO = SIX

135. **Jumbles:** #1. SATURN #2. PLANET #3. GALAXY #4. ECLIPSE #5. SUNSPOT #6. MERCURY
Mystery Answer: ASTRONAUT

136. **Jumbles:** #1. BENCH #2. PENALTY #3. FAIRWAY #4. UNIFORM #5. POSITION #6. GROUNDER
Mystery Answer: THE SUPER BOWL

137. **Jumbles:** #1. MONACO #2. SCRABBLE #3. EGYPT #4. LINCOLN #5. GLASGOW
Mystery Answer: GILA MONSTER

138. **Jumbles:** #1. PRIMP #2. EXCITE #3. EVOLVE #4. HEALTH #5. TRANSIT #6. SERIOUS
Mystery Answer: EXPANSIVE

139. **Jumbles:** #1. BOXER #2. HOUND #3. SPANIEL #4. MALTESE #5. WHIPPET #6. SHEPHERD
Mystery Answer: DOBERMAN

140. **Jumbles:** #1A. NUMERAL #5A. CHOSEN #7A. IDIOM #8A. BALANCE #10A. TRUE #12A. ADMIRAL #13A. OCTANE #1D. NUDIST #2D. ENCORE #3D. LARVA #4D. TONIC #5D. CLOAK #6D. NATURAL #8D. BEYOND #9D. ENERGY #11D. RAYON

141. **Jumbles:** #1. AUTHOR #2. HARVARD #3. LECTURER #4. ATTORNEY #5. PRINCETON
Mystery Person: RALPH NADER

142. **Jumbles:** #1. SPRUCE #2. SEQUOIA #3. CYPRESS #4. HEMLOCK #5. REDWOOD #6. CHESTNUT
Mystery Answer: SYCAMORE

143. **Jumbles:** #1. MOM #2. GIRL #3. FLOCK #4. REFLEX #5. ORCHARD #6. CHESTNUT #7. HUMANKIND #8. SUSPENSION #9. SENTIMENTAL
Mystery Answer: ILLUSTRATION

144. **Jumbles:** #1. ELYSE #2. SKIPPY #3. REAGAN #4. KEATON #5. BROTHER #6. COLUMBUS
Mystery Answer: MALLORY

145. **Jumbles:** #1. GARFIELD #2. COOLIDGE #3. BUCHANAN #4. JEFFERSON
Mystery Answer: HARRISON
Section 2 Answers: 4 2 3 M.A. 1

146. **Jumbles:** #1. DENMARK #2. ELEPHANT #3. WESTERNS #4. TRAVOLTA #5. CUCUMBER
Mystery Answer: SOUND WAVES

147. **Jumbles:** #1A. BLANKET #5A. ANNUAL #7A. THEIR #8A. APOSTLE #10A. RUIN #12A. ACHIEVE #13A. EXCISE #1D. BARTER #2D. NOTION #3D. THUMP #4D. KNEEL #5D. ABYSS #6D. LOVABLE #8D. ACCESS #9D. EXTEND #11D. UPPER

148. **Jumbles:** #1. PATIO #2. FLOOR #3. GUTTER #4. GARAGE #5. WINDOW #6. CHIMNEY #7. DRIVEWAY
Mystery Answer: LIVING ROOM

149. **Jumbles:** #1. WARHOL #2. PICASSO #3. POLLOCK #4. SARGENT #5. WHISTLER
Mystery Answer: EL GRECO

150. **Jumbles:** #1. ALBANY #2. TRENTON #3. BISMARCK #4. NASHVILLE
Mystery Answer: SACRAMENTO
Section 2 Answers: 2 M.A. 3 1 4

151. **Jumbles:** #1. HIPPO #2. BABOON #3. GAZELLE #4. OSTRICH #5. BUFFALO #6. PENGUIN
Mystery Answer: PORCUPINE

152. **Jumbles:** #1. PURITY #2. DERIVE #3. SPIRAL #4. ORCHID #5. LEGEND #6. WALNUT
Mystery Answers: #1. REPORTER #2. INTERVIEW

153. **Jumbles:** #1A. BALDING #5A. WOOFER #7A. KOOKY #8A. APPAREL #10A. PLAT #12. GOURMET #13A. VACANT #1D. BACKUP #2D. DOCKET #3D. GROUP #4D. DODGE #5D. WHEAT #6D. RADIANT #8D. ADDING #9D. LAWMAN #11D. LEAVE

154. **Jumbles:** #1. MOUSE #2. MODEM #3. LAPTOP #4. SURFING #5. ADDRESS #6. KEYBOARD
Mystery Answer: MEGABYTES

155. **Jumbles:** #1. BLUNT #2. UNEVEN #3. NOMADIC #4. DEFINITE #5. DELICATE #6. STUNNING #7. INSECURE #8. DOUBTFUL
Mystery Answer: ELONGATED

156. **Jumbles:** #1. PUDDING #2. POPCORN #3. OATMEAL #4. MEATBALL #5. COLESLAW
Mystery Answer: APPLE PIE

157. **Jumbles:** #1. A ROBIN #2. A CHATTERBOX #3. NOODLE SOUP #4. A CONVERSATION #5. AN ACCOUNTANT #6. DEVILED EGGS

158. **Jumbles:** #1. *GODZILLA* #2. *CAST AWAY* #3. *DEEP IMPACT* #4. *THE FUGITIVE* #5. *NOTTING HILL* #6. *FREAKY FRIDAY*
Mystery Answer: *CITIZEN KANE*

159. **Jumbles:** #1. BATTER—FATTER #2. DIVING—DRIVING #3. PUCKER—TRUCKER #4. SAILING—FAILING
Mystery Answer: BUNT—STUNT

160. **Jumbles:** #1. TAHOE #2. MOUSTACHE #3. GEYSER #4. POLAND #5. OLYMPUS
Mystery Answer: LOS ANGELES

161. **Jumbles:** #1. SIX + SIX = TWELVE
#2. SIXTY × ZERO = ZERO
#3. FIFTEEN / THREE = FIVE
#4. TEN × TEN = ONE HUNDRED
#5. ONE – TWO = NEGATIVE ONE
Mystery Equation: SEVEN × TWO = FOURTEEN

162. **Jumbles:** #1. HAWK #2. RAVEN #3. STARLING #4. BLUEBIRD #5. PHEASANT #6. FLAMINGO
Mystery Answer: KINGFISHER

163. **Jumbles:** #1. BUNKER #2. PRIVATE #3. WARSHIP #4. INFANTRY #5. FLOTILLA #6. GARRISON
Mystery Answer: PURPLE HEART

164. **Jumbles:** #1. FIVE TIMES TWO = TEN
#2. TWO TIMES TWO = FOUR
#3. FOUR MINUS TWO = TWO
#4. SIX PLUS THREE = NINE
#5. ELEVEN MINUS TWO = NINE
Mystery Equation: FOUR TIMES FOUR = SIXTEEN

165. **Jumbles:** #1. AORTA #2. CLINIC #3. SURPASS #4. TELECAST #5. REINDEER #6. WITHDRAW
Mystery Answer: DISSECTED

166. **Jumbles:** #1. RIG #2. OBOE #3. HELLO #4. AUTUMN #5. PACKAGE #6. SHOELACE #7. EXTENSIVE #8. SPELLBOUND #9. PORTERHOUSE
Mystery Answer: KINDERGARTEN

167. **Jumbles:** #1. SODIUM #2. SILICON #3. PLATINUM #4. HYDROGEN
Mystery Answer: POTASSIUM
Section 2 Answers: 4 2 1 M.A. 3

168. **Jumbles:** #1. NORTHWEST #2. ENGLAND #3. MONGOLIA #4. LIBERACE #5. SIBERIA
Mystery Answer: LIGHTNING

169. **Jumbles:** #1. ICELAND #2. HUNGARY #3. DENMARK #4. MOROCCO
Mystery Answer: MONGOLIA
Section 2 Answers: 3 1 M.A. 2 4

170. **Jumbles:** #1A. INVOLVE #5A. ARGUED #7A. CLASS #8A. HEARING #10A. PELT #12A. VOLUMES #13A. EGGNOG #1D. ICECAP #2D. OFFSET #3D. EAGLE #4D. AGAIN #5D. ALARM #6D. DAISIES #8D. HOTDOG #9D. GUNMAN #11D. EATEN

171. **Jumbles:** #1. ARENA #2. SPORTS #3. ATHLETE #4. DEFENSE #5. OFFENSE #6. CONTEST #7. STADIUM #8. COMPETE

172. **Jumbles:** #1. *TOOTSIE* #2. *RUSH HOUR* #3. *GLADIATOR* #4. *ANNIE HALL* #5. *UNFORGIVEN* #6. *RAGING BULL*
Mystery Answer: *THE GODFATHER*

173. **Jumbles:** #1. JUG #2. CHOP #3. JOINT #4. RUCKUS #5. STATION #6. CHLORINE #7. SUPERNOVA #8. RESTAURANT #9. HUMMINGBIRD
Mystery Answer: EARSPLITTING

174. **Jumbles:** #1. MUNICH #2. PHYSICIST #3. PRINCETON #4. DOCTORATE #5. NOBEL PRIZE
Mystery Person: ALBERT EINSTEIN

175. **Jumbles:** #1A. MASSIVE #5A. APIECE #7A. HELLO #8A. BACKHOE #10A. MAIN #12A. ANAGRAM #13A. OBJECT #1D. MAYHEM #2D. STOLEN #3D. ENEMA #4D. HIPPO #5D. AWAKE #6D. EARDRUM #8D. BRANCH #9D. EMERGE #11D. ABHOR

176. **Jumbles:** #1. SUMMIT #2. FEARFUL #3. DEAREST #4. FIGMENT #5. WEALTHY #6. CRUMPET #7. CRACKPOT
Mystery Answer: STRAIGHT

JUMBLE SAMPLERS

TV Jumble: WOODY VARIETY AMAZING LONESOME
Bonus: TONY DANZA

Jumble Crosswords: 1A—SKIMPY 5A—MASON 6A—GRADE 7A—OTTERS 1D—SAMPLE 2D—INSIGHT 3D—PANCAKE 4D—EXCESS
Bonus: DICK CLARK

Jumble See & Search: #1. CHAIR #2. PLANT #3. PHONE #4. BROOM #5. FAUCET #6. SOCKET #7. PLUNGER #8. FLOWERS #9. SCISSORS #10. CALENDAR
Mystery Answers: #1. FIRE #2. SHEAR MADNESS #3. SHORT CUT

JUMBLE® SAMPLERS

We invite you to sample three other great Jumble® products available from Triumph Books.

TV JUMBLE®

Use the clues to help unscramble the four Jumbles, one letter to each square, to form four words.

	Clue
DOWYO	TV bartender
RAYETIV	_____ show
ZGAAIMN	Spider-Man, for example
EEOMLSNO	Dove's adjective

Then arrange the circled letters to form the bonus answer as suggested by the above cartoon and bonus clue.

Bonus  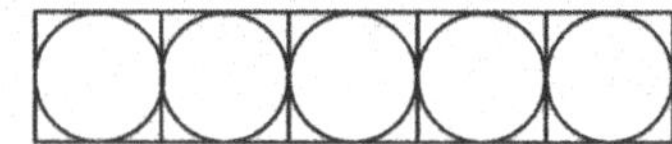

JUMBLE® CROSSWORDS™

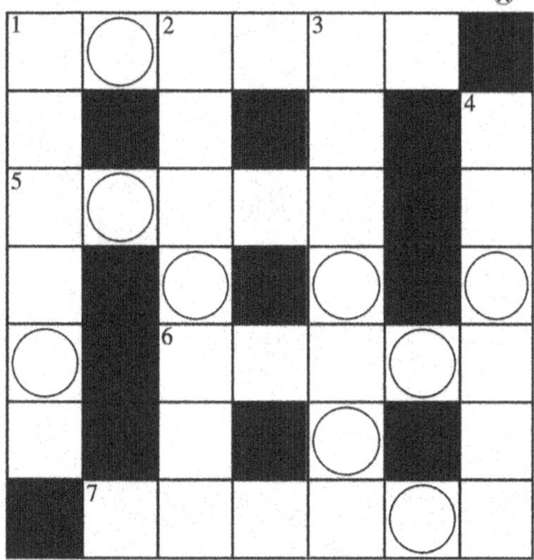

ACROSS

CLUE	ANSWER
1. Insufficient	PIKYSM
5. James _____	AONMS
6. _____ A	EDRAG
7. Weasel relatives	TOETSR

DOWN

CLUE	ANSWER
1. Representative	LMSPEA
2. Intuitiveness	TNIGISH
3. _____ batter	KAPCEAN
4. Surplus	ESXSEC

How to play: Complete the crossword puzzle by looking at the clues and unscrambling the answers. When the puzzle is complete, unscramble the circled letters to solve the bonus.

CLUE: This man, who was born in 1929, was inducted into the Rock and Roll Hall of Fame in 1993.

BONUS 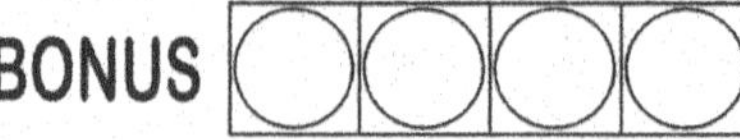 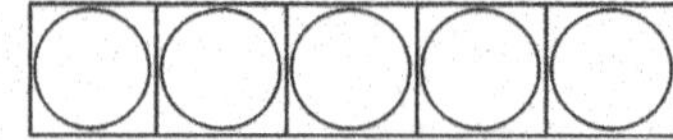

JUMBLE®
SAMPLERS

JUMBLE® SEE & SEARCH #37
LITTLE SHOP OF HAIRSTYLES
Sorry Closed
Call 911!
Call 911!
MAKE UP

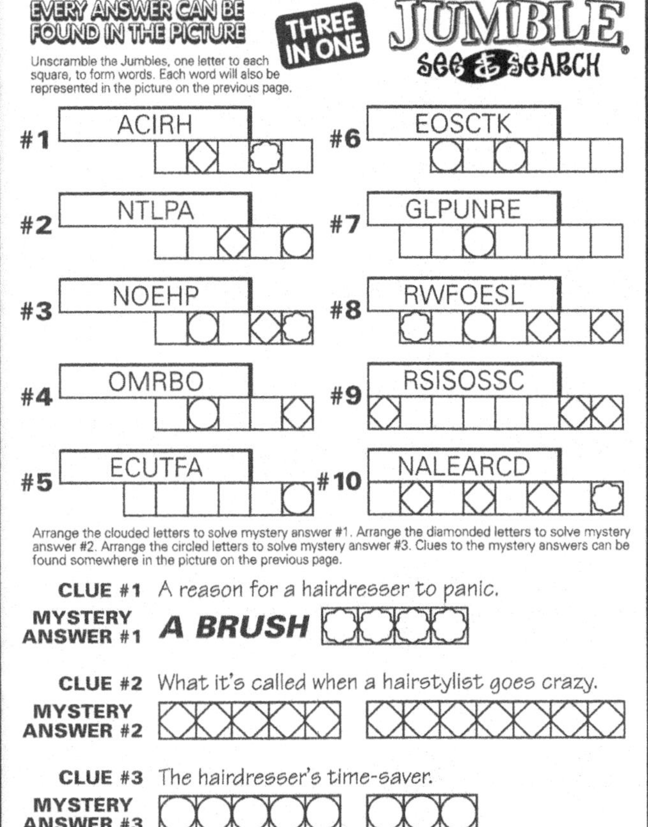
EVERY ANSWER CAN BE FOUND IN THE PICTURE
THREE IN ONE
JUMBLE® SEE & SEARCH
Unscramble the Jumbles, one letter to each square, to form words. Each word will also be represented in the picture on the previous page.
#1 ACIRH
#2 NTLPA
#3 NOEHP
#4 OMRBO
#5 ECUTFA
#6 EOSCTK
#7 GLPUNRE
#8 RWFOESL
#9 RSISOSSC
#10 NALEARCD
Arrange the clouded letters to solve mystery answer #1. Arrange the diamonded letters to solve mystery answer #2. Arrange the circled letters to solve mystery answer #3. Clues to the mystery answers can be found somewhere in the picture on the previous page.
CLUE #1 A reason for a hairdresser to panic.
MYSTERY ANSWER #1 A BRUSH
CLUE #2 What it's called when a hairstylist goes crazy.
MYSTERY ANSWER #2
CLUE #3 The hairdresser's time-saver.
MYSTERY ANSWER #3

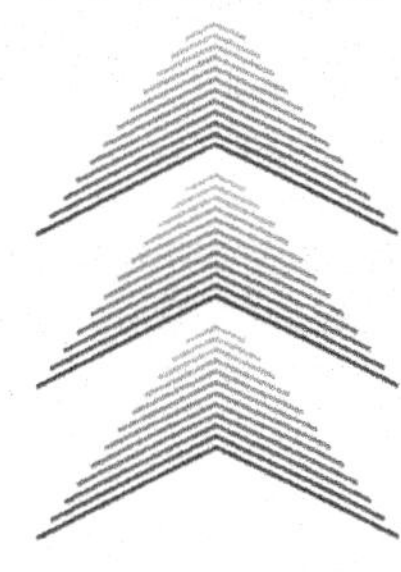
EVERY
ANSWER
CAN BE
FOUND
IN THE
PICTURE

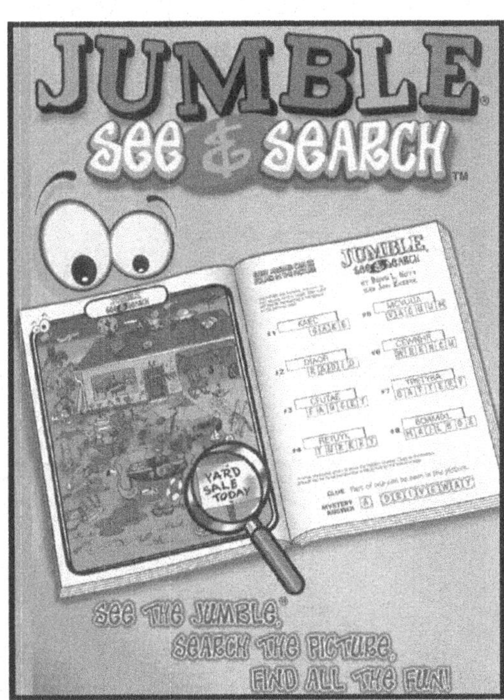
JUMBLE® SEE & SEARCH™
YARD SALE TODAY
SEE THE JUMBLE,
SEARCH THE PICTURE,
FIND ALL THE FUN!